HEALTHCHEQUES™

Carbohydrate, Fat & Calorie Guide

Jane Stephenson, RD, CDE
Diane Bader

Second Edition

Appletree Press, Inc.
Mankato, Minnesota

Appletree Press, Inc.
151 Good Counsel Drive Suite 125
Mankato, MN 56001

Phone: (507) 345-4848
Fax: (507) 345-3002
Website: www.appletree-press.com

The purpose of HealthCheques™: Carbohydrate, Fat & Calorie Guide is to supply authoritative data on the nutritional values of foods in a form for quick and easy reference. The information is not intended as a substitute for treatment prescribed by your physician. Please consult with your licensed health care professional before making any changes to your treatment plan.

CATALOGING-IN-PUBLICATION DATA

Stephenson, Jane, 1960-

HealthCheques™: Carbohydrate, Fat & Calorie Guide / authored by Jane Stephenson and Diane Bader. Mankato, MN : Appletree Press, Inc., c2004.

128 p. ; 13 cm.

Includes index and bibliographical references.

1. Food—Composition—Tables. 2. Nutrition—Tables. 3. Food—Caloric content—Tables. 4. Food—Cholesterol content—Tables. 5. Food—Fat content—Tables. 6. Food—Carbohydrate content—Tables. 7. Convenience foods—Composition—Tables. I. Title. II. Title: HealthCheques. III. Title: Carbohydrate, fat & calorie guide. IV. Title: Carbohydrate, fat and calorie guide. V. Bader, Diane, 1955-

Summary: Values for calories, carbohydrates, carb choices, protein, fat, saturated fat, cholesterol, sodium, and fiber content are provided for more than 4,000 foods, including 17 fast-food chains. A handy nutrition reference and pocket counter.

ISBN 1-891011-065
RA 784.S74 2004   613.28   2004103638

Editor: Linda Hachfeld
Graphic Designer, Second Edition: Kristin Higginbotham
Cover and Book Design: Douglas Allan Graphic Design

Printed in the United States of America

Sincere Thanks

We wish to thank our colleagues and publisher who contributed their time, expertise and inspiration in the development of HealthCheques™: Carbohydrate, Fat & Calorie Guide. We extend a special acknowledgment to Jackie Boucher, MS, RD, CDE, for her endless ideas, encouragement and assistance with the introduction of the book; Bridgett Wagener, RD for co-authoring the first edition of this book; and Janice Abbott and Mary Sassin for their help with the manuscript.

We also thank our families and friends for their patience and understanding during the many hours of research involved in writing this book. Finally, we thank our HealthCheques™ customers who strive to achieve their nutrition and health goals each and every day.

Jane Stephenson, RD, CDE
Diane Bader
Authors

Contents

About This Book

HealthCheques™: Carbohydrate, Fat & Calorie Guide was written as a reference to help you make healthy food choices at home, on the run or in restaurants. It lists the calories, carbohydrate, protein, fat, saturated fat, cholesterol, sodium and fiber content of 4,000 foods and includes carbohydrate choices for persons with diabetes.

The foods in this guide are grouped into easy-to-find categories and then listed alphabetically from A to Z. Within each category you'll find subcategories. For example, under the category of Meats, the subcategories are Beef, Game, Lamb, Pork, Processed & Luncheon Meats and Specialty & Organ Meats. Serving sizes listed for individual foods within a category are consistent for easy comparison. Manufacturer's suggested servings are used in cases when serving sizes varied, such as in the Cereal section. Often two measures are given for foods that are available in more than one portion size; for example, Bagel, blueberry "1 (2 oz.)". Values listed inside parentheses such as Bagel, mini "2 (0.9 oz.)" refer to the value of each item; thus, each of the two mini bagels weigh 0.9 ounces.

Learn how to estimate your daily nutrient goals in three easy steps on page 114. To determine carbohydrate grams and choices by calorie level, please turn to page 115. Use the charts on page 118 and 119 to estimate the number of calories used during 30 minutes of various activities. In addition, you can track your blood lipid levels (Cholesterol, HDL, LDL and Triglycerides) on page 116.

This comprehensive guide is a terrific tool to help you stay healthy—keep it handy in your purse, pocket, desk drawer or glove compartment.

Abbreviations used in HealthCheques™

BBQ . . . . .barbecue
Calif. . . . . . . .California
fl. oz. . . . . . . .fluid ounces
frzn. . . . . .frozen
g . . . . .gram
hmde. . . . . . .homemade
in. . . . . .inch
marg. . . . . . .margarine
mayo. . . . . . .mayonnaise
mg . . . . .milligram
n/a . . . . .not available

oz. . . . . .ounce
pkg. . . . . .package
pkt. . . . . .packet
T. . . . . .tablespoon
tsp. . . . . .teaspoon
veg. . . . . .vegetables
w/ . . . . .with
w/o . . . . .without
/ . . . . .or
Example:
   jam/jelly = jam "or" jelly

Nutrient values have been rounded to the nearest calorie, gram or milligram, with the exception of saturated fat values, which are rounded to the nearest 0.5 gram. Apparent inconsistencies may result from rounding off numbers, values may have been obtained from more than one source or samples of the same food, seasonal differences and slight variations among manufacturers.

Nutrient values change as products and recipes are reformulated and reanalyzed. Menu items listed may not be available at all restaurants and nutrient values for fast food restaurants are meant for general informational purposes only. Nutrient values are subject to change; values are current as of 2004. If the information you find on a label differs significantly from the data in this book, please use the label as your guide.

ALCOHOL

ITEM	AMOUNT	CALORIES	CARBOHYDRATE (g)	CARBOHYDRATE CHOICES	PROTEIN (g)	FAT (g)	SATURATED FAT (g)	CHOLESTEROL (mg)	SODIUM (mg)	FIBER (g)
ALCOHOL										
Alabama slammer	4 fl. oz.	325	29	2	0	0	0.0	0	5	0
B-52	4 fl. oz.	403	43	3	1	8	4.5	19	49	0
Bahama mama	6 fl. oz.	253	21	1½	0	0	0.0	0	19	0
Beer										
light	12 fl. oz.	99	5	0	1	0	0.0	0	11	0
nonalcoholic	12 fl. oz.	73	14	1	1	0	0.0	0	10	0
regular	12 fl. oz.	143	13	1	1	0	0.0	0	7	0
Black Russian	4 fl. oz.	308	20	1	0	0	0.0	0	4	0
Bloody Mary	8 fl. oz.	177	8	½	1	0	0.0	0	651	1
Bourbon & soda	4 fl. oz.	95	0	0	0	0	0.0	0	14	0
Brandy	1 fl. oz.	64	0	0	0	0	0.0	0	0	0
Brandy Alexander	4 fl. oz.	289	15	1	1	8	5.0	26	16	0
Champagne	4 fl. oz.	80	12	1	0	0	0.0	0	10	0
Colorado bulldog	6 fl. oz.	230	21	1½	0	0	0.0	0	4	0
Cordials/liqueurs, 54 proof	1 fl. oz.	100	13	1	0	0	0.0	0	2	0
Cosmopolitan	6 fl. oz.	225	25	1½	0	0	0.0	0	4	0
Daiquiri	6 fl. oz.	337	12	1	0	0	0.0	0	9	0
Fuzzy navel	8 fl. oz.	249	31	2	1	0	0.0	0	2	0
Gimlet	2.5 fl. oz.	146	1	0	0	0	0.0	0	1	0
Gin & tonic	8 fl. oz.	155	16	1	0	0	0.0	0	8	0
Gin/rum/vodka/whiskey										
80 proof	1 fl. oz.	64	0	0	0	0	0.0	0	0	0
86 proof	1 fl. oz.	70	0	0	0	0	0.0	0	0	0
90 proof	1 fl. oz.	73	0	0	0	0	0.0	0	0	0
100 proof	1 fl. oz.	82	0	0	0	0	0.0	0	0	0
Grasshopper	4 fl. oz.	344	31	2	1	7	4.5	24	17	0
Harvey wallbanger	6 fl. oz.	191	18	1	1	0	0.0	0	2	0
Hot toddie	8 fl. oz.	113	5	0	0	0	0.0	0	3	0
Hurricane	8 fl. oz.	221	29	2	1	0	0.0	0	5	0
Irish coffee										
w/ whipped cream	8 fl. oz.	126	2	0	1	3	2.0	10	22	0
w/o whipped cream	8 fl. oz.	97	1	0	0	0	0.0	0	4	0
Irish cream	1 fl. oz.	106	6	½	1	5	2.5	11	26	0
Kahlua	1 fl. oz.	100	13	1	0	0	0.0	0	2	0
Kamikaze	4 fl. oz.	225	20	1	0	0	0.0	0	3	0
Long Island iced tea	6 fl. oz.	241	21	1½	0	0	0.0	0	36	0
Mai tai	4 fl. oz.	274	26	2	0	0	0.0	0	10	0
Manhattan	2.5 fl. oz.	149	2	0	0	0	0.0	0	2	0
Margarita										
w/ salt	6 fl. oz.	375	24	1½	0	0	0.0	0	479	0
w/o salt	6 fl. oz.	375	24	1½	0	0	0.0	0	9	0

ALCOHOL

ITEM	AMOUNT	CALORIES	CARBOHYDRATE (g)	CARBOHYDRATE CHOICES	PROTEIN (g)	FAT (g)	SATURATED FAT (g)	CHOLESTEROL (mg)	SODIUM (mg)	FIBER (g)
Martini										
chocolate	2.5 fl. oz.	190	8	½	0	0	0.0	0	0	0
traditional	2.5 fl. oz.	159	0	0	0	0	0.0	0	1	0
Melon ball	8 fl. oz.	212	26	2	1	0	0.0	0	3	0
Mimosa	8 fl. oz.	123	24	1½	1	0	0.0	0	9	0
Mudslide	4 fl. oz.	358	26	2	1	8	4.5	19	47	0
Old fashioned	4 fl. oz.	265	8	½	0	0	0.0	0	1	0
Piña colada	6 fl. oz.	327	43	3	1	4	3.0	0	12	1
Rob Roy	2.5 fl. oz.	155	1	0	0	0	0.0	0	2	0
Rum & cola	8 fl. oz.	176	20	1	0	0	0.0	0	5	0
Rusty nail	4 fl. oz.	309	17	1	0	0	0.0	0	3	0
Screwdriver	8 fl. oz.	194	20	1	1	0	0.0	0	2	0
Tequila Maria	8 fl. oz.	177	8	½	1	0	0.0	0	651	1
Tequila sunrise	6 fl. oz.	211	26	2	1	0	0.0	0	12	0
Toasted almond	4 fl. oz.	278	19	1	2	15	9.5	51	33	0
Tom Collins	8 fl. oz.	148	17	1	0	0	0.0	0	104	0
Whiskey sour	4 fl. oz.	193	17	1	0	0	0.0	0	26	0
White Russian	4 fl. oz.	292	19	1	0	1	1.0	4	8	0
Wine, cooking										
Marsala	2 T.	45	4	0	0	0	0.0	0	190	0
red/white	2 T.	20	1	0	0	0	0.0	0	190	0
sherry	2 T.	45	2	0	0	0	0.0	0	190	0
Wine, table										
dessert, dry	4 fl. oz.	149	5	0	0	0	0.0	0	11	0
dessert, sweet	4 fl. oz.	181	14	1	0	0	0.0	0	11	0
red/rosé	4 fl. oz.	85	2	0	0	0	0.0	0	6	0
sangria	8 fl. oz.	157	21	1½	0	0	0.0	0	16	0
sherry, dry	4 fl. oz.	82	2	0	0	0	0.0	0	9	0
spritzer	8 fl. oz.	95	2	0	0	0	0.0	0	30	0
white, dry/medium	4 fl. oz.	80	1	0	0	0	0.0	0	6	0
Wine cooler	12 fl. oz.	170	20	1	0	0	0.0	0	29	0

BEVERAGES

ITEM	AMOUNT	CALORIES	CARBOHYDRATE (g)	CARBOHYDRATE CHOICES	PROTEIN (g)	FAT (g)	SATURATED FAT (g)	CHOLESTEROL (mg)	SODIUM (mg)	FIBER (g)
Café latte										
w/ skim milk	8 fl. oz.	80	12	1	8	1	0.5	5	110	0
w/ whole milk	8 fl. oz.	135	11	1	8	7	4.5	30	105	0
Café mocha, w/ whipped cream										
w/ skim milk	8 fl. oz.	145	20	1	7	6	3.0	38	80	1
w/ whole milk	8 fl. oz.	185	20	1	7	11	6.0	55	80	1
Cappuccino										
w/ skim milk	8 fl. oz.	55	8	½	5	0	0.0	3	70	0
w/ water, mix	8 fl. oz.	60	10	½	0	2	0.5	0	50	0

BEVERAGES

ITEM	AMOUNT	CALORIES	CARBOHYDRATE (g)	CARBOHYDRATE CHOICES	PROTEIN (g)	FAT (g)	SATURATED FAT (g)	CHOLESTEROL (mg)	SODIUM (mg)	FIBER (g)
Cappuccino *(continued)*										
w/ whole milk	8 fl. oz.	90	8	½	5	5	3.0	18	68	0
Capri Sun®	6.75 fl. oz.	100	26	2	0	0	0.0	0	20	0
Club soda/seltzer	8 fl. oz.	0	0	0	0	0	0.0	0	50	0
Coffee										
brewed/instant	6 fl. oz.	4	1	0	0	0	0.0	0	4	0
flavored mixes	6 fl. oz.	60	10	½	0	2	0.5	0	40	0
Crystal Light®	8 fl. oz.	5	0	0	0	0	0.0	0	0	0
Espresso	3 fl. oz.	8	1	0	0	0	0.0	0	12	0
Frappuccino®	9.5 fl. oz.	200	37	2½	7	4	2.0	15	110	0
Fruit ₂0®	8 fl. oz.	0	0	0	0	0	0.0	0	5	0
Fruit punch	8 fl. oz.	117	30	2	0	0	0.0	0	55	0
Gatorade®	8 fl. oz.	50	14	1	0	0	0.0	0	110	0
Hi-C®	8 fl. oz.	120	32	2	0	0	0.0	0	140	0
Hot cocoa										
w/ 1% milk, hmde.	8 fl. oz.	182	31	2	9	5	2.0	10	124	1
w/ water, mix	8 fl. oz.	120	22	1½	2	3	1.0	0	130	1
w/ whole milk, hmde.	8 fl. oz.	230	30	2	9	10	5.5	33	120	1
Kool-Aid®										
regular	8 fl. oz.	100	25	1½	0	0	0.0	0	15	0
sugar free	8 fl. oz.	5	0	0	0	0	0.0	0	5	0
Lemonade										
regular	8 fl. oz.	99	26	2	0	0	0.0	0	7	0
sugar free	8 fl. oz.	5	0	0	0	0	0.0	0	0	0
Quinine/tonic water	8 fl. oz.	83	21	1½	0	0	0.0	0	10	0
Soda, diet, most varieties	12 fl. oz.	0	0	0	0	0	0.0	0	35	0
Soda, regular										
7 up®	12 fl. oz.	140	39	2½	0	0	0.0	0	75	0
Cherry Coke®	12 fl. oz.	150	42	3	0	0	0.0	0	35	0
Coca-Cola®	12 fl. oz.	140	39	2½	0	0	0.0	0	50	0
cream	12 fl. oz.	180	46	3	0	0	0.0	0	45	0
Dr. Pepper®	12 fl. oz.	150	40	2½	0	0	0.0	0	55	0
ginger ale	12 fl. oz.	140	36	2½	0	0	0.0	0	50	0
grape	12 fl. oz.	190	53	3½	0	0	0.0	0	35	0
Mountain Dew®	12 fl. oz.	170	46	3	0	0	0.0	0	70	0
Orange Slice®	12 fl. oz.	190	50	3	0	0	0.0	0	55	0
Pepsi®	12 fl. oz.	150	41	3	0	0	0.0	0	35	0
Pepsi® Blue™	12 fl. oz.	150	40	2½	0	0	0.0	0	35	0
root beer	12 fl. oz.	170	46	3	0	0	0.0	0	45	0
Ruby Red Squirt®	12 fl. oz.	180	47	3	0	0	0.0	0	23	0
Sierra Mist™	12 fl. oz.	140	39	2½	0	0	0.0	0	35	0
Sprite®	12 fl. oz.	140	38	2½	0	0	0.0	0	70	0

BEVERAGES

ITEM	AMOUNT	CALORIES	CARBOHYDRATE (g)	CARBOHYDRATE CHOICES	PROTEIN (g)	FAT (g)	SATURATED FAT (g)	CHOLESTEROL (mg)	SODIUM (mg)	FIBER (g)
Soda, regular *(continued)*										
Squirt®	12 fl. oz.	140	39	2½	0	0	0.0	0	50	0
Vanilla Coke®	12 fl. oz.	150	42	3	0	0	0.0	0	35	0
Sunny Delight®	8 fl. oz.	120	29	2	0	0	0.0	0	190	0
Tang®	8 fl. oz.	90	23	1½	0	0	0.0	0	35	0
Tea										
brewed/instant	6 fl. oz.	2	1	0	0	0	0.0	0	5	0
iced, diet, w/ lemon	8 fl. oz.	5	0	0	0	0	0.0	0	0	0
iced, sweetened	8 fl. oz.	70	18	1	0	0	0.0	0	0	0
Water, bottle	8 fl. oz.	0	0	0	0	0	0.0	0	2	0
Yoo-hoo®	8 fl. oz.	130	29	2	2	1	0.5	0	170	0

BREADS & BREAD PRODUCTS
Breads & Muffins

ITEM	AMOUNT	CALORIES	CARBOHYDRATE (g)	CARBOHYDRATE CHOICES	PROTEIN (g)	FAT (g)	SATURATED FAT (g)	CHOLESTEROL (mg)	SODIUM (mg)	FIBER (g)
Bagels										
blueberry										
medium	1 (2 oz.)	150	32	2	5	0	0.0	0	290	1
large	1 (3.7 oz.)	277	59	4	9	1	0.0	0	537	3
cinnamon raisin										
medium	1 (2 oz.)	155	31	2	6	1	0.0	0	183	1
large	1 (3.7 oz.)	287	58	4	10	2	0.5	0	338	2
low carb, Atkins®	1 (2.5 oz.)	200	20	½	20	4	0.5	0	290	11
egg										
medium	1 (2 oz.)	158	30	2	6	1	0.0	14	286	1
large	1 (3.7 oz.)	292	56	4	11	2	0.5	25	530	2
plain										
mini	2 (0.9 oz.)	140	27	2	5	1	0.0	0	273	1
medium	1 (2 oz.)	156	30	2	6	1	0.0	0	303	1
large	1 (3.7 oz.)	288	56	4	11	2	0.0	0	560	2
low carb, Atkins®	1 (2.5 oz.)	190	18	½	20	5	0.5	0	310	11
Bialys	1 (4 in.)	138	32	2	7	0	0.0	0	333	1
Biscuits										
baking powder, can	1 (2 oz.)	190	23	1½	4	9	2.5	0	600	0
baking powder, hmde.	1 (1.4 oz.)	157	25	1½	4	5	1.0	0	451	0
buttermilk, can	1 (2 oz.)	181	24	1½	4	8	1.5	0	573	0
buttermilk, hmde.	1 (1.4 oz.)	141	18	1	3	6	1.5	1	230	1
Breads										
Boston brown, can	1 oz. slice	55	12	1	1	0	0.0	0	179	1
challah/egg	1 oz. slice	81	14	1	3	2	0.5	14	139	1
cracked wheat	1 oz. slice	74	14	1	2	1	0.5	0	153	2
French/Vienna	1 oz. slice	78	15	1	2	1	0.0	0	173	1
fruit	1 oz. slice	92	16	1	1	3	0.5	12	71	0

BREADS & BREAD PRODUCTS
Breads & Muffins

ITEM	AMOUNT	CALORIES	CARBOHYDRATE (g)	CARBOHYDRATE CHOICES	PROTEIN (g)	FAT (g)	SATURATED FAT (g)	CHOLESTEROL (mg)	SODIUM (mg)	FIBER (g)
Breads *(continued)*										
garlic	1 (2 in.)	160	19	1	6	7	2.0	10	260	2
Irish soda	1 oz. slice	82	16	1	2	1	0.5	5	113	1
Italian	1 oz. slice	77	14	1	2	1	0.0	0	166	1
low carb, multigrain, Atkins®	1 oz. slice	70	7	½	7	2	0.0	0	120	4
low carb, white, Atkins®	1 oz. slice	60	8	0	7	1	0.5	5	115	5
low protein	1 oz. slice	73	15	1	0	1	0.0	1	6	2
multigrain	1 oz. slice	71	13	1	3	1	0.0	0	138	2
oatmeal	1 oz. slice	76	14	1	2	1	0.0	0	170	1
pita, white	1 (6 in.)	165	33	2	5	1	0.0	0	322	1
pita, whole wheat	1 (6 in.)	170	35	2	6	2	0.5	0	340	5
pumpernickel	1 oz. slice	71	13	1	2	1	0.0	0	190	2
raisin	1 oz. slice	78	15	1	2	1	0.5	0	111	1
rye	1 oz. slice	73	14	1	2	1	0.0	0	187	2
sourdough	1 oz. slice	78	15	1	2	1	0.0	0	173	1
wheatberry	1 oz. slice	75	13	1	2	1	0.0	0	149	1
white	1 oz. slice	82	14	1	3	1	0.5	0	164	0
white, light	0.8 oz. slice	40	10	½	2	0	0.0	0	130	3
whole wheat	1 oz. slice	70	13	1	3	1	0.5	0	149	2
whole wheat, light	0.8 oz. slice	40	9	½	3	0	0.0	0	120	3
Breadsticks, soft	1 (2 oz.)	150	28	2	7	2	0.5	0	290	1
Cornbread	1 (2 oz.)	178	27	2	4	6	1.5	35	441	1
Croissants	1 (2 oz.)	230	26	2	5	12	6.5	38	422	1
English muffins										
plain	1 medium	134	26	2	4	1	0.0	0	264	2
raisin	1 medium	139	28	2	4	2	0.0	0	255	2
whole wheat	1 medium	127	26	2	5	1	0.0	0	218	3
Melba toast	4	78	15	1	2	1	0.0	0	166	1
Muffins										
banana nut	1 (2 oz.)	190	29	2	3	7	1.5	5	370	1
blueberry	1 (2 oz.)	158	27	2	3	4	1.0	17	255	1
bran	1 (2 oz.)	153	27	2	4	4	0.5	0	223	3
chocolate chip	1 (2 oz.)	184	26	2	4	7	2.5	23	117	1
corn	1 (2 oz.)	173	29	2	3	5	1.0	15	295	2
cranberry nut	1 (2 oz.)	157	27	2	3	4	0.5	17	253	1
lemon poppy seed	1 (2 oz.)	215	34	2	4	8	2.0	24	263	1
low carb, Atkins®	1 (3.5 oz.)	210	17	1	14	10	1.0	0	380	6
pumpkin	1 (2 oz.)	177	33	2	2	4	0.5	26	78	1
Popovers	1 (2 oz.)	146	14	1	5	8	4.0	97	116	0
Rolls										
brown & serve	1 medium	84	14	1	2	2	0.5	0	146	1
crescent	1 medium	110	11	1	2	6	1.5	0	220	0

BREADS & BREAD PRODUCTS
Breads & Muffins

ITEM	AMOUNT	CALORIES	CARBOHYDRATE (g)	CARBOHYDRATE CHOICES	PROTEIN (g)	FAT (g)	SATURATED FAT (g)	CHOLESTEROL (mg)	SODIUM (mg)	FIBER (g)
Rolls *(continued)*										
French	1 medium	105	19	1	3	2	0.5	0	231	1
hamburger/hotdog	1 medium	123	22	1½	4	2	0.5	0	241	1
hard	1 medium	167	30	2	6	2	0.5	0	310	1
kaiser	1 medium	167	30	2	6	2	0.5	0	310	1
rye	1 medium	81	15	1	3	1	0.0	0	253	2
sesame seed	1 medium	140	23	1½	5	3	1.5	0	240	1
sourdough	1 medium	123	23	1½	4	1	0.5	0	274	1
submarine	1 (8 in.)	220	44	3	7	2	0.0	0	460	2
whole wheat	1 medium	75	14	1	2	1	0.0	0	136	2
yeast	1 medium	90	17	1	2	2	0.5	0	130	0
Scones										
commercial	1 large	304	39	2½	8	13	4.0	100	346	1
hmde.	1 medium	150	18	1	4	6	2.0	49	171	1
Bread Products										
Corn fritters	1 (2 oz.)	117	14	1	3	6	2.0	5	279	1
Crêpes	1 (3.5 oz.)	230	22	1½	9	11	3.0	161	77	1
Croutons	¼ cup	47	6	½	1	2	0.5	1	124	1
French toast										
frzn.	1 slice	126	19	1	4	4	1.0	48	292	1
hmde.	1 slice	149	16	1	5	7	2.0	75	311	1
Lefse	1 (2 oz.)	150	30	2	4	2	0.0	0	330	2
Pancakes										
blueberry, mix	2 (4 in.)	169	22	1½	5	7	1.5	43	313	1
buttermilk, mix	2 (4 in.)	173	22	1½	5	7	1.5	44	397	1
plain, frzn.	2 (4 in.)	140	27	2	4	2	0.5	13	373	1
plain, hmde.	2 (4 in.)	173	22	1½	5	7	1.5	45	334	1
plain, lowfat, frzn.	2 (4 in.)	127	23	1½	4	1	0.5	20	253	1
whole wheat, mix	2 (4 in.)	183	26	2	7	6	1.5	54	503	2
Pizza crusts, Boboli®	1 (8 in.)	400	62	4	14	10	2.0	0	800	2
Pretzels, soft										
shopping mall type	1 large	390	84	5½	12	1	0.0	0	1100	3
Super Pretzel®, frzn.	1 medium	180	36	2½	6	1	0.0	0	930	2
Stuffing										
bread, hmde.	½ cup	178	22	1½	3	9	1.5	0	543	3
cornbread, box	½ cup	179	22	1½	3	9	2.0	0	455	3
Stove Top®, box										
reduced sodium	½ cup	180	21	1½	4	9	2.0	0	350	0
regular	½ cup	170	21	1½	4	9	2.0	0	520	0
Taco shells, hard	1 (5 in.)	65	9	½	1	3	0.5	0	95	1
Tortillas										
corn	1 (6 in.)	58	12	1	1	1	0.0	0	42	1

BREADS & BREAD PRODUCTS
Bread Products

ITEM	AMOUNT	CALORIES	CARBOHYDRATE (g)	CARBOHYDRATE CHOICES	PROTEIN (g)	FAT (g)	SATURATED FAT (g)	CHOLESTEROL (mg)	SODIUM (mg)	FIBER (g)
Tortillas *(continued)*										
flour	1 (8 in.)	146	25	1½	4	3	0.5	0	249	1
Waffles										
Belgian, mix	1 (3.6 oz.)	370	47	3	8	17	9.0	130	1020	1
Blueberry Eggo®, frzn.	1 (1.3 oz.)	100	15	1	2	4	1.0	20	205	1
Homestyle Eggo®, frzn.	1 (1.3 oz.)	90	15	1	3	4	1.0	20	220	1
plain, frzn.	1 (1.3 oz.)	80	15	1	2	1	0.5	0	210	1
plain, hmde.	1 (2.5 oz.)	218	25	1½	6	11	2.0	52	383	1
plain, lowfat, frzn.	1 (1.3 oz.)	80	15	1	2	1	0.5	0	210	1

CANDY
Almonds

ITEM	AMOUNT	CALORIES	CARBOHYDRATE (g)	CARBOHYDRATE CHOICES	PROTEIN (g)	FAT (g)	SATURATED FAT (g)	CHOLESTEROL (mg)	SODIUM (mg)	FIBER (g)
candy-coated	10	200	29	2	4	7	0.5	0	5	1
chocolate covered	10	169	15	1	3	12	4.0	0	12	2
Bridge mix	¼ cup	180	27	2	2	9	4.5	5	35	0
Butterfinger BB's®	¼ cup	190	30	2	2	8	5.0	0	75	0
Cadbury Eggs®, creme	1 (1.4 oz.)	170	28	2	2	6	3.5	0	25	0
Candy bars, average size										
3 Musketeers®	1 (2.13 oz.)	260	46	3	2	8	4.5	5	110	1
5th Avenue®	1 (2 oz.)	280	35	2	5	13	3.5	0	125	2
100 Grand®	1 (1.5 oz.)	190	30	2	1	8	5.0	5	85	0
Almond Joy®	1 (1.76 oz.)	240	29	2	2	13	9.0	0	70	2
Baby Ruth®	1 (2.1 oz.)	280	38	2½	4	14	8.0	0	130	1
Bit-o-Honey®	1 (1.7 oz.)	190	40	2½	1	4	2.0	0	125	0
Butterfinger®	1 (2.1 oz.)	270	44	3	3	11	6.0	0	120	1
Caramello®	1 (1.6 oz.)	210	29	2	3	9	6.0	10	55	0
Chunky®	1 (1.4 oz.)	200	24	1½	3	12	6.0	5	15	1
Clark®	1 (1.75 oz.)	220	37	2½	3	8	4.0	0	70	2
Heath Bar®	1 (1.4 oz.)	210	24	1½	1	12	5.0	10	135	0
Hershey's®, w/ almonds	1 (1.45 oz.)	230	20	1	5	14	7.0	5	35	1
Hershey's® milk chocolate	1 (1.55 oz.)	230	25	1½	3	13	9.0	10	40	1
Kit Kat®	1 (1.5 oz.)	220	27	2	3	11	7.0	5	25	0
Mars®	1 (1.76 oz.)	240	31	2	3	13	4.5	5	70	1
Milky Way®	1 (2.05 oz.)	270	41	3	2	10	5.0	5	95	1
Milky Way® lite	1 (1.57 oz.)	170	34	2	2	5	3.0	5	75	0
Mounds®	1 (1.75 oz.)	240	29	2	2	13	10.0	0	70	2
Mr. Goodbar®	1 (1.75 oz.)	270	27	2	5	16	7.0	5	20	2
Nestle's Crunch®	1 (1.55 oz.)	230	29	2	2	12	7.0	10	65	0
Oh Henry!®	1 (1.8 oz.)	240	32	2	4	10	5.0	0	120	1
Pay Day®	1 (1.85 oz.)	260	27	2	6	14	2.0	0	180	2
Pearson's® nut roll	1 (1.8 oz.)	240	27	2	8	11	2.0	0	170	2
Skor®	1 (1.4 oz.)	220	24	1½	1	13	7.0	20	125	0

CANDY

ITEM	AMOUNT	CALORIES	CARBOHYDRATE (g)	CARBOHYDRATE CHOICES	PROTEIN (g)	FAT (g)	SATURATED FAT (g)	CHOLESTEROL (mg)	SODIUM (mg)	FIBER (g)
Candy bars, average size *(continued)*										
Snickers®	1 (2.07 oz.)	280	35	2	4	14	5.0	5	140	1
Twix®	1 (2 oz.)	280	37	2½	3	14	5.0	5	115	1
Whatchamacallit®	1 (1.6 oz.)	230	28	2	4	11	8.0	5	135	0
Candy corn	24	150	37	2½	0	0	0.0	0	110	0
Caramels	6	160	26	2	1	6	4.5	0	70	0
Cherries, chocolate covered	2	110	18	1	0	4	2.5	0	15	2
Circus peanuts	6	163	41	3	0	0	0.0	0	0	0
Cotton candy	1 oz.	120	30	2	0	0	0.0	0	0	0
Divinity, hmde.	2 (0.4 oz.)	77	20	1	0	0	0.0	0	34	0
Dots®	12	150	37	2½	0	0	0.0	0	20	0
Ferrero Rocher®	3	220	17	1	4	15	5.0	0	35	1
Fondant	2 (0.5 oz.)	101	26	2	0	0	0.0	0	11	0
Fudge, hmde.										
chocolate, w/ nuts	1 oz.	121	21	1½	1	5	1.5	4	17	0
chocolate, w/o nuts	1 oz.	108	23	1½	0	2	1.5	4	18	0
vanilla, w/ nuts	1 oz.	118	21	1½	1	4	1.0	4	17	0
vanilla, w/o nuts	1 oz.	105	23	1½	0	2	1.0	5	19	0
Goobers®	¼ cup	220	21	1½	5	14	5.0	5	15	2
Good & Plenty®	33	130	33	2	0	0	0.0	0	90	0
Gum, regular/sugar free	1 stick	10	3	0	0	0	0.0	0	0	0
Gumdrops	10	139	36	2½	0	0	0.0	0	16	0
Gummy bears	15	130	30	2	3	0	0.0	0	10	0
Hard candies										
regular	3 small	35	9	½	0	0	0.0	0	3	0
sugar free	3 small	34	8	½	0	0	0.0	0	0	0
Hershey's Hugs®	9	220	23	1½	3	13	8.0	10	35	0
Hershey's Kisses®	9	230	24	1½	3	13	8.0	10	35	1
Hot Tamales®	19	150	36	2½	0	0	0.0	0	15	0
Jelly beans	35 small	140	37	2½	0	0	0.0	0	15	0
Jolly Rancher®	3	70	17	1	0	0	0.0	0	10	0
Junior® mints	22	210	44	3	0	4	2.5	0	10	0
Licorice, black/red	3 (8 in.)	120	27	2	1	1	0.0	0	85	0
Lifesavers®	2	20	5	0	0	0	0.0	0	0	0
Lollipops										
Blow Pop®	1	60	14	1	0	0	0.0	0	0	0
Dum Dums®	1	30	7	½	0	0	0.0	0	10	0
Safe-T-Pop®	1	43	11	1	0	0	0.0	0	0	0
Tootsie Pop®	1	60	16	1	0	0	0.0	0	10	0
M&M's®										
crispy	52	200	31	2	2	8	5.0	5	60	1
peanut	18	250	30	2	5	13	5.0	5	25	2

CANDY

ITEM	AMOUNT	CALORIES	CARBOHYDRATE (g)	CARBOHYDRATE CHOICES	PROTEIN (g)	FAT (g)	SATURATED FAT (g)	CHOLESTEROL (mg)	SODIUM (mg)	FIBER (g)
M&M's® *(continued)*										
plain	52	240	34	2	2	10	6.0	5	30	1
Malted milk balls	10	180	32	2	1	6	5.0	0	75	0
Marshmallows	4 large	90	23	1½	0	0	0.0	0	30	0
Mary Janes®	7	160	31	2	1	4	1.5	0	45	0
Mike and Ike®	19	150	36	2½	0	0	0.0	0	15	0
Milk Duds®	13	170	28	2	1	6	2.5	0	85	0
Mints										
Altoids®	3	10	2	0	0	0	0.0	0	0	0
Breath Savers®	1	5	2	0	0	0	0.0	0	0	0
butter	6	51	12	1	0	0	0.0	0	21	0
Nips®, caramel	2	60	11	1	0	2	1.0	0	40	0
Orange slices	3	150	38	2½	0	0	0.0	0	15	0
Peanut brittle	½ cup	180	30	2	4	5	1.0	0	130	1
Peanuts, chocolate covered	¼ cup	193	18	1	5	12	5.5	3	15	2
Peeps®	4 bunnies	130	32	2	1	0	0.0	0	15	0
Pez®	12	35	9	½	0	0	0.0	0	0	0
Praline, hmde.	1 (1.4 oz.)	173	22	1½	1	10	3.0	10	40	1
Raisinets®	¼ cup	190	31	2	2	8	5.0	0	15	1
Raisins, yogurt covered	¼ cup	188	35	2	2	6	5.0	0	21	1
Red Raspberry Dollars®	15	140	34	2	0	0	0.0	0	0	0
Reese's Peanut Butter Cups®	2 (0.8 oz.)	250	25	1½	5	14	5.0	0	140	1
Reese's Pieces®	55	220	26	2	5	11	7.0	0	80	1
Rolo®	7	210	29	2	2	9	6.0	5	80	0
Skittles®	¼ cup	170	37	2½	0	2	0.0	0	5	0
Sour Patch Kids®	16	140	36	2½	0	0	0.0	0	30	0
Starburst®	12	240	48	3	0	5	1.0	0	0	0
Sugar Babies®	30	180	39	2½	0	2	0.0	0	70	0
Sugar Daddy®	1 (1.7 oz.)	200	43	3	1	3	0.5	0	100	0
Swedish Fish®										
small	26 (1 inch)	200	51	3½	0	0	0.0	0	40	0
medium	7 (2 inch)	160	41	3	0	0	0.0	0	25	0
Sweet Escapes, Hershey's®										
caramel & peanut butter bar	1 (0.7 oz.)	80	13	1	1	3	1.0	0	70	0
caramel fudge bar	1 (0.7 oz.)	70	13	1	0	2	1.0	0	50	0
chocolate wafer bar	1 (0.7 oz.)	80	13	1	0	3	1.5	0	30	0
Sweet Tarts®	8 small	60	14	1	0	0	0.0	0	0	0
Taffy										
Air Heads®	1 (4 inch)	60	15	1	0	0	0.0	0	5	0
saltwater	8 small	150	36	2½	0	1	1.0	0	10	0
Tic Tac®	2	3	0	0	0	0	0.0	0	0	0
Toblerone®	4 triangles	170	21	1½	2	9	5.0	10	15	0

CANDY

ITEM	AMOUNT	CALORIES	CARBOHYDRATE (g)	CARBOHYDRATE CHOICES	PROTEIN (g)	FAT (g)	SATURATED FAT (g)	CHOLESTEROL (mg)	SODIUM (mg)	FIBER (g)
Tootsie Roll®	6 small	160	33	2	0	3	0.5	0	40	0
Truffles	1 (0.4 oz.)	73	5	0	1	6	4.0	2	7	0
Turtles	2 (0.6 oz.)	160	20	1	2	9	3.0	5	40	0
Whoppers®	18	190	30	2	1	7	7.0	0	100	0
York Peppermint Pattie®	1 (1.4 oz.)	160	32	2	0	3	1.5	0	10	0

CEREAL BARS & CEREALS *(Manufacturer's suggested serving.)*
Cereal Bars

ITEM	AMOUNT	CALORIES	CARBOHYDRATE (g)	CARBOHYDRATE CHOICES	PROTEIN (g)	FAT (g)	SATURATED FAT (g)	CHOLESTEROL (mg)	SODIUM (mg)	FIBER (g)
Crunchy granola										
cinnamon	1 bar	90	15	1	2	3	0.5	0	80	1
maple brown sugar	1 bar	90	15	1	2	3	0.5	0	80	1
oats 'n honey	1 bar	90	15	1	2	3	0.5	0	80	1
peanut butter	1 bar	90	15	1	3	3	0.5	0	85	1
Fruit & Oatmeal										
apple crisp	1 bar	130	26	2	1	3	0.0	0	90	1
iced raspberry	1 bar	130	26	2	1	3	0.0	0	100	1
strawberry	1 bar	130	26	2	1	3	0.0	0	120	0
Kashi® GoLean® Crunchy!										
chocolate caramel karma	1 bar	160	26	1½	8	3	2.0	20	180	5
chocolate peanut bliss	1 bar	170	30	1½	9	4	1.5	0	220	5
sublime lemon lime	1 bar	160	32	2	9	3	2.0	0	150	5
Milk & Cereal										
Cinnamon Toast Crunch®	1 bar	180	31	2	6	4	1.5	0	180	1
Cocoa Puffs®	1 bar	160	26	2	6	4	1.5	0	130	1
Froot Loops®	1 bar	100	16	1	2	3	2.0	0	75	0
Frosted Flakes®	1 bar	110	19	1	2	3	2.5	0	90	0
Honey Nut Cheerio's®	1 bar	160	26	2	6	4	1.5	0	150	1
Nutri-Grain®										
blueberry	1 bar	140	27	2	2	3	0.5	0	110	1
Strawberry	1 bar	140	27	2	2	3	0.5	0	110	1
Nutri-Grain® Twists™										
apple cobbler	1 bar	140	27	2	1	3	0.5	0	105	1
cappuccino & creme	1 bar	140	26	2	1	3	0.5	0	90	1
Power Bar®	1 bar	230	45	3	9	2	0.5	0	90	3
Quaker Chewy® granola										
apple berry	1 bar	110	23	1½	1	2	0.5	0	80	1
Baby Ruth®	1 bar	120	22	1½	2	3	1.0	0	75	0
chocolate chip	1 bar	120	21	1½	2	4	1.5	0	70	1
cookies 'n cream	1 bar	110	22	1½	2	3	0.5	0	80	1
oatmeal raisin	1 bar	110	22	1½	1	2	0.5	0	105	1
peanut butter	1 bar	110	18	1	2	4	0.5	0	105	1
S'mores®	1 bar	110	22	1½	1	2	0.5	0	80	1

CEREAL BARS & CEREALS

Cereal Bars

ITEM	AMOUNT	CALORIES	CARBOHYDRATE (g)	CARBOHYDRATE CHOICES	PROTEIN (g)	FAT (g)	SATURATED FAT (g)	CHOLESTEROL (mg)	SODIUM (mg)	FIBER (g)
Rice Krispies Treats®										
double chocolatey chunk	1 bar	100	15	1	1	4	2.0	0	75	0
original	1 bar	90	18	1	1	2	0.5	0	100	0
Special K®										
blueberry	1 bar	90	18	1	2	2	1.0	0	100	0
strawberry	1 bar	90	18	1	2	2	1.0	0	100	0
Cooked Cereals, prepared w/ water										
Coco Wheats®	1 cup	114	23	1½	4	1	0.0	0	9	1
Cream of Rice®	1 cup	170	38	2½	3	0	0.0	0	0	0
Cream of Wheat®	1 cup	120	25	1½	3	0	0.0	0	90	1
Farina®	1 cup	120	22	1½	3	0	0.0	0	0	0
Grits, corn										
instant	1 pkt.	100	22	1½	2	0	0.0	0	310	1
old fashioned	1 cup	140	32	2	3	1	0.0	0	0	2
quick	1 cup	130	29	2	3	0	0.0	0	0	2
Malt-O-Meal®	1 cup	120	26	2	5	1	0.0	0	0	1
Maypo®	1 cup	180	35	2	5	3	0.5	0	120	4
Oat bran	1 cup	150	25	1	7	3	0.5	0	0	6
Oatmeal										
baked apple, instant	1 pkt.	150	31	2	3	2	0.0	0	230	3
cinnamon roll, instant	1 pkt.	160	33	2	3	3	0.5	0	240	3
maple & brown sugar, instant	1 pkt.	160	32	2	4	2	0.0	0	260	3
raisins & spice, instant	1 pkt.	150	33	2	3	2	0.5	0	240	3
regular, instant	1 pkt.	100	19	1	4	2	0.0	0	80	3
regular, old fashioned/quick	1 cup	150	27	2	5	3	0.5	0	0	4
Wheatena®	1 cup	160	33	2	5	1	0.0	0	0	5
Ready To Eat Cereals										
100% Bran®	⅓ cup	80	23	1	4	1	0.0	0	120	8
All-Bran®										
extra fiber	½ cup	50	20	½	3	1	0.0	0	120	13
original	½ cup	80	23	1	4	1	0.0	0	65	10
Alpha-Bits®										
marshmallow	1 cup	120	27	2	2	1	0.0	0	180	1
original	1 cup	130	27	2	3	2	0.0	0	210	1
Amaranth flakes	¾ cup	100	24	1½	3	0	0.0	0	90	4
Apple Jacks®	1 cup	130	30	2	1	1	0.0	0	150	1
Banana Nut Crunch®	1 cup	240	44	2½	5	6	0.5	0	230	5
Basic 4®	1 cup	200	42	3	4	3	0.0	0	320	3
Blueberry Morning®	1 ¼ cups	230	48	3	4	4	0.0	0	240	2
Bran flakes	¾ cup	100	24	1	3	1	0.0	0	210	5
Cap'n Crunch®										
Crunch Berries®	¾ cup	100	22	1½	1	2	0.5	0	180	1

CEREAL BARS & CEREALS
Ready to Eat Cereals

ITEM	AMOUNT	CALORIES	CARBOHYDRATE (g)	CARBOHYDRATE CHOICES	PROTEIN (g)	FAT (g)	SATURATED FAT (g)	CHOLESTEROL (mg)	SODIUM (mg)	FIBER (g)
Cap'n Crunch® (continued)										
original	¾ cup	110	23	1½	1	2	0.5	0	200	1
Peanut Butter Crunch®	¾ cup	110	21	1½	2	3	0.5	0	200	1
Cheerios®										
apple cinnamon	¾ cup	120	25	1½	2	2	0.0	0	120	1
Berry Burst®	1 cup	110	24	1½	3	2	0.0	0	170	2
frosted	1 cup	120	25	1½	2	1	0.0	0	210	1
honey nut	1 cup	120	24	1½	3	2	0.0	0	270	2
multi-grain	1 cup	110	24	1½	3	1	0.0	0	200	3
original	1 cup	110	22	1½	3	2	0.0	0	280	3
Chex®										
corn	1 cup	110	26	2	2	0	0.0	0	280	0
multi-bran	1 cup	200	49	3	4	2	0.0	0	380	8
rice	1 ¼ cups	120	27	2	2	0	0.0	0	290	0
wheat	1 cup	180	40	2	5	1	0.0	0	420	5
Cinnamon Toast Crunch®	¾ cup	130	24	1½	1	4	0.5	0	210	1
Cocoa Pebbles®	¾ cup	120	25	1½	1	1	1.0	0	180	0
Cocoa Puffs®	1 cup	120	26	2	1	1	0.0	0	170	0
Cocoa Rice Krispies®	¾ cup	120	27	2	1	1	0.5	0	190	1
Cookie Crisp®	1 cup	120	26	2	1	1	0.0	0	180	0
Corn flakes	1 cup	100	24	1½	2	0	0.0	0	200	1
Corn Pops®	1 cup	120	28	2	1	0	0.0	0	120	0
Cracklin' Oat Bran®	¾ cup	200	35	2	4	7	2.0	0	140	5
Cranberry Almond Crunch®	1 cup	210	43	3	4	3	0.0	0	190	3
Crispix®	1 cup	110	25	1½	2	0	0.0	0	210	0
Crunchy Oatmeal Squares	1 cup	230	48	3	6	3	0.5	0	260	5
Fiber One®	½ cup	60	24	½	2	1	0.0	0	130	14
Froot Loops®	1 cup	120	28	2	1	1	0.5	0	150	1
Frosted Flakes®	¾ cup	120	28	2	1	0	0.0	0	150	1
Fruit & Fibre®										
dates, raisins & walnuts	1 cup	200	42	2½	4	3	0.0	0	260	6
peaches, raisins & almonds	1 cup	190	42	2½	4	3	0.0	0	260	6
Fruity Pebbles®	¾ cup	110	24	1½	0	1	1.0	0	160	0
Golden Crisp®	¾ cup	110	25	1½	2	0	0.0	0	25	0
Golden Grahams®	¾ cup	120	25	1½	1	1	0.0	0	270	1
Granola										
lowfat	½ cup	190	39	2½	4	3	0.5	0	120	3
lowfat, w/ raisins	½ cup	170	36	2½	4	2	0.0	0	115	2
regular	½ cup	220	32	2	5	9	4.0	0	25	4
regular, w/ raisins	½ cup	220	35	2	5	8	3.5	0	25	3
Grape-nuts®										
flakes	¾ cup	110	24	1½	3	1	0.0	0	125	3

CEREAL BARS & CEREALS
Ready to Eat Cereals

ITEM	AMOUNT	CALORIES	CARBOHYDRATE (g)	CARBOHYDRATE CHOICES	PROTEIN (g)	FAT (g)	SATURATED FAT (g)	CHOLESTEROL (mg)	SODIUM (mg)	FIBER (g)
Grape-nuts® *(continued)*										
O's™	1 cup	120	28	2	3	0	0.0	0	160	2
original	½ cup	210	47	3	6	1	0.0	0	340	5
Great Grains®										
crunchy pecan	½ cup	220	38	2½	5	6	1.0	0	200	4
raisins, dates, pecans	½ cup	200	39	2½	4	5	0.5	0	135	4
Harmony™	1 ¼ cups	200	44	3	5	1	0.0	0	350	2
Honey Bunches of Oats®										
original	¾ cup	120	25	1½	2	2	0.0	0	170	2
w/ almonds	¾ cup	130	25	1½	3	3	0.0	0	170	2
Honeycomb®	1 ⅓ cups	110	26	2	2	1	0.0	0	220	0
Just Right®, fruit & nut	1 cup	220	49	3	4	2	0.0	0	280	3
Kashi®										
GoLean®	¾ cup	120	28	1	8	1	0.0	0	35	10
GoLean® Crunch!	1 cup	190	36	2	9	3	0.0	0	95	8
Good Friends™	¾ cup	90	24	1	3	1	0.0	0	70	8
Good Friends™ Cinna-Raisin Crunch	1 cup	150	39	2	4	2	0.0	0	95	10
Heart to Heart™	¾ cup	110	25	1	4	2	0.0	0	90	5
Honey Puffed	1 cup	120	25	1½	3	1	0.0	0	6	2
Medley	¾ cup	120	26	2	3	1	0.0	0	60	3
Pillows	¾ cup	200	45	3	3	1	0.0	0	50	2
Kix®										
berry berry	¾ cup	120	25	1½	1	2	0.0	0	180	0
original	1 ⅓ cups	120	26	2	2	1	0.0	0	270	1
Life®	¾ cup	120	25	1½	3	2	0.0	0	160	2
Lucky Charms®	1 cup	120	25	1½	2	1	0.0	0	210	1
Mini-Wheats®										
frosted, big bite	5 biscuits	180	41	2½	5	1	0.0	0	5	5
frosted, bite size	24 biscuits	200	48	3	6	1	0.0	0	5	6
raisin	¾ cup	180	42	2½	5	1	0.0	0	5	5
strawberry	¾ cup	170	40	2	4	1	0.0	0	15	5
Mueslix®	⅔ cup	200	40	2½	5	3	0.0	0	170	4
Oat bran flakes	¾ cup	110	23	1½	3	1	0.0	0	210	4
Oatmeal Crisp®, raisin	1 cup	210	44	3	5	2	0.0	0	220	4
Oreo O's®	¾ cup	110	22	1½	1	2	0.5	0	90	0
Organic flax cereal	¾ cup	190	38	2	6	3	0.0	0	80	6
Organic oat bran flakes	¾ cup	110	23	1½	3	1	0.0	0	90	4
Product 19®	1 cup	100	25	1½	2	0	0.0	0	210	1
Puffed rice	1 cup	50	12	1	1	0	0.0	0	0	0
Puffed wheat	1 ¼ cups	50	11	1	2	0	0.0	0	0	1
Raisin bran	1 cup	190	46	2½	4	1	0.0	0	360	8

CEREAL BARS & CEREALS
Ready to Eat Cereals

ITEM	AMOUNT	CALORIES	CARBOHYDRATE (g)	CARBOHYDRATE CHOICES	PROTEIN (g)	FAT (g)	SATURATED FAT (g)	CHOLESTEROL (mg)	SODIUM (mg)	FIBER (g)
Raisin Bran Crunch®	1 cup	190	45	3	3	1	0.0	0	210	4
Raisin nut bran	½ cup	200	41	3	4	4	0.5	0	250	4
Reese's® Puffs®	½ cup	130	23	1½	2	3	0.5	0	170	0
Rice Krispies®	1 ¼ cups	120	29	2	2	0	0.0	0	320	0
Rice Krispies Treats®	¾ cup	120	26	2	1	2	0.0	0	190	0
Shredded Wheat										
frosted, Spoon Size®	1 cup	180	43	2½	4	1	0.0	0	5	5
original	2 biscuits	160	36	2	5	1	0.0	0	0	6
Wheat 'N Bran, Spoon Size®	1 ¼ cups	200	47	2½	7	1	0.0	0	0	8
Smacks®	¾ cup	100	24	1½	2	1	0.0	0	50	1
Smart Start®	1 cup	180	43	3	3	1	0.0	0	280	2
Special K®										
original	1 cup	110	22	1½	7	0	0.0	0	220	0
red berries	1 cup	110	25	1½	4	0	0.0	0	220	1
Total®										
flakes	1 ⅓ cups	110	24	1½	2	0	0.0	0	210	0
raisin bran	1 cup	170	41	2½	4	1	0.0	0	250	5
whole grain	¾ cup	110	23	1½	2	1	0.0	0	190	3
Trix®	1 cup	120	27	2	1	1	0.0	0	190	1
Waffle Crisp®	1 cup	120	25	1½	2	3	0.0	0	115	0
Wheat bran flakes	¾ cup	90	23	1	3	1	0.0	0	210	5
Wheat germ	2 T.	50	6	½	4	1	0.0	0	0	2
Wheaties®										
Energy Crunch™	1 cup	210	42	3	6	3	0.0	0	310	4
original	1 cup	110	24	1½	3	1	0.0	0	220	3

CHEESE

ITEM	AMOUNT	CALORIES	CARBOHYDRATE (g)	CARBOHYDRATE CHOICES	PROTEIN (g)	FAT (g)	SATURATED FAT (g)	CHOLESTEROL (mg)	SODIUM (mg)	FIBER (g)
American										
fat free	1 oz.	45	4	0	6	0	0.0	7	403	0
reduced fat	1 oz.	51	1	0	7	2	1.5	10	405	0
regular	1 oz.	106	0	0	6	9	5.5	27	405	0
American, singles										
fat free	1 slice	30	2	0	5	0	0.0	0	280	0
reduced fat	1 slice	50	1	0	4	3	2.0	10	290	0
regular	1 slice	70	2	0	4	5	3.0	20	270	0
Blue	1 oz.	100	1	0	6	8	5.0	25	390	0
Brick	1 oz.	105	1	0	7	8	5.5	27	159	0
Brie	1 oz.	95	0	0	6	8	5.0	28	178	0
Camembert	1 oz.	85	0	0	6	7	4.5	20	239	0
Caraway	1 oz.	107	1	0	7	8	5.5	26	196	0
Cheddar										
fat free	1 oz.	40	3	0	7	0	0.0	0	413	0

CHEESE

ITEM	AMOUNT	CALORIES	CARBOHYDRATE (g)	CARBOHYDRATE CHOICES	PROTEIN (g)	FAT (g)	SATURATED FAT (g)	CHOLESTEROL (mg)	SODIUM (mg)	FIBER (g)
Cheddar *(continued)*										
reduced fat	1 oz.	70	1	0	8	5	3.0	15	170	0
regular	1 oz.	110	1	0	7	9	6.0	30	180	0
regular, shredded	¼ cup	114	0	0	7	9	6.0	30	175	0
spread	2 T.	80	1	0	4	7	4.5	22	461	0
Cheez Whiz®	2 T.	90	4	0	3	7	2.5	10	480	0
Colby	1 oz.	110	1	0	7	9	6.0	30	180	0
Colby & Monterey Jack	1 oz.	110	0	0	7	9	5.0	30	180	0
Cottage										
1% fat	½ cup	81	3	0	14	1	0.5	5	459	0
2% fat	½ cup	102	4	0	16	2	1.5	9	459	0
fat free	½ cup	80	6	½	13	0	0.0	5	440	0
Cream										
fat free	2 T.	30	2	0	5	0	0.0	5	200	0
light	2 T.	70	2	0	3	5	3.5	15	150	0
regular	2 T.	101	1	0	2	10	6.5	32	86	0
Cream, flavored										
garden vegetable, regular	2 T.	90	2	0	2	9	6.0	35	150	0
onion & chive, light	2 T.	60	2	0	3	5	3.0	15	170	0
strawberry, light	2 T.	70	6	½	2	4	2.5	15	120	0
Easy Cheese®, cheddar	2 T.	80	2	0	5	6	4.0	20	430	0
Edam	1 oz.	101	0	0	7	8	5.0	25	274	0
Feta	1 oz.	60	1	0	5	5	3.0	10	350	0
Fondue	¼ cup	123	2	0	8	7	4.5	24	71	0
Fontina	1 oz.	98	0	0	6	8	4.0	25	171	0
Goat, soft	1 oz.	76	0	0	5	6	4.0	13	104	0
Gorgonzola	1 oz.	98	1	0	6	8	5.0	30	284	0
Gouda	1 oz.	101	1	0	7	8	5.0	32	232	0
Gruyere	1 oz.	117	0	0	8	9	5.5	31	95	0
Havarti	1 oz.	120	0	0	5	10	7.0	25	150	0
Jarlsberg	1 oz.	100	0	0	7	8	5.0	20	180	0
Limburger	1 oz.	93	0	0	6	8	5.0	26	227	0
Mascarpone	1 oz.	126	1	0	2	13	7.0	36	16	0
Monterey Jack	1 oz.	110	0	0	6	9	6.0	30	190	0
Mozzarella										
part-skim	1 oz.	80	1	0	8	5	3.0	15	180	0
whole milk	1 oz.	90	1	0	6	6	4.0	20	160	0
Muenster	1 oz.	104	0	0	7	9	5.5	27	178	0
Neufchatel	1 oz.	74	1	0	3	7	4.0	22	113	0
Parmesan										
grated	1 T.	30	0	0	3	2	1.5	8	128	0
grated, reduced fat	1 T.	30	3	0	1	1	0.0	0	113	0

CHEESE

ITEM	AMOUNT	CALORIES	CARBOHYDRATE (g)	CARBOHYDRATE CHOICES	PROTEIN (g)	FAT (g)	SATURATED FAT (g)	CHOLESTEROL (mg)	SODIUM (mg)	FIBER (g)
Parmesan *(continued)*										
hard, shredded	1 T.	30	0	0	3	2	1.5	8	113	0
Pepper Jack	1 oz.	110	1	0	7	9	6.0	30	190	0
Port wine, cold pack										
light	2 T.	70	5	0	5	4	2.0	15	190	0
regular	2 T.	90	3	0	5	7	3.0	20	210	0
Provolone	1 oz.	100	1	0	7	8	5.0	20	248	0
Ricotta										
fat free	½ cup	120	10	½	20	0	0.0	0	120	0
lowfat	½ cup	140	6	½	12	6	3.0	32	90	0
part-skim	½ cup	200	4	0	16	12	8.0	60	160	0
whole milk	½ cup	220	4	0	14	16	10.0	60	100	0
Romano, grated	1 T.	20	0	0	1	2	1.0	5	130	0
Roquefort	1 oz.	105	1	0	6	9	5.5	26	513	0
Soy cheese	1 oz.	60	1	0	6	3	0.0	0	390	0
String	1 oz.	80	0	0	7	6	4.0	20	240	0
Swiss										
natural	1 oz.	110	0	0	8	9	5.0	30	50	0
processed	1 oz.	111	0	0	8	9	6.0	30	320	0
Velveeta®										
light	1 oz.	60	4	0	5	3	2.0	15	420	0
regular	1 oz.	80	3	0	5	6	4.0	25	410	0
Yogurt cheese	1 oz.	22	3	0	2	0	0.0	1	22	0

COMBINATION FOODS, FROZEN ENTRÉES & MEALS

(Homemade unless indicated.)

ITEM	AMOUNT	CALORIES	CARBOHYDRATE (g)	CARBOHYDRATE CHOICES	PROTEIN (g)	FAT (g)	SATURATED FAT (g)	CHOLESTEROL (mg)	SODIUM (mg)	FIBER (g)
Bagel Bites®, frzn.										
cheese	4 pieces	200	28	2	8	6	3.0	15	540	2
pepperoni	4 pieces	210	29	2	8	7	3.5	15	580	2
Baked beans, w/ pork, can	½ cup	140	27	1	6	1	0.5	0	460	7
Beans & rice, box	½ cup	110	24	1½	4	0	0.0	0	540	2
Beef goulash, w/ noodles	1 cup	361	27	2	30	14	3.5	95	130	2
Beef Oriental	1 cup	104	12	1	10	2	0.5	12	969	4
Beef stroganoff, w/ noodles	1 cup	344	23	1½	20	19	7.5	74	468	2
Beefaroni®, can	1 cup	260	35	2	10	9	4.5	25	1020	3
Burritos, frzn.										
bean & cheese	1 (6 oz.)	362	53	3½	14	11	5.5	18	1013	4
beef & bean	1 (6 oz.)	386	55	3½	14	12	5.0	18	965	4
chicken & cheese	1 (6 oz.)	199	34	2	8	3	1.5	20	336	3
Casseroles										
chicken & noodles	1 cup	320	32	2	22	11	3.0	81	139	1

COMBINATION FOODS, FROZEN ENTRÉES & MEALS

ITEM	AMOUNT	CALORIES	CARBOHYDRATE (g)	CARBOHYDRATE CHOICES	PROTEIN (g)	FAT (g)	SATURATED FAT (g)	CHOLESTEROL (mg)	SODIUM (mg)	FIBER (g)
Casseroles *(continued)*										
green bean	1 cup	300	22	1½	6	20	6.0	10	1240	4
seafood Newburg	1 cup	613	10	½	30	50	29.5	426	551	0
tuna noodle	1 cup	238	25	1½	17	7	2.0	41	686	1
Chicken cacciatore	6 oz.	320	9	½	29	18	4.5	89	172	1
Chicken cordon bleu	6 oz.	367	8	½	33	22	11.5	140	494	0
Chicken divan	6 oz.	234	6	½	29	10	4.5	97	321	2
Chicken Helper®, box										
chicken & potatoes au gratin	1 cup	270	25	1½	26	7	2.5	65	800	1
chicken & stuffing	1 cup	290	27	2	27	9	2.0	65	820	1
fettuccine Alfredo	1 cup	300	27	2	28	8	2.5	65	800	1
Chicken nuggets, frzn.	4 pieces	210	9	½	11	15	3.5	35	360	1
Chicken parmigiana	6 oz.	299	15	1	27	15	5.0	128	599	1
Chicken tetrazzini	1 cup	366	28	2	19	19	7.0	49	705	2
Chili, w/ beans, can										
beef	1 cup	270	34	2	16	7	3.0	30	1220	7
turkey	1 cup	200	26	1½	17	3	1.0	45	1200	5
Chimichangas, frzn.										
beef	1 (4.5 oz.)	360	37	2½	9	20	5.0	10	470	3
chicken	1 (4.5 oz.)	340	39	2½	11	16	4.0	20	540	2
Chipped beef, creamed	1 cup	327	18	1	18	20	6.0	33	1469	0
Chop suey, can										
beef	1 cup	271	12	1	22	15	3.5	50	924	3
chicken	1 cup	193	10	½	20	8	1.5	50	651	2
pork	1 cup	286	12	1	22	17	4.0	56	926	3
Chow mein, can										
beef	1 cup	271	12	1	22	15	3.5	50	924	3
chicken	1 cup	193	10	½	20	8	1.5	50	651	2
Corn dogs, frzn.	1 (2.7 oz.)	180	15	1	4	12	4.0	15	560	0
Create a Meal!®, stir fry, frzn										
beef & broccoli	1 ⅓ cups	290	15	1	27	13	3.0	60	1150	4
sweet & sour chicken	1 ¼ cups	340	43	3	25	7	1.0	60	620	3
Szechuan chicken	1 ¼ cups	310	20	1	26	14	3.0	60	1390	4
teriyaki chicken	1 ¼ cups	230	18	1	27	6	1.0	55	920	4
Egg rolls										
pork	1 (6 oz.)	220	24	1½	5	11	2.5	10	390	2
shrimp	1 (6 oz.)	180	25	1½	5	7	1.5	15	490	2
Eggplant parmigiana	1 cup	319	17	1	14	22	9.0	55	684	3
Enchiladas										
beef & cheese	1 (6 oz.)	286	27	2	11	16	8.0	36	1169	3
chicken	1 (6 oz.)	193	28	2	10	5	1.5	13	374	3

COMBINATION FOODS, FROZEN ENTRÉES & MEALS

ITEM	AMOUNT	CALORIES	CARBOHYDRATE (g)	CARBOHYDRATE CHOICES	PROTEIN (g)	FAT (g)	SATURATED FAT (g)	CHOLESTEROL (mg)	SODIUM (mg)	FIBER (g)
Fajitas										
beef	1 (6 oz.)	305	27	2	17	14	4.0	34	241	2
chicken	1 (6 oz.)	277	34	2	15	9	1.5	30	262	4
Frozen breakfast bowls, Uncle Bens®										
blueberry pancakes & bacon	1 (6 oz.)	370	66	4½	9	9	2.5	15	910	2
ham, egg & peppers	1 (8.3 oz.)	230	22	1½	17	9	4.5	220	900	3
Frozen breakfasts										
bacon, egg & cheese biscuit	1 (4.2 oz.)	340	24	1½	11	22	8.0	95	750	2
cinnamon French toast,										
w/ sausage	1 (5.5 oz.)	420	46	3	12	21	7.0	100	460	2
egg, ham & cheese bagel	1 (4.5 oz.)	310	35	2	15	12	4.5	135	780	2
pancakes, w/ sausage	1 (6 oz.)	490	52	3½	14	25	11.0	90	950	3
scrambled eggs & bacon,										
w/ home fries	1 (5.3 oz.)	260	17	1	12	17	6.0	265	770	0
scrambled eggs & sausage,										
w/ hashed browns	1 (6.3 oz.)	370	17	1	14	27	9.0	330	670	0
Frozen dinners										
beef tips & gravy	1 (14 oz.)	370	41	2	21	14	4.0	35	1510	8
chicken, barbecue	1 (10 oz.)	330	37	2½	16	13	3.0	50	1210	2
chicken & fettuccini										
Alfredo	1 (16.8 oz.)	570	62	3½	34	21	5.0	50	1420	7
chicken, fried	1 (11.5 oz.)	640	41	3	37	36	8.0	105	1360	2
chicken, Mesquite grilled	1 (10.6 oz.)	380	56	4	23	9	2.5	40	1210	4
chicken Monterey	1 (14.5 oz.)	580	68	4½	29	21	7.0	65	1400	4
chicken parmigiana	1 (16 oz.)	680	63	4	30	34	9.0	55	970	7
chicken teriyaki	1 (11.5 oz.)	340	49	3	20	7	2.0	50	1650	3
fish fillet, breaded	1 (10 oz.)	400	51	3½	16	15	4.0	45	1300	3
meatloaf	1 (17 oz.)	560	38	2	29	32	12.0	95	1420	5
pork rib, boneless	1 (10 oz.)	400	37	2½	17	20	8.0	45	1070	4
Salisbury steak, w/ gravy	1 (16 oz.)	470	49	3	28	18	7.0	60	1010	5
steak, country fried	1 (16 oz.)	670	60	3½	23	37	11.0	40	1690	6
turkey, roasted	1 (11.8 oz.)	420	49	3	22	15	3.5	40	1630	4
veal parmigiana	1 (17.5 oz.)	530	66	4	27	17	4.5	60	1130	7
Frozen dinners, Healthy Choice®										
beef pot roast	1 (11 oz.)	320	39	2	19	9	3.0	45	550	6
roasted chicken, country										
herb	1 (11 oz.)	280	37	2	18	6	2.5	40	600	5
stuffed pasta shells	1 (12 oz.)	380	60	3½	18	6	3.0	20	570	5
Frozen dinners, Lean Cuisine®										
Alfredo pasta primavera	1 (10 oz.)	290	45	3	12	7	3.5	15	560	3
beef portabello	1 (9 oz.)	220	24	1½	14	7	3.5	35	690	2
chicken teriyaki	1 (11.5 oz.)	290	52	3½	16	3	1.0	25	860	3

COMBINATION FOODS, FROZEN ENTRÉES & MEALS

ITEM	AMOUNT	CALORIES	CARBOHYDRATE (g)	CARBOHYDRATE CHOICES	PROTEIN (g)	FAT (g)	SATURATED FAT (g)	CHOLESTEROL (mg)	SODIUM (mg)	FIBER (g)
Frozen dinners, Lean Cuisine® *(continued)*										
penne pasta	1 (11.5 oz.)	270	50	3	9	4	1.0	0	390	5
Frozen dinners, Smart Ones® Bistro Selections™										
chicken carbonara	1 (9.5 oz.)	300	36	2½	21	6	2.0	40	780	2
golden baked garlic chicken	1 (10 oz.)	280	40	2½	19	6	1.5	25	650	3
oven roasted vegetable primavera	1 (10 oz.)	300	46	3	6	8	2.0	10	800	2
pepper steak	1 (10 oz.)	230	32	2	15	5	2.0	30	690	4
Frozen entrées										
chicken à la king	1 (11.5 oz.)	350	45	3	18	11	3.5	45	1150	2
fettuccini Alfredo	1 (11.5 oz.)	520	51	3½	16	28	17.0	80	1090	4
macaroni & beef, w/ tomatoes	1 (11.5 oz.)	350	41	3	20	12	5.0	45	1030	3
manicotti, w/ red sauce	1 (9 oz.)	330	35	2	17	13	8.0	40	810	3
meatloaf	1 (10 oz.)	390	28	2	22	21	11.0	90	840	3
stuffed peppers, w/ beef	1 (15.5 oz.)	200	21	1½	8	9	3.5	25	730	2
Swedish meatballs, w/ pasta	1 (11.5 oz.)	510	43	3	25	26	10.0	100	1150	3
turkey tetrazzini	1 (10 oz.)	370	33	2	20	18	7.0	55	1040	2
Hamburger Helper®, box										
beef pasta	1 cup	280	23	1½	20	12	5.0	60	820	1
cheeseburger macaroni	1 cup	360	32	2	23	16	6.0	65	940	1
four cheese lasagna	1 cup	280	26	2	20	11	4.5	55	850	0
Hot Pockets®, frzn.										
cheeseburger	1 (4.5 oz.)	340	46	3	11	12	4.5	35	570	3
chicken, cheddar & broccoli	1 (4.5 oz.)	300	38	2½	12	11	4.5	30	590	3
ham n' cheese	1 (4.5 oz.)	300	37	2½	12	11	4.5	40	720	2
Lasagna										
w/ meat	6 oz.	272	28	2	16	11	5.5	40	272	2
w/ vegetables	6 oz.	239	31	2	12	7	4.5	25	284	2
Lean Pockets®, frzn.										
pepperoni pizza	1 (4.5 oz.)	280	42	3	14	7	2.5	25	720	4
Philly steak & cheese	1 (4.5 oz.)	280	40	2½	13	7	2.5	25	590	3
turkey, broccoli & cheese	1 (4.5 oz.)	270	39	2½	13	7	2.5	25	530	3
Lo mein, pork	6 oz.	241	18	1	17	12	2.0	36	121	2
Macaroni & cheese										
frzn.	1 cup	330	32	2	15	16	7.0	25	950	2
three cheese, box	1 cup	410	48	3	11	3	1.0	10	610	2
Manicotti, w/ red sauce	2 (5 in.)	330	35	2	17	13	8.0	40	810	3
Meatballs	1 (1 oz.)	60	2	0	5	4	1.5	23	35	0
Meatloaf	3 oz.	182	5	0	14	11	4.0	71	105	0
Moussaka	1 cup	238	13	1	17	13	4.5	97	460	4
Pepper steak	1 cup	320	6	½	28	20	4.0	70	563	1

COMBINATION FOODS, FROZEN ENTRÉES & MEALS

ITEM	AMOUNT	CALORIES	CARBOHYDRATE (g)	CARBOHYDRATE CHOICES	PROTEIN (g)	FAT (g)	SATURATED FAT (g)	CHOLESTEROL (mg)	SODIUM (mg)	FIBER (g)
Pizza, French bread, frzn.										
cheese	1 (5.2 oz.)	370	43	3	14	16	6.0	15	880	3
cheese, Healthy Choice®	1 (6 oz.)	360	57	3½	20	5	1.5	10	600	5
pepperoni	1 (5.6 oz.)	410	47	3	11	20	7.0	25	1020	3
vegetable	1 (6 oz.)	280	44	2½	17	4	1.5	10	480	5
Pizza, frzn.										
cheese	1 (5.2 oz.) slice	360	39	2½	17	15	8.0	30	490	2
pepperoni	1 (5.2 oz.) slice	380	38	2½	17	18	11.0	35	640	2
Pizza Rolls®, frzn.										
cheese	6 rolls	200	26	2	9	7	2.5	10	420	1
pepperoni	6 rolls	230	24	1½	8	11	3.0	10	530	1
Pot pies, frzn.										
beef	1 (7 oz.)	400	42	3	13	21	8.0	60	900	3
beef/chicken, Hungry-Man®	1 cup	520	52	3½	14	29	10.0	40	890	3
chicken	1 (7 oz.)	400	42	3	12	21	8.0	40	880	4
Ravioli, w/ red sauce										
cheese	1 cup	310	41	3	12	11	4.0	20	1150	2
meat	1 cup	352	33	2	19	16	5.5	153	1123	2
Salmon loaf	3 oz.	168	7	½	14	9	2.5	99	410	0
Salmon patties	1 (4.2 oz.)	261	14	1	16	16	3.5	57	506	1
Sandwiches, w/ bread/bun										
BBQ beef	1 (6.8 oz.)	421	43	3	31	13	4.5	70	711	2
BLT, w/ mayo.	1 (4.7 oz.)	341	32	2	11	19	4.5	22	678	2
bologna & cheese	1 (3.9 oz.)	350	28	2	13	20	8.5	35	940	1
cheeseburger	1 (4.9 oz.)	380	28	2	23	19	9.0	65	770	1
chicken, breaded & fried	1 (7.2 oz.)	462	40	2½	26	21	4.5	59	816	2
chicken, broiled	1 (6.5 oz.)	310	30	2	24	10	2.5	50	1040	3
chicken club, w/ mayo.	1 (7.6 oz.)	472	47	3	30	20	4.5	63	935	2
chicken salad, w/ mayo.	1 (4.2 oz.)	395	34	2	11	24	3.0	33	522	2
corned beef & Swiss	1 (5.5 oz.)	427	22	1	28	26	9.5	83	1470	6
egg salad, w/ mayo.	1 (4.4 oz.)	406	34	2	10	26	4.0	165	537	2
grilled cheese	1 (4.5 oz.)	428	32	2	18	25	12.5	57	1240	1
ham & cheese, w/ mustard	1 (5.8 oz.)	446	32	2	25	24	8.5	68	1441	2
ham salad, w/ mayo.	1 (4.9 oz.)	384	39	2½	11	20	4.5	31	997	1
hamburger	1 (4.9 oz.)	290	29	2	17	12	5.0	45	630	2
hot dog	1 (3.5 oz.)	240	19	1	9	14	5.0	25	730	1
peanut butter & jelly	1 (4 oz.)	383	50	3	13	17	3.5	0	472	6
roast beef, w/ mayo.	1 (5.5 oz.)	403	34	2	29	16	3.0	43	1601	1
Rueben, w/ dressing	1 (6.4 oz.)	464	30	2	21	29	10.0	82	1348	3
salami & cheese, w/ mustard	1 (4.1 oz.)	332	28	2	14	18	8.0	40	1113	1
sloppy Joe, beef	1 (6.6 oz.)	358	36	2½	18	15	5.0	46	1008	2
tuna salad, w/ mayo.	1 (4.6 oz.)	350	38	2½	14	15	2.0	14	632	2

COMBINATION FOODS, FROZEN ENTRÉES & MEALS

ITEM	AMOUNT	CALORIES	CARBOHYDRATE (g)	CARBOHYDRATE CHOICES	PROTEIN (g)	FAT (g)	SATURATED FAT (g)	CHOLESTEROL (mg)	SODIUM (mg)	FIBER (g)
Sandwiches, w/ bread/bun *(continued)*										
turkey	1 (5.8 oz.)	316	33	2	27	8	1.0	42	1726	2
Scalloped potatoes & ham	1 cup	252	32	2	13	8	2.5	23	490	2
Shepherd's pie	1 cup	278	32	2	17	9	2.5	37	312	3
Skillet Sensations™, frzn.										
chicken Alfredo	1 cup	250	28	2	15	9	2.5	30	630	1
chicken & grilled vegetables	1 cup	250	26	2	15	9	2.5	30	710	2
homestyle beef	1 cup	170	19	1	11	6	2.5	25	740	2
Skillet Sensations™, Lean Cuisine®, frzn.										
chicken Oriental	1 cup	170	23	1½	12	3	0.5	20	610	2
roasted turkey	1 cup	220	37	2	14	2	0.5	25	790	6
three cheese chicken	1 cup	200	26	2	13	5	2.0	25	460	2
Spaghetti & meatballs	1 cup	370	29	2	19	18	5.0	66	1109	3
SpaghettiO's®, can										
w/ meatballs	1 cup	240	32	2	11	8	3.5	20	990	3
w/ tomato & cheese sauce	1 cup	180	37	2½	6	1	0.5	10	890	3
Stew										
beef, can	1 cup	180	18	1	10	8	3.5	30	920	2
beef, hmde.	6 oz.	158	14	1	8	8	3.5	22	221	2
chicken, can	1 cup	140	19	1	10	3	1.0	20	910	2
turkey, can	1 cup	140	19	1	10	3	1.0	20	910	2
Stuffed cabbage rolls	1 (8.1 oz.)	173	20	1	8	7	1.5	12	607	4
Stuffed green peppers	1 (6.1 oz.)	229	18	1	12	12	5.5	37	233	1
Stuffed shells, w/ red sauce	2 (3 oz.)	388	36	2½	17	21	10.5	100	780	4
Sweet & sour pork	1 cup	231	25	1½	15	8	2.0	39	839	2
Tacos, soft shell										
beef	1 (4 oz.)	289	26	1	19	13	5.5	36	628	7
chicken	1 (4 oz.)	220	23	1½	12	9	3.5	27	531	4
Tamales	1 (2.4 oz.)	107	10	½	2	6	2.5	10	197	2
Tortellini, w/ red sauce										
cheese	1 cup	402	60	3½	16	12	5.0	47	680	5
meat	1 cup	442	44	3	26	17	6.0	240	717	3
Tuna Helper®, box										
au gratin	1 cup	310	38	2½	13	12	3.0	20	920	1
creamy parmesan	1 cup	260	32	2	13	9	2.0	20	900	0
creamy pasta	1 cup	290	32	2	12	13	3.5	15	880	2
Veal Marsala	6 oz.	473	11	1	21	35	15.0	124	254	0
Veal parmigiana	6 oz.	350	21	1½	27	17	6.0	86	1672	2
Veal scallopini	6 oz.	421	3	0	32	30	8.5	114	493	1
Welsh rarebit, frzn.	1 (2.2 oz.)	120	5	0	5	9	4.0	20	280	0
Yorkshire pudding	2 oz.	118	14	1	4	6	2.5	43	335	1
Ziti, w/ meat sauce	6 oz.	272	28	2	16	11	5.5	40	272	2

CONDIMENTS, SAUCES & BAKING INGREDIENTS
Condiments & Sauces

ITEM	AMOUNT	CALORIES	CARBOHYDRATE (g)	CARBOHYDRATE CHOICE	PROTEIN (g)	FAT (g)	SATURATED FAT (g)	CHOLESTEROL (mg)	SODIUM (mg)	FIBER (g)
Alfredo sauce	¼ cup	180	3	0	3	18	7.0	25	600	0
BBQ sauce	1 T.	20	4	0	0	0	0.0	0	212	0
Béarnaise sauce	2 T.	79	2	0	1	8	5.0	58	112	0
Béchamel sauce	2 T.	35	2	0	0	3	2.0	8	287	0
Catsup/ketchup	1 T.	15	4	0	0	0	0.0	0	190	0
Cheese sauce	2 T.	55	2	0	2	4	2.0	9	135	0
Chili sauce	2 T.	30	8	½	0	0	0.0	0	360	0
Chutney	2 T.	52	13	1	0	0	0.0	0	7	1
Clam sauce										
red	½ cup	60	8	½	4	1	0.0	10	350	1
white	½ cup	140	5	0	7	10	1.5	15	510	0
Cocktail sauce	2 T.	30	7	½	1	0	0.0	0	400	1
Cranberry sauce	2 T.	52	13	1	0	0	0.0	0	10	0
Cranberry-orange relish	2 T.	61	16	1	0	0	0.0	0	11	0
Duck sauce	2 T.	80	19	1	0	0	0.0	0	260	0
Enchilada sauce										
green	2 T.	23	2	0	0	2	1.0	5	4	0
red	2 T.	40	1	0	0	4	2.0	11	5	0
Fish sauce	1 T.	6	1	0	1	0	0.0	0	1390	0
Hoisin sauce	1 T.	35	7	½	1	1	0.0	0	258	0
Hollandaise sauce	2 T.	85	0	0	1	9	5.0	90	78	0
Horseradish	1 T.	7	2	0	0	0	0.0	0	47	0
Horseradish sauce	1 T.	30	1	0	0	3	2.0	6	10	0
Lobster sauce	1 T.	24	1	0	1	2	0.5	11	43	0
Manwich® sauce	¼ cup	30	6	½	1	0	0.0	0	380	1
Mole poblana sauce	2 T.	50	4	0	1	3	1.0	0	41	1
Mornay sauce	2 T.	92	3	0	3	8	3.5	40	205	0
Mustard										
brown/yellow	1 tsp.	0	0	0	0	0	0.0	0	55	0
Dijon	1 tsp.	5	0	0	0	0	0.0	0	120	0
honey	1 tsp.	5	1	0	0	0	0.0	0	30	0
Olives										
black	5	25	1	0	0	2	0.5	0	192	1
green, w/ pimento	5	25	0	0	0	3	1.5	0	350	0
Oyster sauce	1 T.	30	6	½	0	0	0.0	0	900	0
Pasta sauce, red										
four cheese, Classico®	½ cup	90	10	½	3	5	1.0	0	570	1
light, Ragú®	½ cup	50	10	½	2	0	0.0	0	370	2
marinara, hmde.	½ cup	71	10	½	2	3	0.5	0	515	2

CONDIMENTS, SAUCES & BAKING INGREDIENTS
Condiments & Sauces

ITEM	AMOUNT	CALORIES	CARBOHYDRATE (g)	CARBOHYDRATE CHOICES	PROTEIN (g)	FAT (g)	SATURATED FAT (g)	CHOLESTEROL (mg)	SODIUM (mg)	FIBER (g)
Pasta sauce, red *(continued)*										
meat flavored, Ragú®	½ cup	80	7	½	2	4	1.0	0	760	2
Sockarooni™, Newman's Own®	½ cup	60	9	½	2	2	0.0	0	590	3
tomato & basil, Barilla®	½ cup	80	12	1	2	3	0.0	0	560	3
traditional, Healthy Choice®	½ cup	50	11	1	3	0	0.0	0	360	3
traditional, Prego®	½ cup	120	18	1	2	5	0.5	0	610	3
w/ meat, hmde.	½ cup	144	11	1	8	8	2.5	23	434	2
Peanut sauce	2 T.	94	4	0	4	8	1.5	0	73	1
Pesto sauce	2 T.	155	2	0	6	14	4.0	10	238	1
Pickles										
bread & butter	3 chips	25	6	½	0	0	0.0	0	170	0
dill	1 medium	5	1	0	0	0	0.0	0	220	1
sweet	1 medium	41	11	1	0	0	0.0	0	329	1
Pico de gallo	2 T.	12	2	0	0	0	0.0	0	191	0
Pizza sauce	¼ cup	30	6	½	1	0	0.0	0	340	1
Plum sauce	2 T.	70	16	1	0	0	0.0	0	205	0
Relish, sweet pickle	1 T.	20	5	0	0	0	0.0	0	124	0
Salsa	2 T.	11	2	0	0	0	0.0	0	251	0
Salt	1 tsp.	0	0	0	0	0	0.0	0	2325	0
Sauerkraut, can	2 T.	6	1	0	0	0	0.0	0	195	1
Soy sauce										
lite	1 T.	15	2	0	1	0	0.0	0	505	0
regular	1 T.	11	2	0	1	0	0.0	0	1315	0
Spices, salt free	¼ tsp.	0	0	0	0	0	0.0	0	0	0
Steak sauce										
A.1.®	1 T.	15	3	0	0	0	0.0	0	280	0
Heinz 57®	1 T.	20	4	0	0	0	0.0	0	190	0
Stir-fry sauce	1 T.	15	3	0	1	0	0.0	0	530	0
Sweet & sour sauce	1 T.	18	5	0	0	0	0.0	0	95	0
Szechuan sauce	1 T.	20	4	0	0	1	0.0	0	520	0
Tabasco® sauce	1 tsp.	0	0	0	0	0	0.0	0	30	0
Taco sauce	1 T.	10	2	0	0	0	0.0	0	125	0
Tamari sauce	1 T.	15	1	0	2	0	0.0	0	960	0
Tartar sauce	1 T.	60	3	0	0	6	1.0	5	100	0
Teriyaki sauce	1 T.	15	3	0	1	0	0.0	0	690	0
Tomato sauce, can	½ cup	37	9	½	2	0	0.0	0	741	2
Vinegar										
balsamic	1 T.	10	2	0	0	0	0.0	0	4	0
cider/white	1 T.	2	1	0	0	0	0.0	0	0	0
raspberry/red wine	1 T.	0	0	0	0	0	0.0	0	0	0
White cream sauce	2 T.	30	2	0	1	2	1.0	3	140	0
Worcestershire sauce	1 tsp.	4	1	0	0	0	0.0	0	56	0

CONDIMENTS, SAUCES & BAKING INGREDIENTS
Baking Ingredients

ITEM	AMOUNT	CALORIES	CARBOHYDRATE (g)	CARBOHYDRATE CHOICES	PROTEIN (g)	FAT (g)	SATURATED FAT (g)	CHOLESTEROL (mg)	SODIUM (mg)	FIBER (g)
Baking Ingredients										
Baking powder	¼ tsp.	0	0	0	0	0	0.0	0	95	0
Baking soda	¼ tsp.	0	0	0	0	0	0.0	0	315	0
Bisquick®, dry										
reduced fat	⅓ cup	140	27	2	3	3	0.5	0	500	0
regular	⅓ cup	160	25	1½	3	6	1.5	0	490	0
Bread crumbs										
plain	¼ cup	110	19	1	4	2	0.0	0	210	1
seasoned	¼ cup	110	21	1½	4	1	0.0	0	795	1
Butterscotch chips	1 T.	80	10	½	0	4	3.5	0	15	0
Carob chips, unsweetened	1 T.	70	8	½	2	3	3.0	0	65	0
Chocolate, baking										
semi-sweet	1 oz.	140	16	1	1	9	5.0	0	0	2
unsweetened	1 oz.	140	8	½	4	14	9.0	0	0	4
Chocolate chips										
milk chocolate	1 T.	80	9	½	0	5	2.5	0	0	0
semi-sweet	1 T.	70	9	½	0	4	2.5	0	0	0
Cocoa powder	1 T.	20	3	0	1	1	0.0	0	0	1
Corn flake crumbs	¼ cup	80	18	1	2	0	0.0	0	160	0
Corn starch	1 T.	30	7	½	0	0	0.0	0	1	0
Corn syrup, dark/light	1 T.	58	16	1	0	0	0.0	0	32	0
Cornmeal	2 T.	55	12	1	1	1	0.0	0	5	1
Flour										
all purpose/white	1 cup	455	95	6	13	1	0.0	0	3	3
bread	1 cup	400	88	6	16	0	0.0	0	0	3
buckwheat	1 cup	400	84	5	16	4	0.0	0	0	12
cake	1 cup	496	107	7	11	1	0.0	0	3	2
carob	1 cup	229	92	3½	5	1	0.0	0	36	41
corn	1 cup	416	87	5	11	4	0.5	0	6	15
potato	1 cup	571	133	8	11	1	0.0	0	88	9
rice, white	1 cup	578	127	8½	9	2	0.5	0	0	4
rye, medium	1 cup	400	88	5	12	0	0.0	0	0	8
soy	1 cup	369	27	1	32	18	2.5	0	11	8
soy, fat free	1 cup	329	38	1	47	1	0.0	0	20	18
white, self-rising	1 cup	443	93	6	12	1	0.0	0	1588	3
whole wheat	1 cup	407	87	5	16	2	0.5	0	6	15
Graham cracker crumbs	¼ cup	122	21	1½	2	4	0.5	0	121	1
Honey	1 T.	64	17	1	0	0	0.0	0	1	0
Lighter Bake™	1 T.	35	9	½	0	0	0.0	0	0	0
Matzo meal, unsalted	2 T.	65	14	1	2	0	0.0	0	0	0
Molasses	1 T.	55	14	1	0	0	0.0	0	8	0
Phyllo dough	3 sheets	180	35	2	5	1	0.0	0	300	1

CONDIMENTS, SAUCES & BAKING INGREDIENTS

Baking Ingredients

ITEM	AMOUNT	CALORIES	CARBOHYDRATE (g)	CARBOHYDRATE CHOICES	PROTEIN (g)	FAT (g)	SATURATED FAT (g)	CHOLESTEROL (mg)	SODIUM (mg)	FIBER (g)
Pie crusts										
graham	⅛ pie	110	14	1	1	5	1.0	0	135	0
graham, chocolate	⅛ pie	110	14	1	1	5	1.0	0	100	0
graham, reduced fat	⅛ pie	90	14	1	1	4	0.5	0	85	0
pastry, double, hmde.	⅛ pie	227	21	1½	3	15	3.5	0	234	2
pastry, single, hmde.	⅛ pie	121	11	1	1	8	2.0	0	125	0
Pie fillings										
apple	⅓ cup	80	20	1	0	0	0.0	0	40	1
cherry	⅓ cup	90	23	1½	0	0	0.0	0	25	1
lemon	⅓ cup	130	28	2	0	2	0.0	0	120	0
Shake 'n Bake®, box	⅛ pkt.	35	7	½	0	1	0.0	0	220	0
Sugar										
brown/raw/white	1 cup	774	200	13	0	0	0.0	0	2	0
powdered	1 cup	467	119	8	0	0	0.0	0	1	0
Yeast	1 pkt.	0	0	0	0	0	0.0	0	0	0

CRACKERS, DIPS & SNACK FOODS

Crackers

ITEM	AMOUNT	CALORIES	CARBOHYDRATE (g)	CARBOHYDRATE CHOICES	PROTEIN (g)	FAT (g)	SATURATED FAT (g)	CHOLESTEROL (mg)	SODIUM (mg)	FIBER (g)
Ak-mak®	5	116	19	1	5	2	0.5	0	214	4
Animal	10	130	23	1½	2	4	0.5	0	150	0
Cheese, w/ peanut butter	8	190	23	1½	4	10	2.0	0	290	1
Cheez-It®										
reduced fat	29	140	20	1	4	5	1.0	0	280	0
regular	27	160	16	1	4	8	2.0	0	240	0
Chicken In A Biskit®	12	170	18	1	2	10	2.0	0	250	0
Club®										
reduced fat	5	70	12	1	1	2	0.0	0	200	0
regular	4	70	9	½	1	3	1.0	0	160	0
Gold Fish®	55	150	20	1	3	6	1.5	0	230	0
Graham										
reduced fat	2 sheets	120	25	1½	2	2	0.0	0	130	1
regular	2 sheets	130	22	1½	2	4	0.5	0	150	1
Harvest Crisps®	13	140	23	1½	3	4	0.5	0	240	1
Matzoh, lightly salted	1 sheet	110	23	1½	3	1	0.0	0	100	1
Melba snacks	5	60	12	1	2	1	0.0	0	140	2
Milk crackers	1	60	8	½	0	2	0.0	0	70	0
Oyster	22	60	11	1	1	2	0.0	0	170	0
Ritz®										
cheese, regular	5	80	11	1	1	4	1.0	0	210	0
original, low sodium	5	80	10	½	1	4	0.5	0	35	0
original, reduced fat	5	70	11	1	1	2	0.0	0	150	0
original, regular	5	80	10	½	1	4	1.0	0	135	0

CRACKERS, DIPS & SNACK FOODS
Crackers

ITEM	AMOUNT	CALORIES	CARBOHYDRATE (g)	CARBOHYDRATE CHOICES	PROTEIN (g)	FAT (g)	SATURATED FAT (g)	CHOLESTEROL (mg)	SODIUM (mg)	FIBER (g)
Ritz® (continued)										
whole wheat, regular	5	70	11	1	1	3	0.0	0	125	0
Ritz Bits® sandwiches										
cheese	14	160	18	1	2	9	2.0	5	280	0
peanut butter	13	160	18	1	3	8	1.5	0	220	1
Saltines										
fat free	5	60	12	1	1	0	0.0	0	170	0
reduced sodium	5	70	11	1	1	2	0.0	0	115	0
regular	5	70	11	1	1	2	0.0	0	220	0
Seasoned Ry Krisp®	2	60	10	½	1	2	0.0	0	90	3
SnackWell's®										
cracked pepper	5	60	10	½	1	2	0.0	0	115	0
wheat	5	70	11	1	1	2	0.0	0	150	0
Sociables®	5	70	9	½	1	4	0.5	0	140	0
Table Water®	5	70	13	1	2	2	0.0	0	95	0
Teddy Grahams®	24	130	23	1½	2	4	1.0	0	150	0
Toasteds®										
buttercrisp	5	80	10	½	1	4	0.5	0	150	0
wheat	5	80	10	½	1	4	0.5	0	150	0
Town House®, original	5	80	9	½	1	5	1.0	0	150	0
Triscuit®										
original	7	140	21	1½	3	5	1.0	0	230	4
reduced fat	7	120	21	1½	3	3	0.5	0	160	3
Wasa®, rye	1	30	7	½	1	1	0.0	0	50	2
Wheat Thins®										
low sodium	16	150	21	1½	3	6	1.0	0	80	1
multi-grain	17	140	21	1½	3	5	1.0	0	290	2
original	16	150	21	1½	2	6	1.0	0	270	1
Dips										
Bean	2 T.	40	5	0	2	1	0.0	0	170	1
Caramel apple	2 T.	150	24	1½	1	5	4.0	5	75	1
Cheese	2 T.	40	4	0	1	3	1.0	5	250	0
Creme cheese fruit dip	2 T.	70	10	½	1	3	2.0	10	85	0
Dill	2 T.	100	2	0	1	10	4.0	10	170	0
French onion	2 T.	60	4	0	1	5	3.0	15	230	0
Marshmallow creme	2 T.	97	11	1	1	5	3.5	17	56	0
Salsa, w/ cheese	2 T.	40	5	0	0	3	1.0	0	280	0
Spinach	2 T.	140	3	0	0	14	2.0	10	200	0
Snack Foods										
Bagel chips	3 large	130	18	1	3	5	0.5	0	55	0
Bugles®	1 ⅓ cups	160	18	1	1	9	8.0	0	310	0

CRACKERS, DIPS & SNACK FOODS

Snack Foods

ITEM	AMOUNT	CALORIES	CARBOHYDRATE (g)	CARBOHYDRATE CHOICES	PROTEIN (g)	FAT (g)	SATURATED FAT (g)	CHOLESTEROL (mg)	SODIUM (mg)	FIBER (g)
Cheetos®										
crunchy	21	160	15	1	2	10	1.5	0	290	0
puffs	13	160	13	1	2	10	1.5	0	350	0
Cheez Balls® Planters®	36	160	14	1	2	11	3.0	5	300	1
Cheez Doodles®	17	150	17	1	2	8	2.5	0	360	0
Chex Mix®	⅔ cup	130	22	1½	2	4	0.5	0	410	1
Combos®										
cheddar, w/ cracker	⅓ cup	140	18	1	2	6	1.0	0	290	0
cheddar, w/ pretzel	⅓ cup	130	19	1	3	5	1.0	0	310	0
Cornnuts®										
original	⅓ cup	120	20	1	3	5	0.5	0	180	2
ranch	⅓ cup	130	19	1	3	5	1.0	0	240	2
Cracker Jack®	¾ cup	140	22	1½	2	4	1.5	0	100	1
Doritos® nacho chips										
3Ds®	27	130	19	1	2	5	1.0	0	280	1
regular	11	140	17	1	2	7	1.0	0	200	1
WOW!®	12	90	20	1	2	1	0.0	0	210	1
Fritos® corn chips	32	160	15	1	2	10	1.5	0	170	1
Funyuns®	13	140	18	1	2	7	1.0	0	270	0
Jax®										
original	25	150	19	1	2	8	1.0	0	380	1
reduced fat	21	130	21	1½	2	4	1.0	0	110	0
Popcorn										
air popped	3 cups	92	19	1	3	1	0.0	0	1	4
caramel, fat free	1 cup	150	35	2	2	0	0.0	0	83	3
caramel & peanuts	1 cup	170	34	2	3	3	0.5	0	125	2
cheddar cheese	3 cups	174	17	1	3	11	2.0	4	293	3
oil popped, salted	3 cups	165	19	1	3	9	1.5	0	292	3
Smartfood®, white cheddar	1¾ cups	160	14	1	3	10	2.0	5	320	1
toffee, fat free	¾ cup	110	26	2	0	0	0.0	0	190	0
Popcorn, microwave										
butter	3 cups	105	12	1	2	8	1.5	0	180	3
Healthy Choice®	3 cups	50	13	1	2	1	0.0	0	70	3
light	3 cups	60	12	1	2	3	0.5	0	145	2
Popcorn cakes	1 (4 in.)	45	9	½	0	0	0.0	0	45	0
Pork rinds	9	80	0	0	8	5	1.5	20	300	0
Potato chips										
baked	11	110	23	1½	2	2	0.0	0	150	2
BBQ	15	150	15	1	2	10	3.0	0	200	1
regular	20	150	15	1	2	10	3.0	0	180	1
WOW!®	15	70	17	1	2	0	0.0	0	190	1
Potato sticks	1 cup	250	23	1½	3	16	2.5	0	270	1

CRACKERS, DIPS & SNACK FOODS
Snack Foods

ITEM	AMOUNT	CALORIES	CARBOHYDRATE (g)	CARBOHYDRATE CHOICES	PROTEIN (g)	FAT (g)	SATURATED FAT (g)	CHOLESTEROL (mg)	SODIUM (mg)	FIBER (g)
Pretzels										
chocolate covered	7 small	200	26	2	3	10	1.5	0	65	1
sourdough, hard	1 large	100	21	1½	2	1	0.0	0	500	1
thin twists, large	9	110	23	1½	2	1	0.0	0	560	1
thin twists, small	18	110	22	1½	3	0	0.0	0	390	1
yogurt covered	11 small	190	28	2	3	8	5.0	0	300	1
Pringles® potato crisps										
BBQ, regular	14	150	15	1	2	10	2.5	0	200	1
fat free	15	70	15	1	2	0	0.0	0	160	2
original, regular	12	150	15	1	1	10	1.5	0	150	1
Rice cakes										
mini, caramel	6 (2 in.)	60	13	1	1	0	0.0	0	35	1
regular, plain	2 (4 in.)	70	14	1	2	0	0.0	0	30	0
Sesame sticks	12 small	140	20	1	3	6	1.0	0	380	1
Sun Chips®	11	140	19	1	2	6	0.5	0	115	2
Tostitos® tortilla chips										
bite size, baked	20	110	24	1½	3	1	0.0	0	200	2
bite size, regular	24	140	17	1	2	8	1.0	0	110	1
crispy rounds	13	140	18	1	2	7	1.0	0	120	1
restaurant style, regular	6	130	19	1	2	6	1.0	0	80	1
restaurant style, WOW!®	6	90	20	1	2	1	0.0	0	105	1
Veggie Stix™	1 oz.	140	18	1	1	7	1.5	0	290	1
Wheat Nuts®	⅓ cup	200	5	0	4	19	3.0	0	190	1

DESSERTS, SWEETS & TOPPINGS
Bars

ITEM	AMOUNT	CALORIES	CARBOHYDRATE (g)	CARBOHYDRATE CHOICES	PROTEIN (g)	FAT (g)	SATURATED FAT (g)	CHOLESTEROL (mg)	SODIUM (mg)	FIBER (g)
Brownies, butterscotch	1 (2 in.)	254	33	2	3	13	2.5	34	151	1
Brownies, chocolate										
fat free, mix	1 (2 in.)	181	42	3	2	0	0.0	0	272	1
regular, w/ nuts	1 (2 in.)	247	35	2	3	11	2.5	9	100	1
regular, w/o nuts	1 (2 in.)	230	37	2½	3	10	3.0	9	145	1
Kudos®, peanut butter	1 (1 oz.)	130	18	1	2	6	2.0	0	90	1
Lemon	1 (2 oz.)	246	36	2½	3	11	2.0	44	149	0
Nutty Bars®	1 (1 oz.)	155	16	1	3	9	2.0	0	55	1
Rice Krispies Treats®										
double chocolatey chunk	1 (0.8 oz.)	100	15	1	1	4	2.0	0	75	0
original	1 (0.8 oz.)	90	18	1	1	2	0.5	0	100	0
Seven layer	1 (2 in.)	224	24	1½	4	14	7.0	18	114	1
Cakes, Pastries & Sweet Breads										
Angel food cake	1/12 cake	146	33	2	3	0	0.0	0	289	0
Apple dumplings	1 (3 oz.)	290	44	3	3	11	2.5	0	160	3
Apple fritters	1 (1 oz.)	103	10	½	2	7	1.5	24	11	0

DESSERTS, SWEETS & TOPPINGS
Cakes, Pastries & Sweet Breads

ITEM	AMOUNT	CALORIES	CARBOHYDRATE (g)	CARBOHYDRATE CHOICES	PROTEIN (g)	FAT (g)	SATURATED FAT (g)	CHOLESTEROL (mg)	SODIUM (mg)	FIBER (g)
Baklava	1 (2 in.)	336	29	2	5	23	9.5	36	293	2
Banana bread	1 (2 oz.)	185	31	2	2	6	1.5	46	224	1
Black forest cake	1/12 cake	280	32	2	3	15	3.0	32	159	4
Caramel rolls	1 (1.7 oz.)	170	24	1½	2	7	1.5	0	330	1
Carrot cake, iced	1 (4 oz.)	444	47	3	4	28	5.5	54	271	2
Cheesecake										
amaretto	1 (3 oz.)	290	20	1	6	21	11.0	105	170	0
chocolate	1 (3 oz.)	336	33	2	6	21	10.5	78	159	1
plain, New York style	1 (3 oz.)	273	22	1½	5	19	8.5	47	176	0
Smart One's®, w/ cherries	1 (3.9 oz.)	170	28	2	7	4	2.0	15	230	2
Chocolate cake, iced	1/12 cake	262	41	3	3	10	2.5	21	193	1
Cinnamon rolls	1 (3 oz.)	320	44	3	5	14	3.5	50	280	2
Cobblers, fruit	1 (3 in.)	163	29	2	2	5	1.0	1	283	2
Coffeecake										
cinnamon, w/ icing	1 (2 oz.)	250	27	2	4	14	3.0	30	200	1
plain, w/ crumb topping	1 (2 oz.)	237	26	2	4	13	3.5	18	199	1
Cream puffs	1 (4 oz.)	293	26	2	8	18	4.0	152	387	0
Crêpes, fruit filled	1 (4 oz.)	211	30	2	5	8	2.0	88	104	2
Crisps, fruit	1 (3 in.)	164	27	2	2	6	3.0	11	90	2
Cupcakes, iced										
chocolate, light	1 (1.5 oz.)	131	29	2	2	2	0.5	0	178	1
chocolate, regular	1 (1.5 oz.)	156	28	2	2	4	1.0	7	191	1
chocolate, regular, w/ filling	1 (1.8 oz.)	180	30	2	2	6	2.5	5	290	1
Danish										
cheese	1 (2.5 oz.)	266	26	2	6	16	5.0	11	320	1
fruit	1 (2.5 oz.)	252	34	2	4	12	2.5	14	251	1
Devil Dogs®	1 (1.7 oz.)	180	26	2	2	7	3.0	0	150	1
Doughnuts										
cake, plain	1 medium	300	28	2	4	19	5.0	25	330	1
holes, glazed	5 medium	200	27	2	3	9	2.0	0	220	1
raised, glazed	1 medium	180	25	1½	3	8	1.5	0	250	1
Eclairs, chocolate	1 (3 oz.)	270	39	2½	3	11	2.5	0	290	1
Funnel cake	1 (6 in.)	278	29	2	7	14	2.5	63	117	1
Funny Bones®	1 (1.3 oz.)	150	21	1½	2	7	2.5	0	110	2
Gingerbread cake	1 (3 in.)	263	36	2½	3	12	3.0	24	242	1
Ho Hos®	1 (1 oz.)	125	17	1	1	6	4.0	10	75	1
Honey buns	1 (1.8 oz.)	230	24	1½	3	13	3.5	0	170	0
Lemon cake, iced	1 (4 oz.)	401	73	5	3	11	2.0	36	373	1
Marble cake, iced	1/12 cake	383	60	4	4	15	6.0	51	323	1
Marshmallow pies	1 (1.5 oz.)	180	28	2	2	7	1.5	0	105	0
Pecan spin rolls	1 (1 oz.)	100	16	1	1	4	1.0	0	65	0
Pineapple upside down cake	1 (3 in.)	362	57	4	4	14	3.5	25	362	1

DESSERTS, SWEETS & TOPPINGS
Cakes, Pastries & Sweet Breads

ITEM	AMOUNT	CALORIES	CARBOHYDRATE (g)	CARBOHYDRATE CHOICES	PROTEIN (g)	FAT (g)	SATURATED FAT (g)	CHOLESTEROL (mg)	SODIUM (mg)	FIBER (g)
Pop Tart®	1 (1.8 oz.)	200	37	2½	2	5	1.0	0	170	1
Pound cake	1/12 cake	220	28	2	3	11	6.5	125	226	0
Pumpkin bread	1 (2 oz.)	176	27	2	2	7	0.5	23	220	1
Ring Dings®	1 (1.4 oz.)	170	22	1½	1	9	3.5	0	110	1
Snow balls	1 (2.1 oz.)	210	36	2½	2	7	2.5	15	200	0
Spice cake, iced	1 (4 oz.)	383	65	4	5	12	3.5	52	292	1
Sponge cake	1/12 cake	164	35	2	3	2	0.5	58	138	0
Strudel, w/ fruit	1 (2 in.)	161	30	2	2	4	1.0	11	82	2
SuzyQ's®	1 (2 oz.)	230	35	2	2	9	4.0	10	270	1
Toaster Strudel™	1 (1.9 oz.)	190	26	2	3	8	2.0	5	190	0
Turnovers, w/ fruit	1 (3 oz.)	301	45	3	4	12	2.5	0	177	3
Twinkies®	1 (1.5 oz.)	150	25	1½	1	5	1.5	15	200	0
White cake, iced	1/12 cake	264	42	3	4	9	2.5	1	242	1
Yodels®	1 (1.1 oz.)	145	17	1	1	8	3.0	0	80	1
Zingers®	1 (1.5 oz.)	160	24	1½	1	7	3.0	5	100	0
Cookies										
Arrowroot biscuit	1	20	4	0	0	1	0.0	0	15	0
Biscotti										
almond	1 med.	100	13	1	2	5	1.0	5	45	1
chocolate almond	1 med.	90	13	1	2	4	1.0	5	40	1
chocolate dipped	1 med.	130	19	1	2	5	2.5	25	65	1
vanilla	1 med.	90	15	1	1	4	0.5	10	55	0
Chocolate chip										
Chips Ahoy®, reduced fat	1	47	7	½	1	2	0.5	0	47	0
Chips Ahoy®, regular	1	53	7	½	1	3	1.0	0	35	0
hmde.	1 (2 in.)	78	9	½	1	5	2.5	11	55	0
Chocolate wafers	1	28	5	0	0	1	0.5	0	46	0
E. L. Fudge®, original	1	65	9	½	1	3	1.0	0	35	0
Fig Newtons®										
fat free	1	45	11	1	1	0	0.0	0	58	1
regular	1	55	11	1	1	1	0.0	0	58	1
Fudge stripes	1	53	7	½	0	3	1.5	0	47	0
Ginger snaps	1	30	6	½	0	1	0.0	0	58	0
Girl Scout Cookies®										
Caramel deLites®	1	70	10	½	1	4	3.0	0	43	1
Do-si-dos®	1	53	7	½	1	2	0.5	0	40	0
Lemon Coolers®, reduced fat	1	26	4	0	0	1	0.5	0	20	0
lemon pastry cremes	1	43	7	½	1	2	0.5	0	33	0
peanut butter patties	1	75	8	½	1	4	2.5	0	58	1
peanut butter sandwich	1	57	8	½	1	2	0.5	0	40	0
Samoas®	1	75	10	½	1	4	2.5	0	28	0
shortbread	1	33	5	0	0	2	0.5	0	34	0

DESSERTS, SWEETS & TOPPINGS
Cookies

ITEM	AMOUNT	CALORIES	CARBOHYDRATE (g)	CARBOHYDRATE CHOICES	PROTEIN (g)	FAT (g)	SATURATED FAT (g)	CHOLESTEROL (mg)	SODIUM (mg)	FIBER (g)
Girl Scout Cookies® *(continued)*										
Tagalongs®	1	70	7	½	1	5	2.0	0	48	1
thin mints	1	35	5	0	0	2	1.0	0	25	0
Iced animal	1	23	4	0	0	1	0.0	0	17	0
Lady fingers	1	23	5	0	1	0	0.0	13	51	0
Lido®	1	90	10	½	0	5	1.5	0	40	0
Lorna Doone® shortbread	1	35	5	0	1	2	0.5	1	33	0
Macaroons	1 (2 in.)	100	14	1	0	5	4.5	0	55	1
Milano®, original	1	60	7	½	1	3	1.0	3	27	0
Molasses	1 med.	65	11	1	1	2	0.5	0	69	0
Mrs. Fields										
chocolate chip	1 (1.2 oz.)	150	21	1½	2	8	4.5	15	100	0
oatmeal raisin, w/ nuts	1 (1.2 oz.)	150	21	1½	2	7	3.0	15	160	0
white chunk macadamia	1 (1.2 oz.)	160	21	1½	2	8	4.5	15	150	0
Nutter Butter®	1	65	10	½	1	3	0.5	0	58	0
Oatmeal raisin	1 med.	65	10	½	1	2	0.5	5	81	0
Oreo®										
Doublestuf®	1	70	10	½	1	4	1.0	0	75	0
reduced fat	1	47	9	½	1	1	0.5	0	67	0
regular	1	53	8	½	0	2	0.5	0	73	0
Peanut butter	1 med.	72	9	½	1	4	0.5	0	62	0
Pecan Sandies®	1	90	9	½	0	5	1.0	0	50	0
Shortbread	1 med.	75	10	½	1	4	1.0	3	68	0
SnackWell's®										
chocolate chip, bite size	13	130	22	1½	2	4	1.5	0	160	0
chocolate chip, sugar free	1	50	8	½	1	3	1.0	0	53	0
chocolate sandwich	1	55	10	½	1	2	0.5	0	105	0
devil's food	1	50	12	1	1	0	0.0	0	30	0
mint creme	1	55	10	½	1	2	0.5	0	35	0
oatmeal, sugar free	1	90	17	1	1	3	0.5	0	80	0
Social Tea® biscuits	1	20	4	0	0	1	0.0	1	19	0
Sugar	1	72	10	½	1	3	1.0	8	54	0
Sugar wafers	1	18	3	0	0	1	0.0	0	5	0
Vanilla wafers										
reduced fat	1	15	3	0	0	0	0.0	0	14	0
regular	1	18	3	0	0	1	0.0	1	14	0
Vienna Fingers®										
reduced fat	1	70	12	1	1	2	0.5	0	53	0
regular	1	75	11	1	1	3	1.0	0	43	0
Frozen Yogurt										
Cherry Garcia®	½ cup	140	27	2	4	3	2.0	5	65	0
Chocolate chip cookie dough	½ cup	180	34	2	4	3	2.0	10	110	0

DESSERTS, SWEETS & TOPPINGS

Frozen Yogurt

ITEM	AMOUNT	CALORIES	CARBOHYDRATE (g)	CARBOHYDRATE CHOICES	PROTEIN (g)	FAT (g)	SATURATED FAT (g)	CHOLESTEROL (mg)	SODIUM (mg)	FIBER (g)
Chocolate fudge brownie	½ cup	150	32	2	4	1	0.0	0	80	1
Chocolate/strawberry/vanilla										
fat free	½ cup	95	19	1	5	0	0.0	2	64	0
regular	½ cup	114	17	1	3	4	2.5	1	63	0
Heath® toffee crunch	½ cup	180	29	2	4	5	2.5	10	100	0
Ice Cream										
Butter pecan	½ cup	290	20	1	4	21	10.0	70	80	1
Cherry Garcia®	½ cup	260	26	2	4	16	11.0	70	65	0
Chocolate chip cookie dough	½ cup	270	31	2	4	15	10.0	70	100	0
Chocolate fudge brownie	½ cup	280	33	2	5	14	9.0	40	85	2
Chocolate/strawberry/vanilla										
fat free	½ cup	100	23	1½	2	0	0.0	0	50	0
fat free, no added sugar	½ cup	80	17	1	4	0	0.0	0	67	0
light	½ cup	110	19	1	3	2	1.0	10	60	0
light, no added sugar	½ cup	100	14	1	3	3	1.5	10	50	0
premium	½ cup	270	22	1½	5	18	11.0	115	60	0
regular	½ cup	150	17	1	3	8	5.0	20	35	0
Mint chocolate chunk	½ cup	220	22	1½	3	15	10.0	65	50	1
Ice Cream Cones, cone only										
Cake/wafer	1 (0.16 oz.)	15	4	0	0	0	0.0	0	20	0
Sugar	1 (0.36 oz.)	50	10	½	1	1	0.0	0	55	0
Waffle	1 (0.9 oz.)	111	21	1½	2	2	0.5	2	35	0
Ice Cream Novelties										
Butterfinger® bars	1 (2.5 oz.)	210	17	1	2	15	10.0	15	50	0
Chipwich®	1 (4 oz.)	250	37	2½	4	11	5.0	15	115	0
Chocolate eclair bars	1 (3 oz.)	160	20	1	2	8	3.0	5	60	0
Creamsicle®	1 (1.8 oz.)	70	13	1	1	2	1.0	5	20	0
Crunch® bars										
reduced fat	1 (2.5 oz.)	150	17	1	2	8	6.0	5	40	0
regular	1 (3 oz.)	220	18	1	2	15	11.0	15	55	0
Dove Bar®	1 (2.7 oz.)	260	25	1½	3	17	11.0	30	50	1
Dove® bite size	5 (0.6 oz.)	320	32	2	4	20	13.0	45	40	0
Drumstick® cones	1 (4.3 oz.)	280	38	2½	3	13	9.0	25	120	0
Eskimo Pie®										
no sugar added	1 (2.5 oz.)	120	13	1	3	8	6.0	10	40	0
regular	1 (2.5 oz.)	160	15	1	2	10	8.0	15	35	0
Frappucino® bars, lowfat	1 (2.5 oz.)	120	22	1½	4	2	1.0	10	50	3
Frozen yogurt bars	1 (2.4 oz.)	90	20	1	2	0	0.0	0	15	0
Fruit juice bars	1 (3 oz.)	80	19	1	0	0	0.0	0	0	0
Fudge bars										
Fudgsicle®, fat free	1 (1.8 oz.)	60	13	1	3	0	0.0	0	50	0
Fudgsicle®, regular	1 (1.8 oz.)	60	11	1	2	1	0.5	0	45	0

DESSERTS, SWEETS & TOPPINGS

Ice Cream Novelties

ITEM	AMOUNT	CALORIES	CARBOHYDRATE (g)	CARBOHYDRATE CHOICES	PROTEIN (g)	FAT (g)	SATURATED FAT (g)	CHOLESTEROL (mg)	SODIUM (mg)	FIBER (g)
Fudge bars *(continued)*										
no sugar added	1 (1.8 oz.)	45	9	½	1	1	0.0	0	45	0
Slim-Fast® fudge bar	1 (3.5 oz.)	110	22	1½	3	2	1.0	10	80	0
Gelato, premium	½ cup	240	40	2½	4	7	3.5	80	75	0
Heath® bars	1 (5 oz.)	300	26	2	3	20	14.0	20	100	0
Ice cream sandwiches	1 (3.3 oz.)	180	27	2	3	7	4.0	20	170	1
Italian ice	½ cup	61	16	1	0	0	0.0	0	5	0
Klondike® bars, original	1 (5 oz.)	280	24	1½	3	19	14.0	20	75	0
M&M's® sandwich cookies	1 (3.1 oz.)	220	29	2	3	11	4.5	25	170	1
Popsicle®										
regular	1 (1.8 oz.)	45	11	1	0	0	0.0	0	0	0
sugar free	1 (1.8 oz.)	10	2	0	0	0	0.0	0	0	0
Push-Ups®, sherbet	1 (2.8 oz.)	90	19	1	1	1	0.5	5	15	0
Reese's® bars	1 (4 oz.)	310	27	2	4	21	13.0	20	90	0
Rice Dream®, nondairy	½ cup	150	23	1½	0	6	0.5	0	100	1
Sherbet	½ cup	130	27	2	1	2	1.0	5	40	0
Snickers® bars	1 (2 oz.)	180	18	1	3	11	6.0	15	60	1
Snow cones	1 (6.7 oz.)	243	62	4	1	0	0.0	0	42	0
Sorbet	½ cup	120	31	2	0	0	0.0	0	5	0
Soy Dream™, nondairy	½ cup	140	17	1	1	7	0.5	0	70	1
Strawberry shortcake bars	1 (3 oz.)	170	21	1½	1	9	2.5	5	60	0
Tofutti®	½ cup	190	20	1	2	11	2.0	0	210	0
Vienetta®	1 slice	190	19	1	3	11	7.0	40	40	0
Other Sweets										
Caramel apples	1 medium	243	54	3½	2	4	3.0	3	102	4
Chocolate mousse, mix	½ cup	107	16	1	1	3	2.0	2	51	2
Crêpe Suzette, w/ sauce	1 (2.5 oz.)	171	17	1	4	10	4.0	89	79	0
Custard	½ cup	140	25	1½	5	3	1.5	10	190	0
Flan, w/ caramel										
hmde.	½ cup	309	38	2½	9	14	8.0	124	160	0
mix	½ cup	150	25	1½	4	4	2.5	16	65	0
Gelatin										
regular	½ cup	80	19	1	2	0	0.0	0	100	0
sugar free	½ cup	8	1	0	1	0	0.0	0	56	0
Marshmallows	3 large	69	18	1	0	0	0.0	0	10	0
Pudding										
bread, hmde.	½ cup	220	45	3	4	3	1.0	4	260	1
chocolate, fat free	½ cup	100	23	1½	2	0	0.0	0	180	0
chocolate, instant, w/ 1%	½ cup	139	28	2	5	2	1.0	5	417	1
chocolate, regular, w/ 1%	½ cup	141	28	2	5	2	1.0	5	150	0
chocolate, regular, w/ skim	½ cup	132	28	2	5	1	0.5	3	151	0
rice, regular, w/ 1%	½ cup	151	30	2	5	1	1.0	5	159	0

DESSERTS, SWEETS & TOPPINGS
Other Sweets

ITEM	AMOUNT	CALORIES	CARBOHYDRATE (g)	CARBOHYDRATE CHOICES	PROTEIN (g)	FAT (g)	SATURATED FAT (g)	CHOLESTEROL (mg)	SODIUM (mg)	FIBER (g)
Pudding *(continued)*										
vanilla, instant, sugar free	½ cup	70	12	1	4	0	0.0	5	400	0
vanilla, instant, w/ 1%	½ cup	143	29	2	4	1	1.0	5	420	0
vanilla, regular, w/ 1%	½ cup	141	28	2	4	1	1.0	5	214	0
vanilla, regular, w/ skim	½ cup	133	28	2	4	0	0.0	2	216	0
Pies										
Apple/cherry	⅛ pie	399	60	4	4	16	4.0	10	444	2
Banana cream	⅛ pie	387	47	3	6	20	5.5	73	346	1
Boston cream	⅛ pie	232	39	2½	2	8	2.5	34	132	1
Chocolate chiffon	⅛ pie	318	41	3	6	15	4.5	107	53	1
Coconut cream	⅛ pie	270	37	2½	3	13	8.0	5	250	1
Grasshopper	⅛ pie	342	33	2	4	19	8.0	96	230	1
Hostess® fruit	1 (4.5 oz.)	470	65	4	3	22	11.0	20	470	1
Key lime	⅛ pie	410	59	4	5	17	11.0	15	290	1
Lemon meringue	⅛ pie	362	50	3	5	16	4.0	67	307	2
Pecan	⅛ pie	503	64	4	6	27	5.0	106	320	6
Pumpkin	⅛ pie	260	34	2	3	13	3.0	55	210	1
Rhubarb	⅛ pie	321	49	3	3	13	3.5	3	195	2
Shoo fly	⅛ pie	397	68	4½	4	13	2.5	37	141	1
Strawberry chiffon	⅛ pie	323	41	3	4	17	8.0	36	187	2
Sweet potato	⅛ pie	295	36	2½	6	14	3.5	58	54	2
Syrups & Toppings										
Apple butter	1 T.	31	8	½	0	0	0.0	0	1	0
Artificial sweeteners										
DiabetiSweet®	1 tsp.	9	4	0	0	0	0.0	0	0	0
Equal®	¼ tsp.	0	0	0	0	0	0.0	0	0	0
Splenda®	1 tsp./1pkt.	0	0	0	0	0	0.0	0	0	0
Sugar Twin®	1 tsp.	0	0	0	0	0	0.0	0	0	0
Sweet 'N Low®	⅒ tsp.	0	0	0	0	0	0.0	0	0	0
Butterscotch/caramel	2 T.	103	27	2	1	0	0.0	0	143	0
Chocolate syrup										
lite	2 T.	50	12	1	0	0	0.0	0	35	0
regular	2 T.	100	24	1½	1	0	0.0	0	50	0
Coffee syrup	2 T.	90	23	1½	0	0	0.0	0	20	0
Frosting/icing										
chocolate	2 T.	140	21	1½	0	6	1.5	0	110	0
reduced fat	2 T.	120	22	1½	0	3	1.0	0	65	0
vanilla	2 T.	150	23	1½	0	6	1.5	0	70	0
Fruit spread	1 T.	40	10	½	0	0	0.0	0	0	0
Grenadine syrup	1 tsp.	18	5	0	0	0	0.0	0	3	0
Honey	1 tsp.	21	6	½	0	0	0.0	0	0	0

DESSERTS, SWEETS & TOPPINGS

Syrups & Toppings

ITEM	AMOUNT	CALORIES	CARBOHYDRATE (g)	CARBOHYDRATE CHOICES	PROTEIN (g)	FAT (g)	SATURATED FAT (g)	CHOLESTEROL (mg)	SODIUM (mg)	FIBER (g)
Hot fudge										
fat free	2 T.	90	23	1½	2	0	0.0	0	95	2
regular	2 T.	140	22	1½	2	4	1.0	0	70	0
Jam/jelly/marmalade	1 T.	50	13	1	0	0	0.0	0	0	0
Maple syrup	1 T.	52	13	1	0	0	0.0	0	2	0
Marshmallow creme	2 T.	120	29	2	0	0	0.0	0	0	0
Pancake syrup										
low calorie	1 T.	25	7	½	0	0	0.0	0	30	0
regular	1 T.	57	15	1	0	0	0.0	0	17	0
Sugar, brown/raw/white	1 tsp.	16	4	0	0	0	0.0	0	0	0
Whipped cream, hmde.	2 T.	52	0	0	0	6	3.5	20	6	0
Whipped toppings										
Cool-Whip®, Free™	2 T.	15	3	0	0	0	0.0	0	5	0
Cool-Whip®, Lite®	2 T.	20	3	0	0	1	1.0	0	0	0
Cool-Whip®, regular	2 T.	25	2	0	0	2	1.5	0	0	0
Reddi Wip®	2 T.	15	0	0	0	1	0.5	0	0	0
sugar free, mix	2 T.	5	1	0	0	1	0.5	0	11	0

EGGS, EGG DISHES & EGG SUBSTITUTES

Eggs
Chicken

ITEM	AMOUNT	CALORIES	CARBOHYDRATE (g)	CARBOHYDRATE CHOICES	PROTEIN (g)	FAT (g)	SATURATED FAT (g)	CHOLESTEROL (mg)	SODIUM (mg)	FIBER (g)
boiled/poached	1 large	75	1	0	6	5	1.5	213	63	0
deviled, w/ filling	½	63	0	0	4	5	1.0	122	50	0
Eggland's Best®	1 large	70	1	0	6	4	1.0	180	65	0
fried, w/ ½ tsp. fat	1 large	92	1	0	6	7	2.0	211	162	0
powdered, whole	2 T.	80	1	0	7	6	2.0	245	75	0
scrambled, w/ 1 tsp. fat	2 large	203	3	0	14	15	4.5	429	342	0
whites	2	33	1	0	7	0	0.0	0	110	0
yolk	1	59	0	0	3	5	1.5	213	7	0
Duck	1	130	1	0	9	10	2.5	619	102	0
Goose	1	266	2	0	20	19	5.0	1227	199	0
Quail	1	14	0	0	1	1	0.5	76	13	0
Turkey	1	135	1	0	11	9	3.0	737	119	0

Egg Dishes

ITEM	AMOUNT	CALORIES	CARBOHYDRATE (g)	CARBOHYDRATE CHOICES	PROTEIN (g)	FAT (g)	SATURATED FAT (g)	CHOLESTEROL (mg)	SODIUM (mg)	FIBER (g)
Frittatas, plain, 10 in.	⅓ pie	233	8	½	16	15	5.0	429	262	0
Omelets										
ham & cheese	1 (2 eggs)	369	2	0	27	28	12.5	479	1155	0
ham & cheese	1 (3 eggs)	585	3	0	43	45	19.0	725	1944	0
vegetable	1 (2 eggs)	214	8	½	14	14	4.0	425	180	2
vegetable	1 (3 eggs)	332	11	1	21	23	6.0	638	294	2
vegetable, low fat	1 (6 whites)	159	11	1	23	2	0.5	0	358	2

EGGS, EGG DISHES & EGG SUBSTITUTES

Egg Dishes

ITEM	AMOUNT	CALORIES	CARBOHYDRATE (g)	CARBOHYDRATE CHOICES	PROTEIN (g)	FAT (g)	SATURATED FAT (g)	CHOLESTEROL (mg)	SODIUM (mg)	FIBER (g)
Quiche										
cheese	4 oz.	366	16	1	10	26	12.5	143	117	0
Lorraine	4 oz.	339	16	1	10	26	12.0	142	142	0
spinach	4 oz.	272	13	1	9	21	9.5	125	89	1
Soufflés										
cheese	1 cup	196	6	½	11	14	5.5	194	298	0
spinach	1 cup	219	3	0	11	18	7.0	184	763	3
Egg Substitutes										
Egg Beaters®	¼ cup	30	1	0	6	0	0.0	0	115	0
Liquid egg whites	¼ cup	33	0	0	7	0	0.0	0	100	0

FAST FOODS & RESTAURANT CHAINS

Arby's®

ITEM	AMOUNT	CALORIES	CARBOHYDRATE (g)	CARBOHYDRATE CHOICES	PROTEIN (g)	FAT (g)	SATURATED FAT (g)	CHOLESTEROL (mg)	SODIUM (mg)	FIBER (g)
Baked potatoes										
deluxe	1 (13 oz.)	650	67	4	20	34	20.0	90	750	6
w/ butter & sour cream	1 (11.2 oz.)	500	65	4	8	24	15.0	55	170	6
Biscuit, w/ butter	1 (2.9 oz.)	280	27	2	5	17	4.0	0	780	1
Chicken finger 4-pack	1 (6.8 oz.)	640	42	3	31	38	8.0	70	1590	0
Chicken finger snack, w/ curly fries	1 (6.4 oz.)	580	55	3½	19	32	7.0	35	1450	3
Chicken sandwiches										
bacon 'n Swiss	1 (7.4 oz.)	610	49	3	31	33	8.0	110	1550	2
breast fillet	1 (7.2 oz.)	540	47	3	24	30	5.0	90	1160	2
cordon bleu	1 (8.4 oz.)	630	47	3	34	35	8.0	120	1820	2
grilled deluxe	1 (8.7 oz.)	450	37	2½	29	22	4.0	110	1050	2
light grilled	1 (6 oz.)	280	30	2	29	5	1.5	55	1170	3
light roast deluxe	1 (7.2 oz.)	260	33	2	23	5	1.0	40	1010	3
roast club	1 (8.4 oz.)	520	38	2½	29	28	7.0	115	1440	2
Croissants										
bacon & egg	1 (4.5 oz.)	410	30	2	13	29	13.0	205	620	0
ham & cheese	1 (4.2 oz.)	355	29	2	16	22	13.0	60	1350	0
Curly fries										
small	1 (3.8 oz.)	310	39	2½	4	15	3.5	0	770	3
medium	1 (4.5 oz.)	400	50	3	5	20	5.0	0	990	4
large	1 (7 oz.)	620	78	5	8	30	7.0	0	1540	7
w/ cheddar	1 (6 oz.)	460	54	3½	6	24	6.0	5	1290	4
Dipping sauces										
Bronco Berry™	1 (1.5 oz.)	90	23	1½	0	0	0.0	0	35	0
Horsey®	1 (0.5 oz.)	60	3	0	0	5	0.5	5	150	0
marinara	1 (1.5 oz.)	35	4	0	1	1	0.0	0	260	0
Tangy Southwest™	1 (1.5 oz.)	250	3	0	0	26	4.5	30	290	0

FAST FOODS & RESTAURANT CHAINS
Arby's®

ITEM	AMOUNT	CALORIES	CARBOHYDRATE (g)	CARBOHYDRATE CHOICES	PROTEIN (g)	FAT (g)	SATURATED FAT (g)	CHOLESTEROL (mg)	SODIUM (mg)	FIBER (g)
French fries, homestyle										
small	1 (4 oz.)	300	42	3	3	13	3.5	0	570	3
medium	1 (5 oz.)	370	53	3½	4	16	4.0	0	710	4
large	1 (7.5 oz.)	560	79	5	6	24	6.0	0	1070	6
French toastix, w/o syrup	1 (4.4 oz.)	370	48	3	7	17	4.0	0	440	4
Hot ham 'n Swiss sub	1 (9.7 oz.)	530	45	3	29	27	8.0	110	1860	3
Italian sub	1 (11 oz.)	780	49	3	29	53	15.0	120	2440	3
Jalapeño Bites™	1 (4 oz.)	330	30	2	7	21	9.0	40	670	2
Mozzarella sticks	4	470	34	2	18	29	14.0	60	1330	2
Onion petals	1 order	410	43	3	4	24	3.5	0	300	2
Potato cakes	2	250	26	2	2	16	4.0	0	490	3
Roast beef sandwiches										
Arby-Q™	1 (6.4 oz.)	360	40	2½	16	14	4.0	70	1530	2
Arby's® melt, w/ cheddar	1 (5.2 oz.)	340	36	2½	16	15	5.0	70	890	2
beef 'n cheddar	1 (6.9 oz.)	480	43	3	23	24	8.0	90	1240	2
Big Montana™	1 (11 oz.)	630	41	3	47	32	15.0	155	2080	3
French dip sub	1 (10 oz.)	440	42	3	28	18	8.0	100	1680	2
giant	1 (7.9 oz.)	480	41	3	32	23	10.0	110	1440	3
junior	1 (4.4 oz.)	310	34	2	16	13	4.5	70	740	2
Philly beef 'n Swiss sub	1 (10.8 oz.)	700	46	3	36	42	15.0	130	1940	4
regular	1 (5.4 oz.)	350	34	2	21	16	6.0	85	950	2
super	1 (8.5 oz.)	470	47	3	22	23	7.0	85	1130	3
Salad dressings										
blue cheese	2 oz. pkt.	300	3	0	2	31	6.0	45	580	0
honey French	2 oz. pkt.	290	18	1	0	24	4.0	0	410	0
Italian, reduced calorie	2 oz. pkt.	25	3	0	0	1	1.0	0	1030	0
Salads, w/o dressing										
light garden	1 (12.3 oz.)	70	14	½	4	1	0.0	0	45	6
light grilled chicken	1 (16.3 oz.)	210	14	½	30	5	1.5	65	800	6
light roast chicken	1 (14.8 oz.)	160	15	½	20	3	0.0	40	700	6
light side	1 (5.7 oz.)	25	5	0	2	0	0.0	0	20	2
Shakes										
chocolate	14 fl. oz.	480	84	5½	10	16	8.0	45	370	0
jamocha	14 fl. oz.	470	82	5½	10	15	7.0	45	390	0
strawberry	14 fl. oz.	500	87	6	11	13	8.0	15	340	0
vanilla	14 fl. oz.	470	83	5½	10	15	7.0	45	360	0
Turkey sandwiches										
light roast deluxe	1 (7.2 oz.)	260	33	2	23	5	0.5	40	980	3
sub	1 (10.6 oz.)	630	51	3½	26	37	9.0	100	2170	2
Turnovers, iced										
apple	1 (4.5 oz.)	420	65	4	4	16	4.5	0	230	2
cherry	1 (4.5 oz.)	410	63	4	4	16	4.5	0	250	1

FAST FOODS & RESTAURANT CHAINS
Burger King®

ITEM	AMOUNT	CALORIES	CARBOHYDRATE (g)	CARBOHYDRATE CHOICES	PROTEIN (g)	FAT (g)	SATURATED FAT (g)	CHOLESTEROL (mg)	SODIUM (mg)	FIBER (g)
Burger King®										
BK Fish Filet™ sandwich	1	520	44	3	18	30	8.0	55	840	2
BK Veggie™ burger	1	330	45	3	14	10	1.5	0	770	4
Chili	1	190	17	1	13	8	3.0	25	1040	5
Chicken sandwiches										
chicken specialty	1	560	52	3½	25	28	6.0	60	1270	3
w/o mayo.	1	460	52	3½	25	17	4.5	55	1190	3
Chicken Whopper®	1	580	48	3	39	26	5.0	75	1370	3
w/o mayo.	1	420	47	3	38	9	2.5	60	1250	3
Chicken Whopper Jr.®	1	350	30	2	26	14	2.5	45	900	2
w/o mayo.	1	270	30	2	25	6	1.5	40	840	2
Chicken Tenders®	4	170	10	½	11	9	2.5	25	420	0
Croissan'wich®										
egg & cheese	1	320	24	1½	12	19	7.0	185	730	0
sausage & cheese	1	420	23	1½	14	31	11.0	45	840	0
sausage, egg & cheese	1	520	24	1½	19	39	14.0	210	1090	1
Dutch apple pie	1	340	52	3½	2	14	3.0	1	470	1
French fries										
small, salted	1 order	230	29	2	3	11	3.0	0	410	2
small, unsalted	1 order	230	29	2	3	11	3.0	0	240	2
medium, salted	1 order	360	46	3	4	18	5.0	0	640	4
medium, unsalted	1 order	360	46	3	4	18	5.0	0	380	4
king size, salted	1 order	600	76	4½	7	30	8.0	0	1070	6
French toast sticks, w/o syrup	5	390	46	3	6	20	4.5	0	440	2
Hamburgers										
bacon cheeseburger	1	400	32	2	22	20	9.0	60	1010	2
bacon double cheeseburger	1	580	32	2	35	34	17.0	110	1240	2
cheeseburger	1	360	31	2	19	17	8.0	50	790	2
double cheeseburger	1	540	32	2	32	31	15.0	100	1050	2
hamburger	1	310	31	2	17	13	5.0	40	580	2
King Supreme™	1	550	32	2	30	34	14.0	100	790	2
Hamburgers, Whopper®										
Double Whopper®	1	980	52	3½	52	62	22.0	160	1070	4
w/o mayo.	1	820	52	3½	52	45	19.0	150	950	4
Double Whopper®, w/ cheese	1	1070	53	3½	57	70	27.0	185	1500	4
w/o mayo.	1	910	53	3½	57	52	25.0	170	1380	4
Whopper®	1	710	52	3½	31	43	13.0	85	980	4
w/o mayo.	1	550	52	3½	31	25	10.0	75	860	4
Whopper®, w/ cheese	1	800	53	3½	36	50	18.0	110	1420	4
w/o mayo.	1	640	53	3½	35	33	16.0	95	1290	4
Whopper Jr.®	1	390	32	2	17	22	7.0	45	570	2
w/o mayo.	1	310	31	2	17	13	5.0	40	510	2

FAST FOODS & RESTAURANT CHAINS
Burger King®

ITEM	AMOUNT	CALORIES	CARBOHYDRATE (g)	CARBOHYDRATE CHOICES	PROTEIN (g)	FAT (g)	SATURATED FAT (g)	CHOLESTEROL (mg)	SODIUM (mg)	FIBER (g)
Hamburgers, Whopper® *(continued)*										
Whopper Jr.® w/ cheese	1	440	32	2	19	26	9.0	55	790	2
w/o mayo.	1	360	32	2	19	17	8.0	50	730	2
Hash brown rounds	small	230	23	1½	2	15	4.0	0	450	2
Onion rings										
small	1 order	180	22	1½	2	9	2.0	0	260	2
medium	1 order	320	40	2½	4	16	4.0	0	460	3
king	1 order	550	70	4	8	27	7.0	5	800	5
Salads, w/o croutons & dressing										
chicken Caesar	1	160	5	0	25	6	3.0	40	730	3
side garden	1	25	5	0	1	0	0.0	0	15	2
Shakes										
chocolate	small	620	72	5	12	32	21.0	95	310	2
chocolate	medium	790	89	6	15	42	27.0	125	380	2
strawberry	small	620	71	5	11	32	21.0	95	230	1
strawberry	medium	780	88	6	15	41	27.0	125	300	1
vanilla	small	560	56	4	11	32	21.0	95	220	1
vanilla	medium	720	73	5	15	41	27.0	125	280	1
Sourdough breakfast sandwiches										
bacon, egg & cheese	1	380	30	2	16	22	8.0	190	990	2
ham, egg & cheese	1	380	30	2	19	20	7.0	195	1560	2
Value meals, king size, w/ king size drink & king size fries										
BK Fish Filet™	1 meal	1550	228	14½	25	60	16.0	55	2060	8
Double Whopper®	1 meal	2010	236	15	59	92	30.0	160	2290	10
Whopper®	1 meal	1740	236	15	38	73	21.0	85	2200	10
Value meals, regular, w/ medium drink & medium fries										
bacon double cheeseburger	1 meal	1170	134	8½	39	52	22.0	110	1962	6
BK Fish Filet™	1 meal	1110	146	9	22	48	13.0	55	1562	6
chicken specialty sandwich	1 meal	1150	154	10	29	46	11.0	60	1992	7
Double Whopper®	1 meal	1570	154	10	56	80	27.0	160	1792	8
Whopper®	1 meal	1300	154	10	35	61	18.0	85	1702	8
Whopper Jr.®	1 meal	980	134	8½	21	40	12.0	45	1292	6
Chili's®										
Guiltless Grill Selections										
Chicken pita	1 order	545	77	4	39	9	n/a	n/a	n/a	15
Chicken platter	1 order	563	83	5½	38	9	3.0	n/a	3284	4
Chicken sandwich	1 order	527	70	4	44	8	2.0	n/a	2923	11
Tomato basil pasta	1 order	671	106	7	28	15	n/a	n/a	n/a	n/a
Veggie pasta	1 order	680	102	6½	34	13	4.0	n/a	760	6

FAST FOODS & RESTAURANT CHAINS
Dairy Queen®

ITEM	AMOUNT	CALORIES	CARBOHYDRATE (g)	CARBOHYDRATE CHOICES	PROTEIN (g)	FAT (g)	SATURATED FAT (g)	CHOLESTEROL (mg)	SODIUM (mg)	FIBER (g)
Dairy Queen®										
Banana split	1	510	96	6½	8	12	8.0	30	180	3
Blizzard®, chocolate chip cookie dough										
small	1	660	99	6½	12	24	13.0	55	440	1
medium	1	950	143	9½	17	36	19.0	75	660	2
Blizzard®, sandwich cookie										
small	1	520	79	5	10	18	9.0	40	380	1
medium	1	640	97	6½	12	23	11.0	45	500	1
Brownie Earthquake™	1	740	112	7½	10	27	16.0	50	350	0
Buster Bar®	1	450	41	3	10	28	12.0	15	280	2
Chicken sandwiches										
chicken breast fillet	1	500	48	3	19	26	4.5	30	1090	4
grilled chicken	1	310	30	2	24	10	2.5	50	1040	3
Chicken Strip Basket™	1	1000	102	6½	35	50	13.0	55	2510	5
Chili 'n' cheese dog	1	330	22	1½	14	21	9.0	45	1090	2
Chocolate Dilly® bar	1	210	21	1½	3	13	7.0	10	75	0
Dipped cone										
small	1	340	42	3	6	17	9.0	20	130	1
medium	1	490	59	4	8	24	13.0	30	190	1
DQ® cakes										
8 in. frozen cake	⅛ cake	370	56	4	7	13	8.0	25	280	0
8 in. round layer cake	⅛ cake	330	49	3	6	12	6.0	15	350	0
DQ® fudge bar, no sugar added	1	50	13	1	4	0	0.0	0	70	0
DQ Homestyle® burgers										
bacon double cheeseburger	1	610	31	2	41	36	18.0	130	1380	2
cheeseburger	1	340	29	2	20	17	8.0	55	850	2
double cheeseburger	1	540	30	2	35	31	16.0	115	1130	2
hamburger	1	290	29	2	17	12	5.0	45	630	2
Ultimate®	1	670	29	2	40	43	19.0	135	1210	2
DQ® ice cream sandwich	1	200	31	2	4	6	3.0	10	140	1
DQ® soft serve, cone, chocolate										
small	1	240	37	2½	6	8	5.0	20	115	0
medium	1	340	53	3½	8	11	7.0	30	160	0
DQ® soft serve, cone, vanilla										
small	1	230	38	2½	6	7	4.5	20	115	0
medium	1	330	53	3½	8	9	6.0	30	160	0
large	1	410	65	4	10	12	8.0	40	200	0
DQ® soft serve, cup										
chocolate	½ cup	150	22	1½	4	5	3.5	15	75	0
vanilla	½ cup	140	22	1½	3	5	3.0	15	70	0
DQ® Treatzza Pizza®, Heath®	⅛ pizza	180	28	2	3	7	3.5	5	160	1

FAST FOODS & RESTAURANT CHAINS

Dairy Queen®

ITEM	AMOUNT	CALORIES	CARBOHYDRATE (g)	CARBOHYDRATE CHOICES	PROTEIN (g)	FAT (g)	SATURATED FAT (g)	CHOLESTEROL (mg)	SODIUM (mg)	FIBER (g)
DQ® vanilla orange bar, no sugar added	1	60	17	1	2	0	0.0	0	40	0
French fries	small	350	42	3	4	18	3.5	0	880	3
Hot dog	1	240	19	1	9	14	5.0	25	730	1
Lemon DQ Freez'r®	½ cup	80	20	1	0	0	0.0	0	10	0
Malts, chocolate										
small	1	650	111	7½	15	16	10.0	55	370	0
medium	1	880	153	10	19	22	14.0	70	500	0
Misty® slush										
small	1	220	56	4	0	0	0.0	0	20	0
medium	1	290	74	5	0	0	0.0	0	30	0
Onion rings	1 order	320	39	2½	5	16	4.0	0	180	3
Peanut Buster® parfait	1	730	99	6½	16	31	17.0	35	400	2
Pecan Mudslide™ treat	1	650	85	5½	11	30	12.0	35	420	2
Shakes, chocolate										
small	1	560	94	6	13	15	10.0	50	310	0
medium	1	770	130	8½	17	20	13.0	70	420	0
Starkiss®	1	80	21	1½	0	0	0.0	0	10	0
Strawberry shortcake	1	430	70	4½	7	14	9.0	60	360	1
Sundaes, chocolate										
small	1	280	49	3	5	7	4.5	20	140	0
medium	1	400	71	5	8	10	6.0	30	210	0
Denny's®										
Appetizers *(Listed w/o condiments or bread.)*										
buffalo chicken strips	5 pieces	734	43	3	48	42	4.0	96	1673	0
buffalo wings	12 pieces	856	1	0	92	54	17.0	500	5552	1
chicken strips	5 pieces	720	56	4	47	33	4.0	95	1666	0
mozzarella sticks	8 pieces	710	49	3	36	41	24.0	48	5220	6
Sampler™	1 (17 oz.)	1405	124	8	47	80	24.0	75	5305	4
smothered cheese fries	1 (9 oz.)	767	69	4½	27	48	17.0	78	875	0
Breakfast *(Listed w/o toppings, bread or sides.)*										
bacon	4 strips	162	1	0	12	18	5.0	36	640	0
bagel, dry	1	235	46	3	9	1	0.0	0	495	0
Belgian waffle	1 (8 oz.)	619	28	2	22	45	22.0	274	1638	0
buttermilk hotcakes	3	466	47	3	20	23	7.0	47	2077	2
country fried steak & eggs	1 (8 oz.)	464	13	½	29	34	9.0	527	828	6
cream cheese	1 oz.	100	1	0	2	10	6.0	31	90	0
English muffin, dry	1	125	24	1½	5	1	0.0	0	198	1
fabulous French toast	3 slices	1146	104	7	26	71	24.0	297	2441	3
fruit mix	3 oz.	36	9	½	1	0	0.0	0	16	1
grits	1 (4 oz.)	80	18	1	2	0	0.0	0	520	0
ham & cheddar omelette	1 (10 oz.)	595	5	0	41	47	16.0	783	1200	0

FAST FOODS & RESTAURANT CHAINS

Denny's®

ITEM	AMOUNT	CALORIES	CARBOHYDRATE (g)	CARBOHYDRATE CHOICES	PROTEIN (g)	FAT (g)	SATURATED FAT (g)	CHOLESTEROL (mg)	SODIUM (mg)	FIBER (g)
Breakfast *(continued)*										
ham & cheddar omelette										
w/ Eggbeaters®	1 (10 oz.)	468	5	0	37	32	11.0	58	1351	0
ham, grilled	1 slice	94	2	0	15	3	1.0	23	761	0
hashed browns	1 (4 oz.)	197	20	1	2	12	2.0	0	446	2
maple-flavored syrup	3 T.	143	36	2½	0	0	0.0	0	26	0
maple-flavored syrup, sugar-free	3 T.	23	9	½	0	0	0.0	0	71	0
margarine, whipped	0.5 oz.	87	0	0	0	10	2.0	0	117	0
meat lover's skillet	1 (14 oz.)	1031	27	1	39	74	24.0	528	2374	10
oatmeal deluxe	1 (19 oz.)	460	95	6	13	6	3.0	11	87	7
one egg	1 (2 oz.)	120	0	0	6	10	3.0	210	120	0
Original Grand Slam®	1 (11 oz.)	665	33	2	26	49	15.0	515	1106	2
sausage	4 links	354	0	0	16	32	12.0	64	944	0
strawberry topping	3 oz.	115	26	2	1	1	0.0	0	12	1
toast, dry	1 slice	90	17	1	3	1	0.0	0	166	1
Ultimate Omelette®	1 (14 oz.)	611	11	1	34	50	17.0	756	1007	3
veggie-cheese omelette	1 (12 oz.)	494	11	1	30	39	12.0	747	719	2
Condiments										
BBQ sauce	1.5 oz.	47	11	1	0	1	0.0	0	595	0
brown gravy	1 oz.	13	2	0	0	0	0.0	0	184	0
chicken gravy	1 oz.	14	2	0	0	1	0.0	2	139	0
country gravy	1 oz.	17	2	0	0	1	0.0	0	93	0
marinara sauce	1.5 oz.	48	7	½	1	2	1.0	0	206	1
sour cream	1.5 oz.	91	2	0	1	9	6.0	19	23	0
tartar sauce	1.5 oz.	225	3	0	0	23	4.0	15	157	0
Dessert Toppings										
blueberry	2 oz.	71	17	1	0	0	0.0	0	10	0
cherry	2 oz.	57	14	1	0	0	0.0	0	3	0
chocolate	2 oz.	317	27	2	2	25	0.0	0	83	0
fudge	2 oz.	201	30	2	1	10	7.0	3	96	1
strawberry	2 oz.	77	17	1	1	1	0.0	0	8	1
whipped cream	2 T.	23	2	0	0	2	0.0	7	3	0
Desserts *(Listed w/o toppings, including sundaes.)*										
apple pie	1 (7 oz.)	470	64	4	3	24	6.0	0	470	1
banana split	1 (19 oz.)	894	121	7½	15	43	19.0	78	177	6
carrot cake	1 (8 oz.)	799	99	6½	9	45	13.0	125	630	2
cheesecake	1 (7 oz.)	580	51	3½	8	38	24.0	174	380	0
chocolate peanut butter pie	1 (6 oz.)	653	64	4	15	39	19.0	27	319	3
double scoop/sundae	1 (6 oz.)	375	29	2	6	27	12.0	74	86	0
Floats, root beer/cola	1 (12 oz.)	280	47	3	3	10	6.0	39	109	0
hot fudge brownie à la mode	1 (10 oz.)	997	147	9½	12	42	6.0	14	82	6
malted milkshake	1 (12 oz.)	583	82	5½	12	26	16.0	100	278	0

FAST FOODS & RESTAURANT CHAINS

Denny's®

ITEM	AMOUNT	CALORIES	CARBOHYDRATE (g)	CARBOHYDRATE CHOICES	PROTEIN (g)	FAT (g)	SATURATED FAT (g)	CHOLESTEROL (mg)	SODIUM (mg)	FIBER (g)
Desserts *(continued)*										
milkshake	1 (12 oz.)	560	76	5	11	26	16.0	100	272	0
Oreo® blender blaster	1 (10 oz.)	580	72	5	11	29	15.0	87	194	1
Oreo® blender blaster	1 (15 oz.)	895	112	7½	16	46	23.0	135	280	2
single scoop/sundae	3 oz.	188	14	1	3	14	6.0	37	43	0
Entrées *(Listed w/o sides, bread or condiments.)*										
chicken strips	1 (10 oz.)	635	55	3½	47	25	1.0	95	1510	0
country fried steak	1 (9 oz.)	644	30	1	28	46	10.0	89	2149	11
fish & chips	1 (17 oz.)	955	77	5	34	57	37.0	97	1497	6
fried shrimp dinner	1 (8 oz.)	219	18	1	17	10	2.0	133	774	1
grilled chicken dinner	1 (4 oz.)	130	0	0	24	4	1.0	67	560	0
pot roast dinner, w/ gravy	1 (7 oz.)	292	5	0	42	11	5.0	87	927	0
roast turkey & stuffing, w/ gravy	1 (14 oz.)	388	38	2½	46	3	1.0	116	2467	2
shrimp scampi skillet dinner	1 (4.5 oz.)	289	3	0	25	19	4.0	192	766	0
sirloin steak dinner	1 (8 oz.)	337	1	0	18	28	8.0	687	344	1
steak & shrimp dinner	1 (9 oz.)	645	31	2	36	42	14.0	150	1143	2
T-bone steak	1 (14 oz.)	860	0	0	65	65	29.0	196	867	0
Salad dressings										
blue cheese	1 oz.	163	1	0	1	18	3.0	20	205	0
Caesar	1 oz.	133	1	0	1	14	2.0	2	380	0
fat free ranch	1 oz.	25	6	½	0	0	0.0	0	300	0
French	1 oz.	106	3	0	0	10	2.0	7	274	0
honey mustard	1 oz.	160	20	1	0	15	8.0	20	123	0
low calorie Italian	1 oz.	15	3	0	0	1	0.0	0	390	0
ranch	1 oz.	129	1	0	0	14	2.0	8	189	0
thousand island	1 oz.	118	5	0	0	11	2.0	15	170	0
Salads *(Listed w/o salad dressing or bread unless indicated.)*										
garden, w/ albacore tuna	1 (19 oz.)	489	41	2	27	29	7.0	66	915	8
garden, w/ fried chicken strips	1 (15 oz.)	438	26	2	33	26	6.0	78	1030	4
garden, w/ grilled chicken	1 (14 oz.)	264	10	½	32	11	5.0	89	714	4
grilled chicken Caesar, w/ dressing	1 (13 oz.)	600	19	1	37	41	10.0	101	1792	4
side Caesar, w/ dressing	1 (6 oz.)	362	20	1	11	26	7.0	23	913	3
side garden, w/o dressing	1 (7 oz.)	113	16	1	3	4	1.0	0	147	3
Sandwiches *(Listed w/o French fries, sides & condiments.)*										
albacore tuna melt	1 (9 oz.)	640	42	3	30	39	13.0	109	1438	3
bacon cheddar burger	1 (14 oz.)	875	58	3½	53	52	19.0	163	1672	5
BBQ Burger™	1 (14 oz.)	953	72	5	52	52	21.0	136	2130	4
BBQ chicken	1 (17 oz.)	1089	86	5½	48	62	14.0	103	1872	5
BLT	1 (7 oz.)	610	50	3	15	38	9.0	35	862	2
Boca Burger®	1 (11 oz.)	601	64	3½	32	27	6.0	14	1446	9

FAST FOODS & RESTAURANT CHAINS

Denny's®

ITEM	AMOUNT	CALORIES	CARBOHYDRATE (g)	CARBOHYDRATE CHOICES	PROTEIN (g)	FAT (g)	SATURATED FAT (g)	CHOLESTEROL (mg)	SODIUM (mg)	FIBER (g)
Sandwiches *(continued)*										
buffalo chicken	1 (11 oz.)	708	80	5	37	28	6.0	74	1733	5
chicken ranch melt	1 (11 oz.)	758	44	3	44	45	14.0	105	2195	3
classic burger	1 (11 oz.)	694	56	4	40	35	12.0	100	785	4
classic burger, w/ cheese	1 (13 oz.)	852	57	4	49	48	20.0	140	1385	4
club	1 (11 oz.)	718	62	4	32	38	7.0	75	1666	3
grilled chicken	1 (9 oz.)	469	53	3½	35	14	3.0	77	1392	4
ham & Swiss on rye	1 (9 oz.)	417	39	2	32	16	8.0	57	1763	5
hoagie chicken melt	1 (12 oz.)	751	43	3	46	44	12.0	93	1834	2
hoagie Philly melt	1 (18 oz.)	874	58	3½	47	50	16.0	114	2444	5
mushroom Swiss burger	1 (16 oz.)	880	63	4	51	49	19.0	137	1619	5
patty melt	1 (10 oz.)	798	37	2½	45	51	21.0	127	1285	4
The Super Bird®	1 (9 oz.)	620	48	3	35	32	5.0	60	1880	2
turkey breast on multigrain, w/o mayo	1 (8 oz.)	277	41	2½	23	4	0.0	15	1607	5
Sides										
applesauce, Musselman's®	3 oz.	60	15	1	0	0	0.0	0	13	1
baked potato, plain	1 (7 oz.)	220	51	3	5	0	0.0	0	16	5
bread stuffing, plain	3 oz.	100	19	1	3	1	0.0	0	405	1
carrots in honey glaze	4 oz.	80	12	1	1	3	1.0	0	220	3
corn in butter sauce	4 oz.	120	19	1	3	4	2.0	5	260	5
cottage cheese	3 oz.	72	2	0	9	3	2.0	10	281	0
French fries, unsalted	1 (6 oz.)	423	57	3½	6	20	5.0	0	221	5
green beans, w/ bacon	4 oz.	60	6	½	1	4	2.0	5	390	3
herb toast	2 oz.	170	15	1	2	11	2.0	0	325	1
mashed potatoes, plain	5 oz.	168	23	1½	3	7	3.0	8	498	2
onion rings	1 (4 oz.)	381	38	2½	5	23	6.0	6	1003	1
seasoned fries	4 oz.	261	35	2	5	12	3.0	0	556	0
Domino's Pizza®										
BBQ wings	1	50	2	0	6	2	0.5	26	175	0
Breadsticks	1	116	18	1	3	4	1.0	0	152	1
Cheese pizza, medium, (12 in.)										
deep dish	1 slice	241	28	2	9	11	4.0	15	562	2
hand tossed	1 slice	187	27	2	8	6	2.5	11	388	1
thin crust	¼ pizza	273	31	2	12	12	4.0	23	835	2
Cheesy bread	1 piece	142	18	1	4	6	2.0	6	183	1
Extra cheese pizza, medium, (12 in.)										
deep dish	1 slice	265	28	2	11	13	5.0	21	643	2
hand tossed	1 slice	211	27	2	10	8	3.5	17	469	1
thin crust	¼ pizza	322	32	2	15	16	6.0	34	998	2
Feast™ pizza, hand tossed, medium, (12 in.)										
Barbeque Feast™	1 slice	253	31	2	11	10	4.5	23	603	1

FAST FOODS & RESTAURANT CHAINS
Domino's Pizza®

ITEM	AMOUNT	CALORIES	CARBOHYDRATE (g)	CARBOHYDRATE CHOICES	PROTEIN (g)	FAT (g)	SATURATED FAT (g)	CHOLESTEROL (mg)	SODIUM (mg)	FIBER (g)
Feast™ pizza *(continued)*										
ExtravaganZZa Feast™	1 slice	288	29	2	13	13	6.0	32	756	2
Hawaiian Feast™	1 slice	225	29	2	11	8	3.5	20	551	2
MeatZZa Feast™	1 slice	280	29	2	13	13	5.5	32	731	2
Vegi Feast™	1 slice	220	29	2	10	8	3.5	17	494	2
Ham pizza, medium, (12 in.)										
deep dish	1 slice	253	28	2	11	11	4.0	20	669	2
hand tossed	1 slice	199	27	2	10	6	2.5	16	495	1
thin crust	¼ pizza	296	31	2	15	13	4.5	32	1050	2
Hot wings	1	45	1	0	5	2	0.5	26	354	0
Pepperoni pizza, medium, (12 in.)										
deep dish	1 slice	278	28	2	11	14	5.5	23	699	2
hand tossed	1 slice	224	27	2	10	9	4.0	19	525	1
thin crust	¼ pizza	347	31	2	15	19	6.5	38	1108	2
Sausage pizza, medium, (12 in.)										
deep dish	1 slice	279	29	2	11	14	5.0	23	682	2
hand tossed	1 slice	225	28	2	10	9	3.5	19	508	1
thin crust	¼ pizza	350	33	2	15	18	6.5	39	1074	2
Dunkin' Donuts®										
Bagels										
berry berry	1	340	69	4½	11	3	0.5	0	540	4
cinnamon raisin	1	330	65	4	10	3	0.5	0	560	3
everything	1	430	75	5	17	7	0.5	0	780	3
onion	1	370	71	5	14	4	1.0	0	650	4
plain	1	360	69	4½	14	3	0.5	0	780	3
sesame	1	450	71	5	18	11	0.5	0	780	3
wheat	1	350	66	4½	13	5	1.0	0	650	4
Breakfast Sandwiches										
bagel, w/ egg, bacon & cheese	1	500	71	5	26	13	6.0	135	1410	2
bagel, w/ egg, sausage & cheese	1	670	71	5	32	28	11.0	170	1700	2
biscuit, w/ egg & cheese	1	360	31	2	14	20	7.0	125	1190	1
croissant, w/ egg, ham & cheese	1	470	38	2½	20	27	9.0	150	940	0
English muffin, w/ egg, ham & cheese	1	310	35	2	21	10	5.0	145	1300	1
Cappuccino, w/ sugar	10 fl. oz.	130	21	1½	4	5	2.5	15	65	0
w/o sugar	10 fl. oz.	80	7	½	4	5	2.5	20	70	0
Coolattas®										
coffee, w/ 2% milk	16 fl. oz.	190	41	3	4	2	1.5	10	80	0
coffee, w/ cream	16 fl. oz.	350	40	2½	3	22	14.0	75	65	0
coffee, w/ skim milk	16 fl. oz.	170	41	3	4	0	0.0	0	80	0
coffee, w/ whole milk	16 fl. oz.	210	42	3	4	4	2.5	15	80	0
lemonade	16 fl. oz.	240	59	4	0	0	0.0	0	35	0
orange mango fruit	16 fl. oz.	270	66	4½	1	0	0.0	0	25	2

ITEM	AMOUNT	CALORIES	CARBOHYDRATE (g)	CARBOHYDRATE CHOICES	PROTEIN (g)	FAT (g)	SATURATED FAT (g)	CHOLESTEROL (mg)	SODIUM (mg)	FIBER (g)
Coolattas® *(continued)*										
strawberry fruit	16 fl. oz.	290	72	5	0	0	0.0	0	30	1
vanilla bean	16 fl. oz.	440	70	4½	1	17	15.0	0	95	1
Cream cheese										
chive	2 oz.	170	4	0	4	17	11.0	45	230	2
garden vegetable	2 oz.	170	4	0	2	15	11.0	45	340	0
lite	2 oz.	110	6	½	4	9	7.0	30	230	0
plain	2 oz.	190	4	0	4	17	13.0	55	190	0
strawberry	2 oz.	190	9	½	4	17	9.0	45	150	0
Donuts										
apple n' spice	1	200	29	2	3	8	1.5	0	270	1
Bavarian kreme	1	210	30	2	3	9	2.0	0	270	1
blueberry cake	1	290	35	2	3	16	3.5	10	400	1
Boston kreme	1	240	36	2½	3	9	2.0	0	280	1
bow tie	1	300	34	2	4	17	3.5	0	340	1
chocolate frosted	1	200	29	2	3	9	2.0	0	260	1
chocolate frosted coffee roll	1	290	36	2½	4	15	3.0	0	340	1
coffee roll	1	270	33	2	4	14	3.0	0	340	1
eclair	1	270	39	2½	3	11	2.5	0	290	1
French cruller	1	150	17	1	2	8	2.0	20	105	1
glazed cake	1	350	41	3	4	19	5.0	25	340	1
glazed raised	1	180	25	1½	3	8	1.5	0	250	1
jelly filled	1	210	32	2	3	8	1.5	0	280	1
lemon burst	1	300	35	2	3	14	5.0	0	300	3
maple frosted	1	210	30	2	3	9	2.0	0	260	1
old fashion cake	1	300	28	2	4	19	5.0	25	330	1
plain cake stick	1	420	35	2	4	29	7.0	35	310	1
powdered cake	1	330	36	2½	4	19	5.0	25	330	1
powdered cake stick	1	450	42	3	4	29	7.0	35	310	1
vanilla kreme	1	270	36	2½	3	13	3.0	0	250	1
Dunkaccino®	10 fl. oz.	230	35	2	2	10	3.0	5	210	0
Espresso, w/ sugar	2 fl. oz.	30	7	½	0	0	0.0	0	5	0
w/o sugar	2 fl. oz.	0	1	0	0	0	0.0	0	5	0
Lattes										
caramel swirl	10 fl. oz.	230	36	2½	8	6	3.5	25	140	0
mocha swirl	10 fl. oz.	230	37	2½	6	7	4.0	25	110	1
regular, w/ sugar	10 fl. oz.	160	22	1½	6	6	3.5	25	95	0
regular, w/o sugar	10 fl. oz.	120	10	½	6	6	3.5	25	95	0
Muffins										
banana nut	1	540	73	5	10	23	6.0	75	550	3
blueberry	1	490	75	5	8	18	6.0	75	630	2
blueberry, reduced fat	1	450	74	5	9	13	3.5	70	650	2

FAST FOODS & RESTAURANT CHAINS

Dunkin' Donuts®

ITEM	AMOUNT	CALORIES	CARBOHYDRATE (g)	CARBOHYDRATE CHOICES	PROTEIN (g)	FAT (g)	SATURATED FAT (g)	CHOLESTEROL (mg)	SODIUM (mg)	FIBER (g)
Muffins *(continued)*										
carrot walnut spice	1	600	81	5½	8	27	8.0	50	430	3
chocolate chip	1	590	85	5½	9	23	10.0	75	570	3
corn	1	510	81	5½	9	17	5.0	85	950	1
cranberry orange	1	460	71	5	8	16	5.0	70	530	3
honey bran raisin	1	490	81	5	10	14	3.5	60	510	5
pumpkin, w/ topping	1	610	83	5½	10	28	6.0	15	690	3
Munchkins										
cinnamon cake	4	270	31	2	3	15	3.5	25	210	1
glazed	5	200	27	2	3	9	2.0	0	220	1
glazed cake	3	280	38	2½	3	13	3.0	20	190	1
jelly filled	5	210	30	2	3	9	2.0	0	240	1
plain cake	4	270	27	2	3	16	4.0	25	240	1
powdered cake	4	270	31	2	3	14	3.5	25	210	1
sugar raised	7	220	26	2	4	12	2.5	0	290	1
Scones										
blueberry	1	410	55	3½	5	19	5.0	40	320	1
cinnamon apple	1	460	67	4½	5	19	5.0	30	340	2
maple walnut	1	470	62	4	6	22	5.0	40	320	1
raspberry white chocolate	1	450	59	4	6	22	7.0	40	330	2
Vanilla chai	10 fl. oz.	230	40	2½	1	8	6.0	5	50	0
Hardee's®										
Apple turnover	1	270	38	2½	4	12	4.0	0	250	n/a
Biscuits										
Apple Cinnamon 'N' Raisin™	1	250	42	3	2	8	2.0	0	350	n/a
bacon, w/ egg & cheese	1	520	45	3	17	30	11.0	210	1420	n/a
Biscuit 'N' Gravy™	1	530	56	4	10	30	9.0	15	1550	n/a
chicken	1	590	62	4	24	27	7.0	45	1820	n/a
country ham	1	440	44	3	14	22	7.0	30	1710	n/a
ham	1	410	45	3	13	20	6.0	25	1200	n/a
loaded omelet	1	540	45	3	20	32	12.0	225	1350	n/a
plain, made from scratch	1	390	44	3	6	21	6.0	0	1000	n/a
sausage	1	550	44	3	12	36	11.0	25	1310	n/a
sausage & egg	1	620	45	3	19	41	13.0	225	1370	n/a
steak	1	580	56	4	15	32	10.0	30	1580	n/a
Chicken, fried										
breast	1	370	29	2	29	15	4.0	75	1190	n/a
leg	1	170	15	1	13	7	2.0	45	570	n/a
thigh	1	330	30	2	19	15	4.0	60	1000	n/a
wing	1	200	23	1½	10	8	2.0	30	740	n/a
Chicken sandwiches										
big chicken fillet	1	716	65	4	41	34	6.0	93	1942	n/a

FAST FOODS & RESTAURANT CHAINS

Hardee's®

ITEM	AMOUNT	CALORIES	CARBOHYDRATE (g)	CARBOHYDRATE CHOICES	PROTEIN (g)	FAT (g)	SATURATED FAT (g)	CHOLESTEROL (mg)	SODIUM (mg)	FIBER (g)
Chicken sandwiches *(continued)*										
grilled chicken	1	350	28	2	23	16	3.0	65	860	n/a
slammer	1	278	35	2	17	8	2.0	40	743	n/a
Cole slaw	small	240	13	1	2	20	3.0	10	340	n/a
Fish supreme sandwich	1	520	47	3	20	28	7.0	75	1120	n/a
French fries										
small	1 order	340	45	3	4	16	2.0	0	390	n/a
medium	1 order	440	59	4	5	21	3.0	0	520	n/a
large	1 order	510	67	4½	6	24	3.0	0	590	n/a
Frisco™ breakfast sandwich	1	450	42	3	22	22	8.0	225	1290	n/a
Hamburgers										
1/3 lb. Bacon Cheese Thickburger™	1	800	41	3	39	55	18.0	120	1413	n/a
1/3 lb. cheeseburger	1	613	45	3	34	35	14.0	92	1382	n/a
1/3 lb. Chili Cheese Thickburger™	1	855	48	3	42	57	23.0	121	1704	n/a
1/3 lb. Monster Thickburger™	1	856	38	2½	41	61	22.0	136	1716	n/a
1/2 lb. Six Dollar™ burger	1	900	45	3	45	62	22.0	129	1777	n/a
2/3 lb. Bacon Cheese Thickburger™	1	1148	42	3	63	82	31.0	198	2042	n/a
2/3 lb. Monster Thickburger™	1	1201	38	2½	66	88	34.0	228	2337	n/a
2/3 lb. Thickburger™	1	1088	44	3	59	76	29.0	183	2027	n/a
slammer	1	271	27	2	11	13	5.0	30	400	n/a
slammer, w/ cheese	1	318	28	2	14	17	7.0	35	626	n/a
Hash Rounds™	16	230	24	1½	3	14	3.0	0	560	n/a
Hot dog, w/ chili	1	450	25	1½	15	32	12.0	55	1240	n/a
Hot Ham 'N' Cheese™ sandwich	1	300	34	2	16	12	6.0	50	1390	n/a
Mashed potatoes, w/ gravy	small	90	17	1	2	0	0.0	0	590	n/a
Peach cobbler	small	310	60	4	2	7	1.0	0	360	n/a
Roast beef sandwiches										
Big Roast Beef™	1	410	26	2	24	24	9.0	40	1140	n/a
regular	1	310	26	2	17	16	6.0	40	800	n/a
KFC®										
BBQ baked beans	1 (5.5 oz.)	190	33	2	6	3	1.0	5	760	6
Biscuit	1 (2 oz.)	180	20	1	4	10	2.5	0	560	0
Chicken sandwiches										
honey BBQ flavored	1 (5.3 oz.)	310	37	2½	28	6	2.0	125	560	2
Original Recipe®, w/ sauce	1 (7.3 oz.)	450	33	2	29	22	5.0	70	940	2
Chunky chicken pot pie	1 (13 oz.)	770	69	4	29	42	13.0	70	2160	5
Cole slaw	1 (5 oz.)	232	26	2	2	14	2.0	8	284	3
Colonel's Crispy Strips®	3 pieces	340	20	1	28	16	4.5	70	1140	0
Corn on the cob	1 (5.7 oz.)	150	35	2	5	2	0.0	0	20	2
Extra Crispy™ chicken										
breast	1 (5.7 oz.)	470	19	1	34	28	8.0	135	1230	0
drumstick	1 (2.1 oz.)	160	5	0	12	10	2.5	70	415	0

FAST FOODS & RESTAURANT CHAINS

KFC®

ITEM	AMOUNT	CALORIES	CARBOHYDRATE (g)	CARBOHYDRATE CHOICES	PROTEIN (g)	FAT (g)	SATURATED FAT (g)	CHOLESTEROL (mg)	SODIUM (mg)	FIBER (g)
Extra Crispy™ chicken *(continued)*										
thigh	1 (4 oz.)	370	12	1	21	26	7.0	120	710	0
whole wing	1 (1.8 oz.)	190	10	½	10	12	3.5	55	390	0
Green beans	1 (4.7 oz.)	45	7	½	1	2	0.5	5	730	3
Hot & spicy chicken										
breast	1 (6.3 oz.)	450	20	1	33	27	8.0	130	1450	0
drumstick	1 (2.1 oz.)	140	4	0	13	9	2.5	65	380	0
thigh	1 (4.5 oz.)	390	14	1	22	28	8.0	125	1240	0
whole wing	1 (1.9 oz.)	180	9	½	11	11	3.0	60	420	0
Hot Wings™	6 pieces	471	18	1	27	33	8.0	150	1230	2
Macaroni & cheese	1 (5.4 oz.)	180	21	1½	7	8	3.0	10	860	2
Mashed potatoes, w/ gravy	1 (4.8 oz.)	120	17	1	1	6	1.0	0	440	2
Mean Greens®	1 (5.4 oz.)	70	11	½	4	3	1.0	10	650	5
Original Recipe® chicken										
breast	1 (5.7 oz.)	370	11	1	40	19	6.0	145	1145	0
drumstick	1 (2.1 oz.)	140	4	0	14	8	2.0	75	440	0
thigh	1 (3.2 oz.)	360	12	1	22	25	7.0	165	1060	0
whole wing	1 (1.7 oz.)	145	5	0	11	9	2.5	60	370	0
Popcorn chicken										
small	1 order	362	21	1½	17	23	6.0	43	610	0
large	1 order	620	36	2½	30	40	10.0	73	1046	0
Potato salad	1 (5.6 oz.)	230	23	1½	4	14	2.0	15	540	3
Potato wedges	1 (5.5 oz.)	376	53	3	6	15	4.0	4	1323	5
McDonald's®										
Apple pie	1 (2.7 oz.)	260	34	2	3	13	3.5	0	200	0
Biscuits										
bacon, egg & cheese	1 (5.4 oz.)	480	31	2	21	31	10.0	250	1360	1
plain	1 (2.4 oz.)	240	30	2	4	11	2.5	0	640	1
sausage	1 (4 oz.)	410	30	2	10	28	8.0	35	930	1
sausage & egg	1 (5.7 oz)	490	31	2	16	33	10.0	245	1010	1
Breakfast burrito, sausage	1 (4 oz.)	290	24	1½	13	16	6.0	170	680	2
Chicken McNuggets®										
4 piece	1 (2.5 oz.)	210	12	1	10	13	2.5	35	460	1
6 piece	1 (3.8 oz.)	310	18	1	15	20	4.0	50	680	2
Chicken sandwiches										
Chicken McGrill®	1 (7.5 oz.)	400	37	2½	25	17	3.0	60	890	2
crispy chicken	1 (7.7 oz.)	500	46	3	22	26	4.5	50	1100	2
Cinnamon roll	1 (3.5 oz.)	340	52	3½	5	15	5.0	35	250	3
Danish										
apple	1 (3.7 oz.)	340	47	3	5	15	3.0	20	340	2
cheese	1 (3.7 oz.)	400	45	3	7	21	5.0	40	400	2
Egg McMuffin®	1 (4.9 oz.)	300	29	2	18	12	5.0	235	840	1

FAST FOODS & RESTAURANT CHAINS
McDonald's®

ITEM	AMOUNT	CALORIES	CARBOHYDRATE (g)	CARBOHYDRATE CHOICES	PROTEIN (g)	FAT (g)	SATURATED FAT (g)	CHOLESTEROL (mg)	SODIUM (mg)	FIBER (g)
Filet-O-Fish®	1 (5.5 oz.)	470	45	3	15	26	5.0	50	730	1
French fries										
small	1 (2.4 oz.)	210	26	2	3	10	1.5	0	135	2
medium	1 (5.2 oz.)	450	57	3½	6	22	4.0	0	290	5
large	1 (6.2 oz.)	540	68	4	8	26	4.5	0	350	6
Super Size®	1 (7 oz.)	610	77	4½	9	29	5.0	0	390	7
Fruit 'n yogurt parfait										
original	1 (11.9 oz.)	380	76	5	10	5	2.0	15	240	2
snack size	1 (5.3 oz.)	160	30	2	4	2	1.0	5	85	0
Hamburgers										
Big Mac®	1 (7.6 oz.)	590	47	3	24	34	11.0	85	1070	3
Big N' Tasty®	1 (8.2 oz.)	530	37	2½	24	32	10.0	80	790	2
Big N' Tasty®, w/ cheese	1 (8.7 oz.)	580	37	2½	26	37	12.0	95	1030	2
cheeseburger	1 (4.2 oz.)	330	35	2	15	14	6.0	45	800	2
double cheeseburger	1 (6.1 oz.)	480	37	2½	25	27	12.0	85	1220	2
hamburger	1 (3.7 oz.)	280	35	2	12	10	4.0	30	560	2
Quarter Pounder®	1 (6.1 oz.)	420	36	2½	23	21	8.0	70	780	2
Quarter Pounder®, w/cheese	1 (7 oz.)	530	38	2½	28	30	13.0	95	1250	2
Hash browns	1 (1.9 oz.)	130	14	1	1	8	1.5	0	330	1
Hot cakes, w/ margarine & syrup	1 (8 oz.)	600	104	7	9	17	3.0	20	770	0
Ice cream cone, vanilla,										
reduced fat	1 (3.2 oz.)	150	23	1½	4	5	3.0	20	75	0
McDonaldland® cookies	1 pkt.	230	38	2½	3	8	2.0	0	250	1
McFlurry™										
Butterfinger®	1 (12 oz.)	620	90	6	16	22	14.0	70	260	0
M&M®	1 (12 oz.)	630	90	6	16	23	15.0	75	210	1
Nestle Crunch®	1 (12 oz.)	630	89	6	16	24	16.0	75	230	0
Oreo®	1 (12 oz.)	570	82	5½	15	20	12.0	70	280	0
McGriddle™										
bacon, egg & cheese	1 (5.9 oz.)	450	43	3	19	23	8.0	240	1270	1
sausage	1 (4.7 oz.)	420	42	3	11	23	7.0	35	970	1
sausage, egg & cheese	1 (7 oz.)	550	43	3	20	33	11.0	260	1290	1
Salad dressings, Newman's Own®										
balsamic vinaigrette, light	1 pkt.	90	4	0	0	8	1.0	0	950	0
Caesar	1 pkt.	190	4	0	2	18	3.5	20	500	0
cobb	1 pkt.	120	9	½	1	9	1.5	10	440	0
ranch	1 pkt.	290	4	0	1	30	4.5	20	530	0
Salads										
Caesar, crispy chicken	1 (10 oz.)	310	20	1	23	16	4.5	50	890	3
Caesar, grilled chicken	1 (9.8 oz.)	210	11	1	26	7	3.5	60	680	3
Caesar, w/o chicken	1 (6.7 oz.)	90	7	½	7	4	2.5	10	170	3
Calif. cobb, crispy chicken	1 (10.9 oz.)	380	20	1	27	23	7.0	125	1170	3

FAST FOODS & RESTAURANT CHAINS

McDonald's®

ITEM	AMOUNT	CALORIES	CARBOHYDRATE (g)	CARBOHYDRATE CHOICES	PROTEIN (g)	FAT (g)	SATURATED FAT (g)	CHOLESTEROL (mg)	SODIUM (mg)	FIBER (g)
Salads *(continued)*										
Calif. cobb, grilled chicken	1 (10.7 oz.)	280	11	1	30	14	6.0	130	960	3
Calif. cobb, w/o chicken	1 (7.6 oz.)	160	7	½	11	11	4.5	85	450	3
garden, side salad	1 (3 oz.)	15	3	0	1	0	0.0	0	10	1
Sausage McMuffin®, w/ egg	1 (5.8 oz.)	450	29	2	20	28	10.0	260	930	2
Scrambled eggs (2)	1 order	160	1	0	13	11	3.5	425	170	0
Shakes, Triple Thick™										
chocolate	1 (12 oz.)	430	70	4½	11	12	8.0	50	210	1
strawberry	1 (12 oz.)	420	67	4½	11	12	8.0	50	140	0
vanilla	1 (12 oz.)	430	67	4½	11	12	8.0	50	300	0
Sundaes										
hot caramel	1 (6.4 oz.)	360	61	4	7	10	6.0	35	180	0
hot fudge	1 (6.3 oz.)	340	52	3½	8	12	9.0	30	170	1
strawberry	1 (6.3 oz.)	290	50	3	7	7	5.0	30	95	0
Value meals, regular, w/ medium drink & medium fries										
Big Mac®	1 meal	1250	162	10	30	56	15.0	85	1380	8
Chicken McNuggets®, 10 piece	1 meal	1170	145	9	31	55	10.0	85	1450	8
crispy chicken	1 meal	1160	161	10	28	48	8.5	50	1410	7
double cheeseburger	1 meal	1140	152	9½	31	49	16.0	85	1530	7
Filet-O-Fish®	1 meal	1130	160	10	21	48	9.0	50	1140	6
Quarter Pounder®	1 meal	1080	151	9½	29	43	12.0	70	1090	7
Value meals®, Super Size®, w/ large drink & Super Size® fries										
Big Mac®	1 meal	1610	237	15	33	63	16.0	85	1500	10
crispy chicken	1 meal	1520	236	15	31	55	9.5	50	1530	9
Filet-O-Fish®	1 meal	1490	235	15	24	55	10.0	50	1160	8
Olive Garden										
Garden Fare Selections *(Carbohydrate choices were calculated without adjusting for fiber.)*										
Lunch Entrées										
capellini pomodoro	1 order	350	52	3½	10	11	1.5	5	720	n/a
chicken giardino	1 order	350	40	2½	26	7	3.0	50	1180	n/a
linguine alla marinara	1 order	280	48	3	8	6	1.0	0	510	n/a
shrimp primavera	1 order	490	65	4	26	15	2.0	140	820	n/a
Dinner Entrées										
capellini pomodoro	1 order	560	84	5½	17	18	3.0	10	1130	n/a
chicken giardino	1 order	460	59	4	36	8	3.0	60	1180	n/a
linguine alla marinara	1 order	450	79	5	14	9	1.5	0	770	n/a
shrimp primavera	1 order	730	84	5½	44	25	4.0	270	1220	n/a
Soups & Breadsticks										
minestrone soup	1 order	100	18	1	5	1	0.0	0	610	n/a
plain breadstick	1 stick	140	26	2	5	2	0.0	0	270	n/a

ITEM	AMOUNT	CALORIES	CARBOHYDRATE (g)	CARBOHYDRATE CHOICES	PROTEIN (g)	FAT (g)	SATURATED FAT (g)	CHOLESTEROL (mg)	SODIUM (mg)	FIBER (g)
P.F. Chang's China Bistro®										
Appetizers										
Chang's chicken in soothing lettuce wraps (Servings per dish = ~3½)	1 serving	128	14	1	10	4	n/a	n/a	n/a	4
Chang's vegetarian lettuce wraps (Servings per dish = ~3½)	1 serving	175	15	1	8	9	n/a	n/a	n/a	2
Crab wontons (Servings per dish = ~2½)	1 serving	290	26	2	10	16	6.0	n/a	1660	1
Harvest spring rolls (Servings per dish = ~2)	1 serving	170	14	1	2	12	2.5	n/a	890	3
Peking dumplings (Servings per dish = ~2)	1 serving	170	11	1	10	9	2.0	n/a	930	1
Salt & pepper calamari (Servings per dish = ~1½)	1 serving	320	21	1½	16	19	1.0	n/a	1670	2
Seared Ahi tuna (Servings per dish = ~2)	1 serving	130	5	0	20	3	0.5	n/a	1680	3
Shanghai cucumbers (Servings per dish = ~2)	1 serving	50	3	0	4	3	1.0	n/a	1860	2
Shrimp dumplings (Servings per dish = ~2)	1 serving	120	11	1	9	4	1.0	n/a	1330	1
Vegetable dumplings (Servings per dish = ~2)	1 serving	110	18	1	5	2	0.0	n/a	940	4
Entrées										
Almond & cashew chicken (Servings per dish = ~3)	1 serving	164	20	1	7	6	1.0	n/a	n/a	4
Beef à la Szechuan (Servings per dish = ~3)	1 serving	260	33	2	17	7	1.5	n/a	2560	2
Beef w/ broccoli (Servings per dish = ~3)	1 serving	230	17	1	13	12	5.0	n/a	2970	3
Buddha's feast, steamed (Servings per dish = ~3)	1 serving	60	10	0	4	1	0.0	n/a	200	5
Buddha's feast, stir-fried (Servings per dish = ~3½)	1 serving	110	13	½	7	3	0.5	n/a	2160	5
Cantonese pork medallions (Servings per dish = ~1)	1 serving	190	18	1	20	5	2.5	n/a	1390	3
Cantonese roasted duck (Servings per dish = ~3½)	1 serving	260	18	1	19	12	3.5	n/a	250	2
Cantonese scallops (Servings per dish = ~3)	1 serving	107	5	0	15	3	0.0	n/a	n/a	1
Cantonese shrimp (Servings per dish = ~3)	1 serving	106	3	0	16	3	0.0	n/a	n/a	1

FAST FOODS & RESTAURANT CHAINS

P.F. Chang's China Bistro®

ITEM	AMOUNT	CALORIES	CARBOHYDRATE (g)	CARBOHYDRATE CHOICS	PROTEIN (g)	FAT (g)	SATURATED FAT (g)	CHOLESTEROL (mg)	SODIUM (mg)	FIBER (g)
Chang's lemon scallops (Servings per dish = ~3½)	1 serving	230	24	1½	15	8	1.5	n/a	600	3
Chang's spicy chicken (Servings per dish = ~2½)	1 serving	329	33	2	n/a	14	1.5	n/a	880	2
Chicken chow mein (Servings per dish = ~4)	1 serving	210	24	1½	12	7	1.0	n/a	1610	3
Chicken w/ black bean sauce (Servings per dish = ~3)	1 serving	150	7	½	22	4	1.0	n/a	n/a	1
Coconut curry vegetables (Servings per dish = ~5½)	1 serving	170	12	1	6	11	8.0	n/a	1290	3
Combo double pan fried noodles (Servings per dish = ~6)	1 serving	190	22	1½	10	7	1.0	n/a	1930	1
Crispy honey chicken (Servings per dish = ~3)	1 serving	380	31	2	20	19	1.5	n/a	850	2
Crispy honey shrimp (Servings per dish = ~2)	1 serving	400	25	1½	20	24	4.5	n/a	1460	4
Dan-Dan noodles (Servings per dish = ~6)	1 serving	200	25	1½	11	7	1.0	n/a	1540	2
Garlic noodles (Servings per dish = ~3½)	1 serving	250	30	2	8	11	1.0	n/a	1440	2
Garlic snap peas (Servings per dish = ~1½)	1 serving	260	55	3	5	2	0.0	n/a	670	5
Ginger chicken & broccoli (Servings per dish = ~4½)	1 serving	126	9	½	16	3	0.0	n/a	n/a	2
Hot fish (Servings per dish = ~4½)	1 serving	200	15	1	13	10	1.0	n/a	1580	2
Kung pao chicken (Servings per dish = ~2½)	1 serving	290	14	1	31	12	2.5	n/a	860	3
Lemon pepper shrimp (Servings per dish = ~3)	1 serving	190	13	1	12	10	2.0	n/a	1250	3
Ma po totu (Servings per dish = ~5)	1 serving	93	10	½	6	3	0.0	n/a	878	3
Malaysian chicken (Servings per dish = ~3)	1 serving	180	10	½	13	10	8.0	n/a	1460	2
Mongolian beef (Servings per dish = ~2½)	1 serving	360	17	1	28	20	5.0	n/a	3010	2
Moo goo gai pan (Servings per dish = ~4½)	1 serving	101	4	0	15	5	0.0	n/a	n/a	3
Mu shu chicken (Servings per dish = ~4½)	1 serving	240	19	1	11	13	2.5	n/a	1440	2
Mu shu pork (Servings per dish = ~5½)	1 serving	160	11	1	10	5	2.0	n/a	740	4

FAST FOODS & RESTAURANT CHAINS
P.F. Chang's China Bistro®

ITEM	AMOUNT	CALORIES	CARBOHYDRATE (g)	CARBOHYDRATE CHOICES	PROTEIN (g)	FAT (g)	SATURATED FAT (g)	CHOLESTEROL (mg)	SODIUM (mg)	FIBER (g)
Oolong marinated sea bass (Servings per dish = ~3)	1 serving	220	8	½	14	14	n/a	n/a	n/a	2
Orange peel beef (Servings per dish = ~2½)	1 serving	449	43	3	n/a	25	3.5	n/a	1870	3
Orange peel chicken (Servings per dish = ~2½)	1 serving	340	28	2	21	16	3.0	n/a	1370	3
Orange peel shrimp (Servings per dish = ~3)	1 serving	270	26	2	16	11	2.0	n/a	2040	4
P.F. Chang's fried rice (Servings per dish = ~6)	1 serving	280	33	2	9	13	1.5	n/a	1010	2
Paul's catfish (Servings per dish = ~2½)	1 serving	260	6	½	25	15	3.0	n/a	2390	2
Philip's better lemon chicken (Servings per dish = ~4)	1 serving	270	24	1½	17	11	4.5	n/a	150	2
Poached baby bok choy (Servings per dish = ~3½)	1 serving	70	13	1	3	1	0.0	n/a	1740	3
Scallion pancakes (Servings per dish = ~2)	1 serving	180	21	1½	5	9	3.5	n/a	550	1
Shanghai snow peas (Servings per dish = ~2)	1 serving	90	15	½	4	2	0.0	n/a	390	6
Shrimp w/ lobster sauce (Servings per dish = ~3½)	1 serving	175	24	1½	13	3	0.0	n/a	n/a	1
Singapore street noodles (Servings per dish = ~3)	1 serving	210	27	2	5	9	0.5	n/a	1430	3
Spicy ground chicken & eggplant (Servings per dish = ~4½)	1 serving	220	13	1	8	15	2.5	n/a	1580	2
Spinach w/ garlic (Servings per dish = ~3½)	1 serving	110	5	0	4	10	2.5	n/a	520	3
Stir-fried spicy eggplant (Servings per dish = ~2)	1 serving	220	18	1	2	16	3.0	n/a	1500	2
Sweet & sour pork (Servings per dish = ~4)	1 serving	320	23	1½	9	21	5.0	n/a	550	3
Szechwan asparagus (Servings per dish = ~2)	1 serving	170	12	½	5	11	1.0	n/a	3070	5
Szechwan chicken chow fun (Servings per dish = ~4)	1 serving	290	16	1	9	21	9.0	n/a	2970	2
Szechwan from the sea (Servings per dish = ~2½)	1 serving	230	19	1	20	8	1.5	n/a	1720	2
Szechwan long beans (Servings per dish = ~1½)	1 serving	190	23	1½	6	8	1.5	n/a	3790	0
Temple long beans (Servings per dish = ~3)	1 serving	160	12	1	11	7	1.0	n/a	2520	2

FAST FOODS & RESTAURANT CHAINS

P.F. Chang's China Bistro®

ITEM	AMOUNT	CALORIES	CARBOHYDRATE (g)	CARBOHYDRATE CHOICES	PROTEIN (g)	FAT (g)	SATURATED FAT (g)	CHOLESTEROL (mg)	SODIUM (mg)	FIBER (g)
Vegetable chow fun										
(Servings per dish = ~3½)	1 serving	180	30	1½	4	5	1.0	n/a	2100	6
Soups & salads										
Hot & sour soup										
(Servings per dish = ~4½)	1 serving	80	3	0	4	6	1.5	n/a	2110	2
Oriental chicken salad										
(Servings per dish = ~3½)	1 serving	218	14	1	n/a	14	1.5	n/a	340	1
Peanut chicken salad										
(Servings per dish = ~3½)	1 serving	230	6	½	18	14	3.0	n/a	520	3
Warm duck spinach salad										
(Servings per dish = ~4)	1 serving	216	9	½	16	13	n/a	n/a	n/a	3
Wonton soup										
(Servings per dish = ~4½)	1 serving	70	5	0	4	4	1.0	n/a	1330	2
Pizza Hut®										
Beef pizza										
hand tossed	1 slice	330	29	2	16	17	8.0	25	880	3
pan	1 slice	330	29	2	14	18	7.0	20	690	3
Thin 'N Crispy®	1 slice	270	22	1½	13	15	7.0	25	750	2
Breadstick	1	130	20	1	3	4	1.0	0	170	1
Buffalo wings										
hot	4	210	4	0	22	12	3.0	130	900	0
mild	5	200	0	0	23	12	3.5	150	510	0
Cheese pizza										
hand tossed	1 slice	240	28	2	12	10	5.0	10	650	2
pan	1 slice	290	28	2	12	14	6.0	10	590	2
Personal Pan® pizza	1 pizza	630	71	4	28	28	12.0	25	1370	6
stuffed crust	1 slice	360	39	2½	18	16	8.0	25	1090	3
The Big New Yorker™	1 slice	410	46	2½	20	18	9.0	20	1210	8
Thin 'N Crispy®	1 slice	200	22	1½	10	9	5.0	10	590	2
Chicken supreme pizza										
hand tossed	1 slice	230	29	2	13	7	3.5	15	650	2
pan	1 slice	270	29	2	13	12	4.0	15	580	2
stuffed crust	1 slice	350	41	3	21	13	6.0	35	1130	3
Thin 'N Crispy®	1 slice	200	23	1½	12	7	3.5	20	620	2
Dessert pizza										
apple	1 slice	250	48	3	3	5	1.0	0	230	2
cherry	1 slice	250	47	3	3	5	1.0	0	220	3
Garlic bread	1 slice	150	16	1	3	8	1.5	0	240	1
Ham pizza										
hand tossed	1 slice	260	28	2	14	10	5.0	20	800	2
pan	1 slice	260	28	2	11	12	4.0	15	610	2
stuffed crust	1 slice	330	39	2½	18	13	6.0	30	1130	3

ITEM	AMOUNT	CALORIES	CARBOHYDRATE (g)	CARBOHYDRATE CHOICES	PROTEIN (g)	FAT (g)	SATURATED FAT (g)	CHOLESTEROL (mg)	SODIUM (mg)	FIBER (g)
Ham pizza (continued)										
Thin 'N Crispy®	1 slice	170	21	1½	9	7	3.5	15	610	2
Meat Lover's® pizza										
hand tossed	1 slice	320	28	2	14	17	7.0	30	900	2
pan	1 slice	360	29	2	14	21	7.0	30	840	3
stuffed crust	1 slice	470	40	2½	22	25	11.0	50	1430	3
The Chicago Dish™	1 slice	470	35	2	21	27	12.0	30	630	3
Thin 'N Crispy®	1 slice	310	22	1½	14	19	8.0	35	910	2
P'Zone®										
classic	½ order	640	74	5	34	23	12.0	55	1270	3
pepperoni	½ order	630	69	4½	35	24	12.0	60	1340	3
Pasta										
Cavatini® pasta	1 order	480	66	4	21	14	6.0	8	1170	9
Cavatini Supreme® pasta	1 order	560	73	4	24	19	8.0	10	1400	10
spaghetti, w/ marinara	1 order	490	91	5½	18	6	1.0	0	730	8
spaghetti, w/ meat sauce	1 order	600	98	6	23	13	5.0	8	910	9
spaghetti, w/ meatballs	1 order	850	120	7	37	24	10.0	17	1120	10
Pepperoni Lover's® pizza										
hand tossed	1 slice	280	27	2	11	11	4.5	15	730	2
pan	1 slice	330	29	2	14	18	7.0	20	760	2
stuffed crust	1 slice	420	40	2½	21	21	9.0	40	1350	3
Thin 'N Crispy®	1 slice	250	22	1½	12	13	6.0	20	760	2
Pepperoni pizza										
hand tossed	1 slice	280	28	2	13	13	6.0	20	790	2
pan	1 slice	280	28	2	11	14	5.0	15	610	2
Personal Pan® pizza	1 pizza	620	70	4	26	28	11.0	30	1430	5
stuffed crust	1 slice	360	39	2½	17	16	7.0	30	1120	3
The Big New Yorker®	1 slice	390	46	2½	18	17	7.0	20	1215	8
The Chicago Dish™	1 slice	390	34	2	18	20	9.0	10	390	3
Thin 'N Crispy®	1 slice	190	21	1½	9	9	4.0	15	610	2
Sausage pizza										
hand tossed	1 slice	340	28	2	16	18	8.0	30	910	2
pan	1 slice	340	29	2	13	20	7.0	25	720	2
stuffed crust	1 slice	400	40	2½	19	20	8.0	35	1180	3
Thin 'N Crispy®	1 slice	290	22	1½	12	17	7.0	30	800	2
Super supreme pizza										
hand tossed	1 slice	290	29	2	13	14	6.0	25	850	2
pan	1 slice	340	30	2	14	18	6.0	25	780	3
stuffed crust	1 slice	430	41	3	21	22	9.0	40	1360	3
Thin 'N Crispy®	1 slice	280	23	1½	13	15	6.0	25	840	2
Supreme pizza										
hand tossed	1 slice	270	29	2	13	12	5.0	20	730	3

FAST FOODS & RESTAURANT CHAINS

Pizza Hut®

ITEM	AMOUNT	CALORIES	CARBOHYDRATE (g)	CARBOHYDRATE CHOICES	PROTEIN (g)	FAT (g)	SATURATED FAT (g)	CHOLESTEROL (mg)	SODIUM (mg)	FIBER (g)
Supreme pizza *(continued)*										
pan	1 slice	320	29	2	13	17	6.0	20	670	3
stuffed crust	1 slice	410	41	3	20	20	9.0	35	1220	3
The Big New Yorker®	1 slice	470	48	2½	23	23	10.0	35	1410	9
The Chicago Dish™	1 slice	420	36	2½	20	23	10.0	15	460	3
Thin 'N Crispy®	1 slice	250	23	1½	12	13	6.0	20	710	2
Supreme sandwich	1	640	62	4	34	28	10.0	28	2150	4
Veggie Lover's® pizza										
hand tossed	1 slice	220	29	2	9	8	3.0	5	580	2
pan	1 slice	270	30	2	10	12	4.0	5	510	3
stuffed crust	1 slice	340	42	3	16	14	6.0	20	1030	3
The Chicago Dish™	1 slice	370	36	2½	17	18	8.0	0	310	3
Thin 'N Crispy®	1 slice	190	24	1½	8	7	3.0	5	520	2
Starbuck's® Coffee Company										
Bagels										
cinnamon raisin	1	440	96	6½	13	1	0.0	0	570	3
plain	1	430	92	6	15	1	0.0	0	660	3
sesame	1	440	92	6	16	3	0.0	0	630	6
Bars										
caramel apple	1	310	38	2½	3	16	8.0	40	150	2
caramel brownie	1	580	60	4	5	36	12.0	100	230	2
carrot cake	1	420	46	3	4	25	9.0	85	440	0
enrobed espresso brownie	1	430	48	3	5	25	16.0	75	140	3
espresso brownie	1	370	43	3	4	21	13.0	85	115	2
lemon	1	310	44	3	4	14	8.0	140	130	0
milk chocolate peanut butter brownie	1	460	45	3	6	29	9.0	50	170	2
oatmeal cranberry mountain	1	430	49	3	7	24	13.0	60	320	3
Oreo® dream	1	420	33	2	5	30	15.0	65	200	2
pecan diamond	1	490	38	2½	4	37	12.0	40	170	2
raspberry Sammy	1	300	41	3	3	14	9.0	35	115	1
toffee cream cheese chew	1	440	38	2½	5	31	10.0	65	400	2
toffee crunch	1	430	56	4	4	21	8.0	50	420	1
Biscotti										
chocolate hazelnut	1	110	15	1	2	5	2.0	25	80	1
vanilla almond	1	110	15	1	2	5	1.5	25	75	1
Brewed coffees, black										
coffee of the week	12 fl. oz.	5	1	0	0	0	0.0	0	0	0
decaf coffee of the week	12 fl. oz.	5	1	0	0	0	0.0	0	0	0
Cakes										
apple walnut coffee	1	320	41	3	4	17	5.0	55	330	1
banana pound	1	360	47	3	4	18	11.0	100	380	1
banana pullman	1	400	57	4	5	17	5.0	65	320	2

FAST FOODS & RESTAURANT CHAINS

Starbuck's® Coffee Company

ITEM	AMOUNT	CALORIES	CARBOHYDRATE (g)	CARBOHYDRATE CHOICES	PROTEIN (g)	FAT (g)	SATURATED FAT (g)	CHOLESTEROL (mg)	SODIUM (mg)	FIBER (g)
Cakes *(continued)*										
blueberry walnut coffee	1	340	43	3	4	18	5.0	60	360	1
chocolate big baby bundt	1	330	45	3	5	15	7.0	25	380	4
chocolate pullman	1	380	54	3½	5	17	7.0	55	270	2
cinnamon walnut coffee	1	360	46	3	4	18	5.0	65	390	1
classic coffee	1	570	75	5	7	28	10.0	75	310	2
cranberry walnut pound	1	390	45	3	6	21	9.0	110	310	1
cranberry walnut pullman	1	360	53	3½	5	15	4.0	25	240	2
crumb	1	670	89	6	8	32	15.0	115	360	1
crumble berry coffee	1	520	69	4½	6	26	10.0	75	350	2
hazelnut coffee	1	630	74	5	9	35	14.0	125	460	2
iced carrot pound	1	540	101	7	5	13	2.5	35	320	3
iced lemon pound	1	500	69	4½	6	23	12.0	145	390	0
key lime crumb	1	550	71	5	8	27	10.0	190	370	1
lemon glazed pullman	1	370	55	3½	5	15	9.0	90	180	0
lemon yogurt bundt	1	350	56	4	4	13	4.5	55	250	0
marble chocolate chip pullman	1	440	61	4	6	20	12.0	95	250	1
marble pound	1	400	49	3	6	21	11.0	130	370	0
orange poppy cheese pullman	1	450	55	3½	7	22	13.0	110	290	1
orange poppy pound	1	490	55	3½	8	27	12.0	140	380	2
pumpkin pound	1	310	47	3	5	12	1.5	65	360	2
pumpkin pullman	1	370	51	3½	4	17	3.0	60	340	2
sour cream coffee	1	420	43	3	5	25	12.0	95	260	1
zucchini pound	1	370	47	3	5	19	2.0	55	250	2
Classic favorite beverages										
(All beverages were calculated as "tall." For Grande, multiply all values by 1.33.)										
apple juice	12 fl. oz.	180	45	3	0	0	0.0	0	15	0
caramel apple cider										
w/ whipped cream	12 fl. oz.	340	59	4	0	9	6.0	40	25	0
w/o whipped cream	12 fl. oz.	230	56	4	0	0	0.0	0	15	0
chocolate milk										
w/ nonfat milk	12 fl. oz.	190	35	2	13	2	0.0	5	170	1
w/ soy milk	12 fl. oz.	230	38	2½	9	6	1.0	0	120	3
w/ whole milk	12 fl. oz.	270	33	2	12	12	7.0	40	150	1
hot chocolate, w/ whipped cream										
w/ nonfat milk	12 fl. oz.	280	36	2½	13	10	6.0	45	170	1
w/ soy milk	12 fl. oz.	320	40	2½	9	15	7.0	35	125	3
w/ whole milk	12 fl. oz.	360	34	2	12	21	13.0	80	160	1
hot chocolate, w/o whipped cream										
w/ nonfat milk	12 fl. oz.	190	35	2	13	2	0.0	5	170	1
w/ soy milk	12 fl. oz.	230	38	2½	9	6	1.0	0	120	3
w/ whole milk	12 fl. oz.	270	33	2	12	12	7.0	40	150	1

FAST FOODS & RESTAURANT CHAINS
Starbuck's® Coffee Company

ITEM	AMOUNT	CALORIES	CARBOHYDRATE (g)	CARBOHYDRATE CHOICES	PROTEIN (g)	FAT (g)	SATURATED FAT (g)	CHOLESTEROL (mg)	SODIUM (mg)	FIBER (g)
milk, nonfat	12 fl. oz.	130	19	1	13	0	0.0	5	190	0
milk, whole	12 fl. oz.	210	16	1	12	12	7.0	50	170	0
steamed apple cider	12 fl. oz.	180	45	3	0	0	0.0	0	15	0
steamed milk, nonfat	12 fl. oz.	130	19	1	13	0	0.0	5	190	0
steamed milk, whole	12 fl. oz.	210	16	1	12	12	7.0	50	170	0
vanilla créme, w/ whipped cream										
w/ nonfat milk	12 fl. oz.	260	33	2	12	8	5.0	40	180	0
w/ soy milk	12 fl. oz.	300	37	2½	8	12	6.0	30	130	1
w/ whole milk	12 fl. oz.	340	31	2	10	18	12.0	75	160	0
vanilla créme, w/o whipped cream										
w/ nonfat milk	12 fl. oz.	180	32	2	12	0	0.0	5	170	0
w/ soy milk	12 fl. oz.	210	35	2	8	5	0.5	0	120	1
w/ whole milk	12 fl. oz.	260	30	2	10	11	7.0	45	160	0
white hot chocolate, w/ whipped cream										
w/ nonfat milk	12 fl. oz.	380	52	3½	15	12	8.0	40	260	0
w/ soy milk	12 fl. oz.	420	56	4	11	16	9.0	35	210	1
w/ whole milk	12 fl. oz.	460	50	3	13	22	15.0	75	250	0
white hot chocolate, w/o whipped cream										
w/ nonfat milk	12 fl. oz.	300	51	3½	15	5	3.5	10	250	0
w/ soy milk	12 fl. oz.	330	54	3½	11	9	4.0	0	210	1
w/ whole milk	12 fl. oz.	370	49	3	13	15	10.0	45	240	0
Cookies										
black & white	1	430	68	4½	4	17	3.0	50	210	2
crisp cinnamon twist	1	60	9	½	0	2	0.5	0	25	0
dark chocolate graham	1	140	17	1	2	8	4.5	0	60	0
double chocolate chunk	1	430	58	4	5	21	7.0	15	350	3
homestyle oatmeal raisin	1	390	65	4	6	15	2.0	15	340	3
Madeline	1	80	11	1	1	4	1.5	25	30	0
milk chocolate graham	1	140	17	1	2	8	4.5	0	60	0
shortbread	1	100	12	1	1	6	3.0	15	65	0
white chocolate macadamia nut	1	470	54	3½	6	27	8.0	15	350	2
Croissants										
almond filled	1	330	39	2½	6	18	7.0	30	230	2
butter croissant, w/ apricot glaze	1	320	37	2½	5	17	1.5	25	280	1
chocolate filled	1	350	43	3	5	19	8.0	30	210	2
raspberry & cream cheese filled	1	260	34	2	4	12	7.0	30	270	1
Espresso, hot										
caffé Americano	12 fl. oz.	10	2	0	1	0	0.0	0	10	0
caffé latte										
w/ breve	12 fl. oz.	420	15	1	10	36	23.0	115	130	0
w/ nonfat milk	12 fl. oz.	120	18	1	12	0	0.0	5	170	0
w/ soy milk	12 fl. oz.	160	21	1½	8	5	0.5	0	120	1

FAST FOODS & RESTAURANT CHAINS

Starbuck's® Coffee Company

ITEM	AMOUNT	CALORIES	CARBOHYDRATE (g)	CARBOHYDRATE CHOICES	PROTEIN (g)	FAT (g)	SATURATED FAT (g)	CHOLESTEROL (mg)	SODIUM (mg)	FIBER (g)
Caffé latte *(continued)*										
w/ whole milk	12 fl. oz.	200	16	1	11	11	7.0	45	160	0
caffé misto/caffé au lait										
w/ breve	12 fl. oz.	220	8	½	5	19	12.0	65	70	0
w/ nonfat milk	12 fl. oz.	60	9	½	6	0	0.0	0	90	0
w/ soy milk	12 fl. oz.	80	12	1	4	3	0.0	0	65	0
w/ whole milk	12 fl. oz.	110	8	½	6	6	3.5	25	85	0
caffé mocha, w/ whipped cream										
w/ breve	12 fl. oz.	510	32	2	9	39	24.0	130	110	1
w/ nonfat milk	12 fl. oz.	280	34	2	11	11	7.0	45	140	1
w/ soy milk	12 fl. oz.	300	37	2½	8	15	7.0	40	105	2
w/ whole milk	12 fl. oz.	340	33	2	10	19	12.0	75	130	1
caffé mocha, w/o whipped cream										
w/ breve	12 fl. oz.	400	30	2	9	30	18.0	90	105	1
w/ nonfat milk	12 fl. oz.	170	33	2	11	2	0.0	5	135	1
w/ soy milk	12 fl. oz.	200	35	2	8	5	1.0	0	95	2
w/ whole milk	12 fl. oz.	240	31	2	10	10	5.0	35	125	1
cappuccino										
w/ breve	12 fl. oz.	250	9	½	6	22	14.0	70	80	0
w/ nonfat milk	12 fl. oz.	80	11	1	7	0	0.0	0	100	0
w/ soy milk	12 fl. oz.	100	13	1	5	3	0.0	0	75	0
w/ whole milk	12 fl. oz.	120	10	½	7	6	4.0	25	95	0
caramel macchiato										
w/ breve	12 fl. oz.	350	19	1	7	28	17.0	90	105	0
w/ nonfat milk	12 fl. oz.	130	22	1½	9	1	0.0	5	135	0
w/ soy milk	12 fl. oz.	160	24	1½	6	4	1.0	0	100	0
w/ whole milk	12 fl. oz.	190	20	1	8	9	5.0	35	125	0
caramel mocha, w/ whipped cream										
w/ breve	12 fl. oz.	530	47	3	9	36	22.0	115	105	1
w/ nonfat milk	12 fl. oz.	320	49	3	11	9	5.0	35	130	1
w/ soy milk	12 fl. oz.	360	52	3½	8	15	7.0	40	105	2
w/ whole milk	12 fl. oz.	370	48	3	10	17	10.0	65	120	1
caramel mocha, w/o whipped cream										
w/ breve	12 fl. oz.	450	46	3	9	28	17.0	85	100	1
w/ nonfat milk	12 fl. oz.	230	48	3	11	2	0.0	5	125	1
w/ soy milk	12 fl. oz.	260	50	3	8	5	1.0	0	95	2
w/ whole milk	12 fl. oz.	290	46	3	10	9	5.0	30	115	1
cinnamon spice mocha, w/ whipped cream										
w/ breve	12 fl. oz.	510	31	2	9	40	25.0	135	120	0
w/ nonfat milk	12 fl. oz.	260	33	2	11	8	5.0	40	150	0
w/ soy milk	12 fl. oz.	290	36	2½	8	12	6.0	30	115	2

FAST FOODS & RESTAURANT CHAINS

Starbuck's® Coffee Company

ITEM	AMOUNT	CALORIES	CARBOHYDRATE (g)	CARBOHYDRATE CHOICES	PROTEIN (g)	FAT (g)	SATURATED FAT (g)	CHOLESTEROL (mg)	SODIUM (mg)	FIBER (g)
Cinnamon spice mocha, w/ whipped cream *(continued)*										
w/ whole milk	12 fl. oz.	320	31	2	10	17	11.0	70	140	0
cinnamon spice mocha, w/o whipped cream										
w/ breve	12 fl. oz.	430	29	2	9	32	20.0	100	115	0
w/ nonfat milk	12 fl. oz.	170	32	2	11	1	0.0	5	150	0
w/ soy milk	12 fl. oz.	200	35	2	8	5	0.5	0	105	2
w/ whole milk	12 fl. oz.	240	30	2	10	10	6.0	35	135	0
white chocolate mocha, w/ whipped cream										
w/ breve	12 fl. oz.	580	44	3	11	40	26.0	125	190	0
w/ nonfat milk	12 fl. oz.	340	46	3	12	11	8.0	40	220	0
w/ soy milk	12 fl. oz.	350	50	3	10	12	6.0	20	200	1
w/ whole milk	12 fl. oz.	410	44	3	11	20	13.0	70	210	0
white chocolate mocha, w/o whipped cream										
w/ breve	12 fl. oz.	500	42	3	11	33	21.0	95	180	0
w/ nonfat milk	12 fl. oz.	260	45	3	12	4	3.0	5	210	0
w/ soy milk	12 fl. oz.	290	47	3	9	7	3.5	0	170	1
w/ whole milk	12 fl. oz.	320	43	3	11	12	8.0	35	200	0
Espresso, iced										
iced caffé Americano	12 fl. oz.	10	2	0	1	0	0.0	0	10	0
iced caffé latte										
w/ nonfat milk	12 fl. oz.	70	11	1	7	0	0.0	0	105	0
w/ soy milk	12 fl. oz.	90	13	1	5	3	0.0	0	75	0
w/ whole milk	12 fl. oz.	120	10	½	6	6	4.0	25	95	0
iced caffé mocha, w/ whipped cream										
w/ nonfat milk	12 fl. oz.	230	28	2	7	10	6.0	40	85	1
w/ soy milk	12 fl. oz.	240	30	2	5	12	6.0	35	65	2
w/ whole milk	12 fl. oz.	260	27	2	7	15	9.0	55	80	1
iced caffé mocha, w/o whipped cream										
w/ nonfat milk	12 fl. oz.	130	27	2	7	2	0.0	0	80	1
w/ soy milk	12 fl. oz.	150	28	2	5	4	0.5	0	60	2
w/ whole milk	12 fl. oz.	170	26	2	7	6	3.0	20	75	1
iced caramel macchiato										
w/ nonfat milk	12 fl. oz.	140	25	1½	8	1	0.5	5	120	0
w/ soy milk	12 fl. oz.	160	28	2	5	4	1.0	0	90	0
w/ whole milk	12 fl. oz.	190	24	1½	7	8	4.5	30	110	0
iced white chocolate mocha, w/ whipped cream										
w/ nonfat milk	12 fl. oz.	330	44	3	9	13	9.0	40	170	0
w/ soy milk	12 fl. oz.	350	45	3	7	15	9.0	40	150	0
w/ whole milk	12 fl. oz.	370	43	3	8	17	12.0	55	170	0
iced white chocolate mocha, w/o whipped cream										
w/ nonfat milk	12 fl. oz.	240	42	3	9	4	3.5	0	170	0

FAST FOODS & RESTAURANT CHAINS
Starbuck's® Coffee Company

ITEM	AMOUNT	CALORIES	CARBOHYDRATE (g)	CARBOHYDRATE CHOICES	PROTEIN (g)	FAT (g)	SATURATED FAT (g)	CHOLESTEROL (mg)	SODIUM (mg)	FIBER (g)
Iced white chocolate mocha, w/o whipped cream *(continued)*										
w/ soy milk	12 fl. oz.	250	44	3	7	6	3.5	0	150	0
w/ whole milk	12 fl. oz.	270	42	3	8	9	6.0	20	160	0
Frappucino® blended coffees										
caramel, w/ whipped cream	12 fl. oz.	320	47	3	4	12	8.0	50	200	0
caramel, w/o whipped cream	12 fl. oz.	210	43	3	4	3	1.5	10	180	0
chocolate brownie, w/ whipped cream	12 fl. oz.	370	54	3½	5	15	10.0	45	220	1
chocolate brownie, w/o whipped cream	12 fl. oz.	270	51	3½	5	7	4.5	10	220	1
coffee	12 fl. oz.	190	38	2½	4	3	1.5	10	180	0
espresso	12 fl. oz.	160	33	2	4	2	1.5	10	160	0
mocha, coconut, w/ whipped cream	12 fl. oz.	410	61	4	5	16	11.0	45	230	2
mocha, coconut, w/o whipped cream	12 fl. oz.	300	58	4	5	7	5.0	10	220	2
mocha, w/ whipped cream	12 fl. oz.	310	46	3	5	12	7.0	45	190	0
mocha, w/o whipped cream	12 fl. oz.	220	44	3	5	3	1.5	10	180	0
white chocolate mocha, w/ whipped cream	12 fl. oz.	340	50	3	5	12	8.0	45	220	0
white chocolate mocha, w/o whipped cream	12 fl. oz.	240	48	3	5	4	2.5	10	210	0
Frappucino® blended créme										
chocolate, w/ whipped cream	12 fl. oz.	380	54	3½	13	13	7.0	40	310	0
chocolate, w/o whipped cream	12 fl. oz.	290	52	3½	13	5	1.0	0	300	0
vanilla, w/ whipped cream	12 fl. oz.	360	49	3	11	12	7.0	40	290	0
vanilla, w/o whipped cream	12 fl. oz.	260	47	3	11	4	1.0	0	280	0
Frappucino® blended teas										
Tazo® chai créme, w/ whipped cream	12 fl. oz.	370	52	3½	11	12	7.0	40	290	0
Tazo® chai créme, w/o whipped cream	12 fl. oz.	280	51	3½	11	4	1.0	0	280	0
Tazoberry®	12 fl. oz.	140	36	2½	0	0	0.0	0	30	0
Tazoberry® chai créme, w/ whipped cream	12 fl. oz.	330	55	3½	4	10	6.0	35	135	0
Tazoberry® chai créme, w/o whipped cream	12 fl. oz.	240	54	3½	4	1	0.0	0	125	0
Iced shaken refreshments										
iced shaken coffee	12 fl. oz.	60	15	1	0	0	0.0	0	0	0
Tazo® iced tea	12 fl. oz.	60	15	1	0	0	0.0	0	0	0
Muffins										
blueberry	1	380	49	3	5	19	3.5	70	380	1

FAST FOODS & RESTAURANT CHAINS

Starbuck's® Coffee Company

ITEM	AMOUNT	CALORIES	CARBOHYDRATE (g)	CARBOHYDRATE CHOICES	PROTEIN (g)	FAT (g)	SATURATED FAT (g)	CHOLESTEROL (mg)	SODIUM (mg)	FIBER (g)
Muffins *(continued)*										
chocolate cream cheese	1	450	53	3½	5	24	6.0	80	420	1
cranberry orange	1	410	53	3½	5	20	4.0	70	400	2
morning sunrise	1	330	54	3½	5	12	5.0	35	550	2
Scones										
apricot currant	1	450	67	4½	7	17	8.0	60	360	3
blueberry	1	460	68	4½	5	18	8.0	50	400	3
butterscotch pecan	1	520	64	4	7	27	11.0	50	390	2
cinnamon chip, w/ icing	1	510	71	5	6	23	10.0	50	480	2
maple oat, w/ icing	1	490	69	4½	7	22	9.0	45	430	2
raspberry	1	440	65	4	7	18	8.0	50	360	2
Sweet rolls										
apple Danish, w/ mocha swirls	1	370	44	3	5	19	1.5	25	330	2
caramel pecan sticky roll	1	730	75	4½	10	40	7.0	40	860	7
cheese Danish, w/ mocha swirls	1	460	44	3	7	28	7.0	50	400	1
cinnamon flavored twist	1	320	37	2½	5	17	1.5	25	280	1
cinnamon roll	1	620	80	5	9	29	7.0	45	740	3
raspberry Danish, w/ mocha swirls	1	370	45	3	5	19	1.5	25	380	1
Tazo® teas										
chai, hot										
w/ nonfat milk	12 fl. oz.	170	37	2½	6	0	0.0	5	95	0
w/ soy milk	12 fl. oz.	190	39	2½	4	2	0.0	0	70	0
w/ whole milk	12 fl. oz.	210	36	2½	6	5	3.5	20	85	0
chai, iced										
w/ nonfat milk	12 fl. oz.	170	36	2½	6	0	0.0	5	90	0
w/ soy milk	12 fl. oz.	180	38	2½	4	2	0.0	0	65	0
w/ whole milk	12 fl. oz.	200	36	2½	5	5	3.0	20	80	0
Subway®										
(Subs, salads & sandwiches do not include cheese, mayonnaise, oil or sauce unless specified.)										
Atkins® friendly & premium salads, w/o dressing										
classic club	1	390	13	1	37	21	10.0	210	1820	4
garden fresh	1	60	11	½	3	1	0.0	0	80	5
grilled chicken & spinach	1	420	10	0	38	26	10.0	215	970	5
Mediterranean chicken	1	170	11	½	22	5	2.0	55	520	5
Atkins® friendly wraps										
chicken bacon ranch	1	480	19	½	40	27	9.0	90	1340	11
turkey bacon melt	1	430	22	½	32	25	9.0	65	1650	12
Bread										
deli style roll	1	170	32	2	6	3	1.0	0	280	3
honey oat	1 (6 in.)	250	48	3	10	4	1.0	0	380	4
Italian herbs & cheese	1 (6 in.)	240	40	2½	10	6	3.0	10	490	3
parmesan oregano	1 (6 in.)	210	40	2½	8	4	1.5	0	530	3

FAST FOODS & RESTAURANT CHAINS
Subway®

ITEM	AMOUNT	CALORIES	CARBOHYDRATE (g)	CARBOHYDRATE CHOICES	PROTEIN (g)	FAT (g)	SATURATED FAT (g)	CHOLESTEROL (mg)	SODIUM (mg)	FIBER (g)
Bread *(continued)*										
wheat	1 (6 in.)	200	40	2½	8	3	1.0	0	360	3
white	1 (6 in.)	200	38	2½	7	3	1.5	0	340	3
Breakfast sandwiches, on deli round										
bacon & egg	1	320	34	2	15	15	4.5	185	520	3
ham & egg	1	310	34	2	16	13	3.5	190	720	3
steak & egg	1	330	35	2	19	14	4.0	190	570	3
western & egg	1	300	36	2½	14	12	3.5	180	530	3
Classic salads, w/ cheese, w/o dressing										
Cold Cut Trio™	1	230	12	1	14	15	6.0	55	1370	3
Italian BMT®	1	280	12	1	16	19	8.0	55	1590	3
meatball	1	330	18	1	16	20	10.0	45	980	3
steak & cheese	1	180	13	1	17	8	3.5	35	890	4
Subway Melt®	1	200	12	1	18	10	4.5	45	1410	3
Subway Seafood & Crab®	1	200	17	1	9	11	3.5	25	970	4
tuna	1	240	11	1	13	16	4.0	40	880	3
Classic sandwiches, w/ cheese										
Cold Cut Trio™, w/ oil	1 (6 in.)	440	47	3	21	21	7.0	55	1680	4
Italian BMT®, w/ oil	1 (6 in.)	480	47	3	23	24	9.0	55	1900	4
meatball	1 (6 in.)	540	53	3	23	26	11.0	45	1300	5
steak & cheese	1 (6 in.)	390	48	3	24	14	5.0	35	1210	5
Subway Melt®	1 (6 in.)	410	47	3	25	15	6.0	45	1720	4
Subway Seafood & Crab®	1 (6 in.)	410	52	3	16	16	4.5	25	1280	5
tuna	1 (6 in.)	450	46	3	20	22	6.0	40	1190	4
Cookies										
chocolate chip	1	220	30	2	2	10	4.0	15	160	1
chocolate chunk	1	220	30	2	2	10	4.0	10	105	1
double chocolate	1	210	30	2	2	10	4.0	15	170	1
M&M®	1	220	30	2	2	10	4.0	15	105	1
oatmeal raisin	1	200	30	2	3	8	2.5	15	180	2
peanut butter	1	220	26	2	4	12	4.0	10	200	1
sugar	1	230	28	2	2	12	4.0	15	135	0
white macadamia nut	1	220	28	2	2	11	4.0	15	160	1
Condiments & extras										
American cheese	2 triangles	40	1	0	2	4	2.0	10	200	0
bacon	2 strips	45	0	0	3	4	1.5	10	180	0
mayonnaise, light	1 T.	45	1	0	0	5	1.0	10	100	0
mayonnaise, regular	1 T.	110	0	0	0	12	3.0	10	80	0
Deli round sandwiches										
ham	1	210	35	2	11	4	1.5	10	770	3
roast beef	1	220	35	2	13	5	2.0	15	660	3
tuna	1	330	36	2½	13	16	4.5	25	830	3

FAST FOODS & RESTAURANT CHAINS

Subway®

ITEM	AMOUNT	CALORIES	CARBOHYDRATE (g)	CARBOHYDRATE CHOICES	PROTEIN (g)	FAT (g)	SATURATED FAT (g)	CHOLESTEROL (mg)	SODIUM (mg)	FIBER (g)
Deli round sandwiches *(continued)*										
turkey breast	1	220	36	2½	13	4	1.5	15	730	3
Salad dressings, fat free										
French	2 oz.	70	17	1	0	0	0.0	0	390	0
Italian	2 oz.	20	4	0	0	0	0.0	0	610	0
ranch	2 oz.	60	14	1	0	0	0.0	0	530	0
Select sandwiches, w/ sauce										
chipotle southwest										
turkey bacon	1 (6 in.)	410	48	3	22	16	4.5	40	1260	4
Dijon horseradish melt	1 (6 in.)	470	48	3	26	21	7.0	55	1620	5
honey mustard ham	1 (6 in.)	310	52	3½	18	5	1.5	25	1260	4
red wine vinaigrette club	1 (6 in.)	350	53	3½	24	6	2.5	35	1520	4
sweet onion chicken teriyaki	1 (6 in.)	380	59	4	26	5	1.5	50	1100	4
Seven salads under 6 grams of fat										
ham	1	110	11	1	11	3	1.0	25	1070	3
roast beef	1	120	10	½	12	3	1.5	20	720	3
roasted chicken breast	1	140	12	1	16	3	1.0	45	800	3
Subway Club®	1	150	12	1	17	4	1.5	35	1110	3
turkey breast	1	100	11	1	11	2	0.0	20	820	3
turkey breast & ham	1	120	11	1	13	3	0.5	25	1030	3
Veggie Delite®	1	50	9	½	2	1	0.0	0	310	3
Seven sandwiches under 6 grams of fat										
ham	1 (6 in.)	290	46	3	18	5	1.5	25	1270	4
roast beef	1 (6 in.)	290	45	3	19	5	2.0	20	910	4
roasted chicken breast	1 (6 in.)	320	47	3	23	5	2.0	45	1000	5
Subway Club®	1 (6 in.)	320	46	3	24	6	2.0	35	1300	4
turkey breast	1 (6 in.)	280	46	3	18	5	1.5	20	1010	4
turkey breast & ham	1 (6 in.)	290	46	3	20	5	1.5	25	1220	4
Veggie Delite®	1 (6 in.)	230	44	3	9	3	1.0	0	510	4
Soups										
black bean	1 cup	180	27	1	9	5	2.0	10	1160	15
brown & wild rice, w/ chicken	1 cup	190	17	1	6	11	4.5	20	990	2
cheese with ham & bacon	1 cup	230	13	1	8	16	6.0	20	1270	2
chicken & dumpling	1 cup	130	16	1	7	5	2.5	30	1030	1
chili con carne	1 cup	310	28	1	17	14	5.0	35	900	9
cream of broccoli	1 cup	130	15	1	5	6	0.0	10	860	2
cream of potato, w/ bacon	1 cup	210	20	1	5	12	4.0	20	970	4
golden broccoli cheese	1 cup	180	12	0	6	12	4.0	10	910	9
minestrone	1 cup	70	11	1	3	1	0.0	10	1030	2
New England style clam chowder	1 cup	140	19	1	5	5	1.0	15	900	7
potato cheese chowder	1 cup	210	22	1½	7	10	7.0	25	1010	2

ITEM	AMOUNT	CALORIES	CARBOHYDRATE (g)	CARBOHYDRATE CHOICES	PROTEIN (g)	FAT (g)	SATURATED FAT (g)	CHOLESTEROL (mg)	SODIUM (mg)	FIBER (g)
Soups *(continued)*										
roasted chicken noodle	1 cup	90	7	½	7	4	1.0	20	1180	1
tomato bisque	1 cup	90	15	1	1	3	0.5	0	750	3
vegetable beef	1 cup	90	14	1	5	2	0.5	10	1340	2
Taco Bell®										
Burritos										
7-Layer	1	530	67	4	18	22	8.0	25	1360	10
bean	1	370	55	3	14	10	3.5	10	1200	8
breakfast	1	510	48	3	22	25	9.0	345	1490	6
Burrito Supreme®, beef	1	440	51	3	18	18	8.0	40	1330	7
Burrito Supreme®, chicken	1	410	50	3	21	14	6.0	45	1270	5
Burrito Supreme®, steak	1	420	50	3	19	16	7.0	35	1260	6
chili cheese	1	390	40	2½	16	18	9.0	40	1080	3
grilled stuft chicken	1	680	76	4½	35	26	7.0	70	1950	7
Chalupas, Baja®										
beef	1	430	32	2	14	27	8.0	30	750	3
chicken	1	400	30	2	17	24	6.0	40	690	2
steak	1	400	30	2	15	25	7.0	30	680	2
Chalupas, nacho cheese										
beef	1	380	33	2	12	22	7.0	20	740	3
chicken	1	350	31	2	16	18	5.0	25	670	1
steak	1	350	31	2	14	19	5.0	20	670	2
Chalupas, Supreme®										
beef	1	390	31	2	14	24	10.0	40	600	3
chicken	1	370	30	2	17	20	8.0	45	530	1
steak	1	370	29	2	15	22	8.0	35	520	2
Cinnamon twists	1 order	160	28	2	0	5	1.0	0	150	0
Gorditas, Baja®										
beef	1	350	31	2	14	19	5.0	30	750	4
chicken	1	320	29	2	17	15	3.5	40	690	2
steak	1	320	29	2	15	16	4.0	30	680	2
Gorditas, nacho cheese										
beef	1	300	32	2	13	13	4.0	20	740	3
chicken	1	270	30	2	16	10	2.5	25	670	2
steak	1	270	30	2	14	11	3.0	20	660	2
Gorditas, Supreme®										
beef	1	310	30	2	14	16	7.0	35	590	3
chicken	1	290	28	2	17	12	5.0	45	530	2
steak	1	290	28	2	16	13	6.0	35	520	2
Guacamole	¾ oz.	35	2	0	0	3	0.0	0	100	0
Mexican pizza	1	550	46	2½	21	31	11.0	45	1030	7
Mexican rice	1 order	210	23	1½	6	10	4.0	15	740	3

FAST FOODS & RESTAURANT CHAINS

Taco Bell®

ITEM	AMOUNT	CALORIES	CARBOHYDRATE (g)	CARBOHYDRATE CHOICES	PROTEIN (g)	FAT (g)	SATURATED FAT (g)	CHOLESTEROL (mg)	SODIUM (mg)	FIBER (g)
MexiMelt®	1	290	23	1½	15	16	8.0	45	880	3
Nachos										
Nachos BellGrande®	1 order	780	80	4½	20	43	13.0	35	1300	12
Nachos Supreme®	1 order	450	42	2	13	26	9.0	35	800	7
regular	1 order	320	33	2	5	19	4.5	0	530	2
Pintos 'n cheese	1 order	180	20	1	10	7	3.5	15	700	6
Quesadillas										
breakfast	1	400	38	2½	17	20	9.0	190	1050	3
breakfast, w/ steak & green sauce	1	460	39	2½	24	23	10.0	205	1310	3
cheese	1	490	39	2½	19	28	13.0	55	1150	3
chicken	1	540	40	2½	28	30	13.0	80	1380	3
Taco salad, w/ salsa, w/o dressing										
w/ shell	1	790	73	4	31	42	15.0	65	1670	13
w/o shell	1	420	33	1½	24	21	11.0	65	1400	11
Tacos, hard										
Double Decker®	1	340	39	2	15	14	5.0	25	800	6
regular	1	170	13	1	8	10	4.0	25	350	3
Taco Supreme®	1	220	14	1	9	14	7.0	40	360	3
Tacos, soft										
beef	1	210	21	1½	10	10	4.5	25	620	2
chicken	1	190	19	1	14	6	2.5	30	550	0
grilled steak	1	280	21	1½	12	17	4.5	30	650	1
Supreme®, beef	1	260	22	1½	11	14	7.0	40	630	3
Supreme®, chicken	1	230	21	1½	15	10	5.0	45	570	1
Tostada	1	250	29	1½	11	10	4.0	15	710	7
Wendy's®										
Baked potatoes										
bacon & cheese	1	580	79	5	18	22	6.0	40	950	7
broccoli & cheese	1	480	81	5	9	14	3.0	5	510	9
plain	l	310	72	4	7	0	0.0	0	25	7
sour cream & chives	1	370	73	4½	7	6	4.0	15	40	7
Chicken nuggets	5	220	13	1	11	14	3.0	35	480	0
Chicken sandwiches										
chicken breast fillet	1	430	46	3	27	16	3.0	55	750	2
chicken club	1	470	47	3	30	19	4.0	65	920	2
grilled chicken	1	300	36	2½	24	7	1.5	55	740	2
spicy chicken	1	430	47	3	27	15	3.0	60	1240	3
Chicken strips, homestyle	3	410	33	2	28	18	3.5	60	1470	0
Chili	small	200	21	1	17	6	2.5	35	870	5
French fries										
medium	1 order	390	56	3	4	17	3.0	0	340	6

FAST FOODS & RESTAURANT CHAINS
Wendy's®

ITEM	AMOUNT	CALORIES	CARBOHYDRATE (g)	CARBOHYDRATE CHOICES	PROTEIN (g)	FAT (g)	SATURATED FAT (g)	CHOLESTEROL (mg)	SODIUM (mg)	FIBER (g)
French fries, (continued)										
Biggie®	1 order	440	63	4	5	19	3.5	0	380	7
Great Biggie®	1 order	530	75	4½	6	23	4.5	0	450	8
Frosty™ dairy dessert										
small	1	330	56	4	8	8	5.0	35	200	0
medium	1	440	73	5	11	11	7.0	50	260	0
Hamburgers										
Big Bacon Classic®	1	570	46	3	34	29	12.0	100	1460	3
Classic Single®, plain	1	360	31	2	24	16	6.0	65	590	2
Classic Single®, w/ works	1	410	37	2½	24	19	7.0	70	890	2
Jr. bacon cheeseburger	1	380	34	2	20	18	7.0	55	890	2
Jr. cheeseburger	1	310	34	2	17	12	5.0	45	820	2
Jr. cheeseburger deluxe	1	350	37	2½	17	16	6.0	45	890	2
Jr. hamburger	1	270	34	2	14	9	3.0	30	600	2
Salad dressings										
Caesar	1 pkt.	150	1	0	1	16	2.5	20	240	0
creamy ranch	1 pkt.	230	5	0	1	23	4.0	15	580	0
French, fat free	1 pkt.	80	19	1	0	0	0.0	0	210	0
honey mustard	1 pkt.	280	11	1	1	26	4.0	25	350	0
Oriental sesame	1 pkt.	250	19	1	1	19	2.5	0	560	0
Salads, w/o dressing										
Caesar side, w/o croutons	1	70	2	0	7	4	2.0	15	250	1
chicken BLT, w/o croutons	1	310	10	½	33	16	8.0	60	1100	4
Mandarin Chicken™, w/o almonds										
& noodles	1	150	17	1	20	2	0.0	10	650	3
side	1	35	7	½	2	0	0.0	0	20	3
taco, w/ chips	1	580	54	3	30	28	11.0	65	1240	10
FATS, OILS, CREAM & GRAVY										
Bacon fat	1 T.	125	0	0	0	14	6.5	14	76	0
Beef fat/tallow	1 T.	108	0	0	0	12	6.0	13	0	0
Benecol® spread										
light	1 tsp.	15	0	0	0	2	0.0	0	37	0
regular	1 tsp.	27	0	0	0	3	0.5	0	37	0
Butter										
butter oil	1 T.	112	0	0	0	13	8.0	33	0	0
stick	1 tsp.	33	0	0	0	4	2.5	10	39	0
stick	1 T.	100	0	0	0	11	7.0	31	116	0
stick, unsalted	1 tsp.	33	0	0	0	4	2.5	10	1	0
whipped	1 tsp.	23	0	0	0	2	1.5	7	17	0
whipped, light	1 tsp.	12	0	0	0	1	1.0	3	15	0
Butter flavored sprinkles	1 tsp.	5	2	0	0	0	0.0	0	180	0

FATS, OILS, CREAM & GRAVY

ITEM	AMOUNT	CALORIES	CARBOHYDRATE (g)	CARBOHYDRATE CHOICES	PROTEIN (g)	FAT (g)	SATURATED FAT (g)	CHOLESTEROL (mg)	SODIUM (mg)	FIBER (g)
Chicken fat	1 T.	115	0	0	0	13	4.0	11	0	0
Coffee-Mate®										
fat free	1 T.	10	2	0	0	0	0.0	0	0	0
regular	1 T.	20	2	0	0	1	0.0	0	0	0
regular, flavored	1 T.	40	5	0	0	2	0.0	0	5	0
Coffee Rich®										
fat free	1 T.	15	2	0	0	0	0.0	0	10	0
regular	1 T.	20	2	0	0	2	0.0	0	10	0
Cooking spray	⅓ second	0	0	0	0	0	0.0	0	0	0
Cooking spray	2 seconds	14	0	0	0	2	0.0	0	0	0
Cream										
heavy	1 T.	51	0	0	0	6	3.5	20	6	0
light	1 T.	30	0	0	0	3	1.5	10	10	0
Gravy, beef										
au jus, jar	¼ cup	20	1	0	1	1	0.0	0	360	0
brown, mix	¼ cup	20	4	0	0	0	0.0	0	180	0
fat free, can	¼ cup	20	5	0	0	0	0.0	5	310	0
hmde.	¼ cup	53	4	0	1	4	1.0	1	389	0
regular, can	¼ cup	31	3	0	2	1	0.5	2	326	0
Gravy, chicken										
fat free, can	¼ cup	15	3	0	1	0	0.0	5	320	0
giblet, hmde.	¼ cup	49	3	0	3	3	0.5	28	341	0
mix	¼ cup	25	4	0	0	1	0.0	0	180	0
regular, can	¼ cup	47	3	0	1	3	1.0	1	343	0
Gravy, other										
mushroom, can	¼ cup	30	3	0	1	2	0.0	0	339	0
onion, mix	¼ cup	19	4	0	1	0	0.0	0	251	0
pork, can	¼ cup	25	3	0	1	1	0.0	0	350	0
sausage, can	¼ cup	98	4	0	4	7	2.5	14	204	0
turkey, can	¼ cup	30	3	0	2	1	0.5	1	344	0
turkey, mix	¼ cup	25	4	0	0	1	0.0	0	160	0
Half & half										
fat free	1 T.	10	2	0	0	0	0.0	0	15	0
regular	1 T.	20	1	0	0	2	1.0	6	6	0
Lard/pork fat	1 T.	115	0	0	0	13	5.0	12	0	0
Margarine										
fat free	1 tsp.	2	0	0	0	0	0.0	0	30	0
light	1 tsp.	15	0	0	0	2	0.5	0	33	0
regular, soft/tub	1 tsp.	33	0	0	0	4	0.5	0	35	0
regular, soft/tub, unsalted	1 tsp.	34	0	0	0	4	0.5	0	1	0
regular, stick	1 tsp.	30	0	0	0	3	0.5	0	37	0
regular, stick	1 T.	90	0	0	0	10	2.0	0	110	0

FATS, OILS, CREAM & GRAVY

ITEM	AMOUNT	CALORIES	CARBOHYDRATE (g)	CARBOHYDRATE CHOICES	PROTEIN (g)	FAT (g)	SATURATED FAT (g)	CHOLESTEROL (mg)	SODIUM (mg)	FIBER (g)
Mayonnaise										
fat free	1 T.	11	2	0	0	0	0.0	2	120	0
imitation, soy	1 T.	35	1	0	0	4	0.5	0	115	0
light	1 T.	50	1	0	0	5	1.0	5	120	0
regular	1 T.	100	0	0	0	11	1.5	5	75	0
Miracle Whip®										
Free®	1 T.	15	2	0	0	0	0.0	0	125	0
light	1 T.	30	3	0	0	2	0.0	0	140	0
regular	1 T.	60	2	0	0	6	1.0	0	100	0
Mocha Mix®										
fat free	1 T.	10	1	0	0	0	0.0	0	5	0
regular	1 T.	20	1	0	0	2	0.0	0	5	0
Oils										
avocado	1 T.	124	0	0	0	14	1.5	0	0	0
canola	1 T.	124	0	0	0	14	1.0	0	0	0
chili, flavored	1 T.	130	0	0	0	14	3.0	0	0	0
coconut	1 T.	117	0	0	0	14	12.0	0	0	0
cod liver/fish	1 T.	123	0	0	0	14	3.0	78	0	0
corn	1 T.	120	0	0	0	14	1.5	0	0	0
cottonseed	1 T.	120	0	0	0	14	3.5	0	0	0
flaxseed/linseed	1 T.	120	0	0	0	14	1.5	0	0	0
grapeseed	1 T.	120	0	0	0	14	1.5	0	0	0
olive	1 T.	119	0	0	0	14	2.0	0	0	0
palm	1 T.	120	0	0	0	14	6.5	0	0	0
palm kernel	1 T.	117	0	0	0	14	11.0	0	0	0
peanut	1 T.	119	0	0	0	14	2.5	0	0	0
safflower	1 T.	120	0	0	0	14	1.0	0	0	0
sesame	1 T.	120	0	0	0	14	2.0	0	0	0
soybean	1 T.	120	0	0	0	14	2.0	0	0	0
sunflower	1 T.	120	0	0	0	14	1.5	0	0	0
walnut	1 T.	120	0	0	0	14	1.0	0	0	0
wheat germ	1 T.	120	0	0	0	14	2.5	0	0	0
Popcorn topping	1 T.	120	0	0	0	14	2.0	0	0	0
Shortening, vegetable	1 T.	113	0	0	0	13	3.0	0	0	0
Sour cream										
fat free	1 T.	15	2	0	1	0	0.0	1	12	0
imitation, soy	1 T.	25	1	0	1	3	1.0	0	60	0
light	1 T.	20	1	0	1	1	1.0	5	10	0
regular	1 T.	31	1	0	0	3	2.0	6	8	0

FISH & SEAFOOD

ITEM	AMOUNT	CALORIES	CARBOHYDRATE (g)	CARBOHYDRATE CHOICES	PROTEIN (g)	FAT (g)	SATURATED FAT (g)	CHOLESTEROL (mg)	SODIUM (mg)	FIBER (g)
FISH & SEAFOOD										
(Cooked w/o fat unless indicated.)										
Abalone										
baked/broiled	3 oz.	119	7	½	19	1	0.0	96	341	0
flour fried	3 oz.	161	9	½	17	6	1.5	80	503	0
Anchovies, oil pack, can	3	25	0	0	3	1	0.5	10	440	0
Anchovy paste	1 tsp.	10	1	0	1	0	0.0	3	624	0
Bass										
freshwater	3 oz.	124	0	0	21	4	1.0	74	77	0
sea/striped	3 oz.	105	0	0	19	3	0.5	88	75	0
Bluefish	3 oz.	135	0	0	22	5	1.0	65	65	0
Burbot	3 oz.	98	0	0	21	1	0.0	65	105	0
Butterfish	3 oz.	159	0	0	19	9	2.5	71	97	0
Calamari/squid										
baked/broiled	3 oz.	118	3	0	16	4	1.0	240	76	0
flour fried	3 oz.	149	7	½	15	6	1.5	221	260	0
Carp										
baked/broiled	3 oz.	138	0	0	19	6	1.0	71	54	0
flour fried	3 oz.	239	11	1	18	13	3.0	84	175	0
Catfish, farmed										
baked/broiled	3 oz.	144	0	0	17	8	2.0	50	51	0
flour fried	3 oz.	248	11	1	16	15	3.5	68	181	0
Catfish, wild	3 oz.	89	0	0	16	2	0.5	61	43	0
Caviar, black/red	1 T.	40	1	0	4	3	0.5	94	240	0
Cisco, smoked	3 oz.	151	0	0	14	10	1.5	27	409	0
Clams										
breaded & fried	10 small	190	10	½	13	10	2.5	57	342	0
raw	6 large	89	3	0	15	1	0.0	41	67	0
stuffed, frzn.	1 (2.5 oz.)	120	14	1	6	5	0.0	0	440	2
Cod, Atlantic/Pacific										
baked/broiled	3 oz.	89	0	0	19	1	0.0	47	66	0
breaded & fried	3 oz.	149	6	½	15	7	1.5	43	78	0
dried, salted	3 oz.	247	0	0	53	2	0.5	129	5976	0
Crab										
Alaska king	3 oz.	83	0	0	16	1	0.0	45	912	0
blue, can	½ cup	67	0	0	14	1	0.0	60	225	0
blue, fresh	3 oz.	87	0	0	17	2	0.0	85	237	0
dungeness	3 oz.	94	1	0	19	1	0.0	65	321	0
imitation	3 oz.	87	9	½	10	1	0.0	17	715	0
snow	3 oz.	117	0	0	16	5	1.0	80	270	0
soft shell, flour fried	3 oz.	284	15	1	17	17	3.5	105	283	0
Crab cakes	1 (2 oz.)	160	5	0	11	10	2.0	82	491	0

FISH & SEAFOOD

ITEM	AMOUNT	CALORIES	CARBOHYDRATE (g)	CARBOHYDRATE CHOICES	PROTEIN (g)	FAT (g)	SATURATED FAT (g)	CHOLESTEROL (mg)	SODIUM (mg)	FIBER (g)
Crawdads/crayfish	3 oz.	70	0	0	14	1	0.0	113	80	0
Croaker, breaded & fried	3 oz.	188	6	½	15	11	3.0	71	296	0
Cusk	3 oz.	95	0	0	21	1	0.0	45	34	0
Cuttlefish	3 oz.	134	1	0	28	1	0.0	191	633	0
Dolphinfish/mahi mahi	3 oz.	93	0	0	20	1	0.0	80	96	0
Drum, freshwater	3 oz.	130	0	0	19	5	1.0	70	82	0
Eel	3 oz.	201	0	0	20	13	2.5	137	55	0
Escargot/snails	6	82	5	0	14	0	0.0	39	105	0
Fish cakes, breaded, frzn.	1 (3 oz.)	231	15	1	8	15	6.0	22	152	1
Fish fillets, frzn.	1 (4 oz.)	220	16	1	15	11	2.0	35	310	0
Fish sticks, frzn.	6 (0.6 oz.)	260	20	1	11	15	2.5	25	360	0
Flounder										
baked/broiled	3 oz.	100	0	0	21	1	0.5	58	89	0
breaded & fried	3 oz.	189	7	½	17	10	2.0	59	157	0
Gefiltefish	3 oz.	71	6	½	8	1	0.5	26	446	0
Grouper	3 oz.	100	0	0	21	1	0.5	40	45	0
Haddock										
baked/broiled	3 oz.	95	0	0	21	1	0.0	63	74	0
breaded & fried	3 oz.	186	7	½	17	9	2.0	66	146	0
smoked	3 oz.	99	0	0	21	1	0.0	65	649	0
Halibut										
Atlantic/Pacific	3 oz.	119	0	0	23	3	0.5	35	59	0
Greenland	3 oz.	203	0	0	16	15	2.5	50	88	0
Herring, Atlantic										
baked/broiled	3 oz.	173	0	0	20	10	2.0	65	98	0
pickled	1 (0.7 oz.)	52	2	0	3	4	0.5	3	174	0
Herring, Pacific	3 oz.	213	0	0	18	15	3.5	84	81	0
Ling/lingcod	3 oz.	93	0	0	19	1	0.0	57	65	0
Lobster										
northern, breaded & fried	3 oz.	180	7	½	16	9	2.0	66	300	0
northern, broiled/steamed	3 oz.	99	1	0	17	3	1.5	65	335	0
spiny, steamed	3 oz.	122	3	0	22	2	0.5	77	193	0
Lox/smoked salmon	3 oz.	100	0	0	16	4	1.0	20	1701	0
Mackerel										
Atlantic	3 oz.	223	0	0	20	15	3.5	64	71	0
Jack/Pacific	3 oz.	171	0	0	22	9	2.5	51	94	0
king	3 oz.	114	0	0	22	2	0.5	58	173	0
Spanish	3 oz.	134	0	0	20	5	1.5	62	56	0
Milkfish	3 oz.	162	0	0	22	7	2.0	57	78	0
Mollusks/whelk	3 oz.	234	13	1	41	1	0.0	111	350	0
Monkfish	3 oz.	83	0	0	16	2	0.5	27	20	0
Mullet, striped	3 oz.	128	0	0	21	4	1.0	54	60	0

FISH & SEAFOOD

ITEM	AMOUNT	CALORIES	CARBOHYDRATE (g)	CARBOHYDRATE CHOICES	PROTEIN (g)	FAT (g)	SATURATED FAT (g)	CHOLESTEROL (mg)	SODIUM (mg)	FIBER (g)
Mussels	3 oz.	146	6	½	20	4	0.5	48	314	0
Octopus	3 oz.	139	4	0	25	2	0.5	82	391	0
Orange roughy	3 oz.	76	0	0	16	1	0.0	22	69	0
Oysters										
eastern, breaded & fried	6 (0.5 oz.)	173	10	½	8	11	3.0	71	367	0
eastern, raw	6 (0.5 oz.)	50	5	0	4	1	0.5	21	150	0
Pacific, raw	3 (1.8 oz.)	122	7	½	14	3	1.0	75	159	0
smoked, oil pack, can	3 oz.	150	9	½	15	9	3.0	60	315	0
Perch										
baked/broiled	3 oz.	103	0	0	20	2	0.5	46	82	0
breaded & fried	3 oz.	192	7	½	17	10	2.0	54	152	0
Pollock, Atlantic	3 oz.	96	0	0	20	1	0.0	82	99	0
Pompano, Florida	3 oz.	179	0	0	20	10	4.0	54	65	0
Pout	3 oz.	87	0	0	18	1	0.5	57	66	0
Rockfish, Pacific	3 oz.	103	0	0	20	2	0.5	37	65	0
Roe	3 oz.	174	2	0	24	7	1.5	407	100	0
Sablefish	3 oz.	213	0	0	15	17	3.5	54	61	0
Salmon										
Atlantic	3 oz.	155	0	0	22	7	1.0	60	48	0
Chinook	3 oz.	196	0	0	22	11	2.5	72	51	0
coho	3 oz.	151	0	0	21	7	1.5	54	44	0
pink, can	3 oz.	122	0	0	16	7	1.5	54	365	0
sockeye, can	3 oz.	130	0	0	17	6	1.5	37	458	0
Sardines, oil pack, can	2	50	0	0	6	3	0.5	34	121	0
Scallops										
bay, baked/broiled	3 oz.	122	2	0	22	1	0.0	56	263	0
imitation	3 oz.	84	9	½	11	0	0.0	19	676	0
sea, baked/broiled	6 large	120	2	0	22	1	0.0	55	260	0
sea, breaded & fried	6 large	200	9	½	17	10	2.5	57	432	0
Scup	3 oz.	115	0	0	21	3	1.0	57	46	0
Shad	3 oz.	214	0	0	18	15	4.0	82	55	0
Shad roe	½ cup	183	2	0	24	10	2.5	400	139	0
Shark	3 oz.	153	0	0	21	7	1.5	51	108	0
Shrimp										
baked/broiled/raw	10 large	54	0	0	12	1	0.0	107	123	0
breaded & fried	10 large	182	9	½	16	9	1.5	133	258	0
Smelt, rainbow										
baked/broiled	3 oz.	105	0	0	19	3	0.5	77	65	0
flour fried	3 oz.	217	11	1	18	11	2.5	88	188	0
Snapper	3 oz.	109	0	0	22	1	0.5	40	48	0
Sole										
baked/broiled	3 oz.	100	0	0	21	1	0.5	58	89	0

FISH & SEAFOOD

ITEM	AMOUNT	CALORIES	CARBOHYDRATE (g)	CARBOHYDRATE CHOICES	PROTEIN (g)	FAT (g)	SATURATED FAT (g)	CHOLESTEROL (mg)	SODIUM (mg)	FIBER (g)
Sole *(continued)*										
breaded & fried	3 oz.	189	7	½	17	10	2.0	59	157	0
Sturgeon										
baked/broiled	3 oz.	115	0	0	18	4	1.0	65	59	0
flour fried	3 oz.	199	7	½	15	12	2.5	68	133	0
smoked	3 oz.	147	0	0	27	4	1.0	68	629	0
Sucker, white	3 oz.	101	0	0	18	3	0.5	45	43	0
Sunfish	3 oz.	97	0	0	21	1	0.0	73	88	0
Sushi, w/ rice & vegetables	½ cup	116	23	1½	4	0	0.0	6	46	1
Swordfish	3 oz.	132	0	0	22	4	1.0	43	98	0
Tilefish	3 oz.	125	0	0	21	4	0.5	54	50	0
Trout, rainbow										
baked/broiled	3 oz.	128	0	0	19	5	1.5	59	48	0
flour fried	3 oz.	230	9	½	20	13	2.5	72	151	0
Tuna, can										
light, oil pack	¼ cup	110	0	0	13	6	1.0	30	250	0
light, water pack	¼ cup	60	0	0	13	1	0.0	30	250	0
low sodium, water pack	¼ cup	70	0	0	15	1	0.0	25	35	0
white, oil pack	¼ cup	90	0	0	14	3	0.5	25	250	0
white, water pack	¼ cup	70	0	0	15	1	0.0	25	250	0
Tuna, fresh										
bluefin	3 oz.	156	0	0	25	5	1.5	42	43	0
yellowfin	3 oz.	118	0	0	25	1	0.5	49	40	0
Turbot	3 oz.	104	0	0	18	3	0.5	53	163	0
Walleye	3 oz.	101	0	0	21	1	0.5	94	55	0
Whitefish	3 oz.	146	0	0	21	6	1.0	65	55	0
Whiting	3 oz.	99	0	0	20	1	0.5	71	112	0
Wolffish, Atlantic	3 oz.	105	0	0	19	3	0.5	50	93	0
Yellowtail	3 oz.	159	0	0	25	6	1.0	60	43	0

FRUIT & VEGETABLE JUICES
Fruit Juices & Nectars

ITEM	AMOUNT	CALORIES	CARBOHYDRATE (g)	CARBOHYDRATE CHOICES	PROTEIN (g)	FAT (g)	SATURATED FAT (g)	CHOLESTEROL (mg)	SODIUM (mg)	FIBER (g)
Apple cider/juice	1 cup	117	29	2	0	0	0.0	0	7	0
Apple-cherry	1 cup	117	29	2	1	0	0.0	0	6	1
Apricot nectar	1 cup	141	36	2½	1	0	0.0	0	8	2
Cranberry cocktail										
reduced calorie	1 cup	40	10	½	0	0	0.0	0	75	0
regular, red	1 cup	130	33	2	0	0	0.0	0	35	0
regular, white	1 cup	120	29	2	0	0	0.0	0	35	0
Cran-raspberry cocktail										
light	1 cup	40	10	½	0	0	0.0	0	75	0
regular	1 cup	140	34	2	0	0	0.0	0	35	0

FRUIT & VEGETABLE JUICES
Fruit Juices & Nectars

ITEM	AMOUNT	CALORIES	CARBOHYDRATE (g)	CARBOHYDRATE CHOICES	PROTEIN (g)	FAT (g)	SATURATED FAT (g)	CHOLESTEROL (mg)	SODIUM (mg)	FIBER (g)
Five Alive®	1 cup	110	30	2	0	0	0.0	0	0	0
Grape										
purple	1 cup	170	42	3	0	0	0.0	0	20	0
white	1 cup	160	39	2½	0	0	0.0	0	20	0
Grapefruit										
red	1 cup	120	30	2	0	0	0.0	0	65	0
white	1 cup	100	24	1½	1	0	0.0	0	35	0
Guava nectar	1 cup	149	38	2½	0	0	0.0	0	7	2
Lemon	2 T.	8	3	0	0	0	0.0	0	0	0
Lime	2 T.	8	3	0	0	0	0.0	0	0	0
Mango	1 cup	130	31	2	0	0	0.0	0	25	0
Orange	1 cup	110	27	2	1	0	0.0	0	15	0
Peach juice/nectar	1 cup	134	35	2	1	0	0.0	0	17	1
Pear juice/nectar	1 cup	150	39	2½	0	0	0.0	0	10	2
Pineapple, unsweetened	1 cup	140	34	2	1	0	0.0	0	3	1
Prune	1 cup	182	45	3	2	0	0.0	0	10	3
Twister®										
kiwi strawberry	1 cup	130	33	2	0	0	0.0	0	15	0
mango tangerine	1 cup	140	34	2	0	0	0.0	0	15	0
passion fruit	1 cup	130	31	2	0	0	0.0	0	10	0
tropical fruit	1 cup	140	34	2	0	0	0.0	0	30	0
Vegetable Juices										
Carrot	1 cup	94	22	1½	2	0	0.0	0	68	2
Clamato®	1 cup	60	11	1	1	0	0.0	0	880	1
Tomato	1 cup	50	9	½	2	0	0.0	0	860	1
V-8®										
regular	1 cup	50	10	½	2	0	0.0	0	620	2
regular, low sodium	1 cup	50	11	1	1	0	0.0	0	140	2
Splash®, tropical blend	1 cup	110	27	2	0	0	0.0	0	40	0
Splash®, tropical blend, diet	1 cup	10	3	0	0	0	0.0	0	25	0

FRUITS

Apples										
dried	4 rings	62	17	1	0	0	0.0	0	22	2
fresh	1 medium	81	21	1½	0	1	0.0	0	0	4
Applesauce										
natural/unsweetened	½ cup	52	14	1	0	0	0.0	0	2	1
sweetened	½ cup	97	25	1½	0	0	0.0	0	4	1
Apricots										
dried	4 medium	80	23	1½	1	0	0.0	0	8	3
fresh	1 medium	17	4	0	0	0	0.0	0	0	1
heavy syrup, can	½ cup	107	28	2	1	0	0.0	0	5	2

FRUITS

ITEM	AMOUNT	CALORIES	CARBOHYDRATE (g)	CARBOHYDRATE CHOICES	PROTEIN (g)	FAT (g)	SATURATED FAT (g)	CHOLESTEROL (mg)	SODIUM (mg)	FIBER (g)
Apricots *(continued)*										
light syrup, can	½ cup	80	21	1½	1	0	0.0	0	5	2
Avocados	½ medium	162	7	0	2	15	2.5	0	10	5
Banana chips	¼ cup	119	13	1	1	8	6.5	0	1	2
Bananas, fresh	1 medium	109	28	2	1	1	0.0	0	1	3
Blackberries, fresh	1 cup	75	18	½	1	1	0.0	0	0	8
Blueberries, fresh/frzn.	1 cup	81	20	1	1	1	0.0	0	9	4
Boysenberries, fresh	1 cup	75	18	½	1	1	0.0	0	0	8
Breadfruit, fresh	¼ medium	99	26	1½	1	0	0.0	0	2	5
Cantaloupe, fresh	1 cup	56	13	1	1	0	0.0	0	14	1
Casaba melon, fresh	1 cup	44	11	1	2	0	0.0	0	20	1
Cherries, red										
maraschino	1 medium	10	3	0	0	0	0.0	0	0	0
sour, fresh	½ cup	39	9	½	1	0	0.0	0	2	1
sour, heavy syrup, can	½ cup	116	30	2	1	0	0.0	0	9	1
sweet, fresh	12 medium	59	14	1	1	1	0.0	0	0	2
sweet, heavy syrup, can	½ cup	105	27	2	1	0	0.0	0	4	2
Coconut, shredded										
fresh	¼ cup	71	3	0	1	7	6.0	0	4	2
sweetened, dried	¼ cup	116	11	1	1	8	7.5	0	61	1
Cranberries										
Craisins®/sweetened, dried	¼ cup	98	25	1½	0	0	0.0	0	0	2
fresh/frzn.	½ cup	23	6	½	0	0	0.0	0	0	2
Currants, fresh	½ cup	35	9	½	1	0	0.0	0	1	4
Dates, dried	¼ cup	122	33	2	1	0	0.0	0	1	3
Figs										
dried	2 medium	105	25	1	1	0	0.0	0	5	5
fresh	2 medium	74	19	1	1	0	0.0	0	1	3
Fruit cocktail										
heavy syrup, can	½ cup	91	23	1½	0	0	0.0	0	7	1
light syrup, can	½ cup	69	18	1	0	0	0.0	0	7	1
Gooseberries, fresh	1 cup	66	15	½	1	1	0.0	0	2	6
Grapefruit										
light syrup, can	½ cup	76	20	1	1	0	0.0	0	3	1
sections, fresh	1 cup	74	19	1	1	0	0.0	0	0	3
whole, fresh	½ medium	39	10	½	1	0	0.0	0	0	1
Grapes, fresh	15 medium	53	13	1	1	0	0.0	0	2	1
Guavas, fresh	1 medium	46	11	½	1	1	0.0	0	3	5
Honeydew melon, fresh	1 cup	60	16	1	1	0	0.0	0	17	1
Kiwifruit, fresh	1 medium	46	11	1	1	0	0.0	0	4	3
Kumquats, fresh	1 medium	12	3	0	0	0	0.0	0	1	1
Lemons, fresh	½ medium	8	3	0	0	0	0.0	0	1	1

FRUITS

ITEM	AMOUNT	CALORIES	CARBOHYDRATE (g)	CARBOHYDRATE CHOICES	PROTEIN (g)	FAT (g)	SATURATED FAT (g)	CHOLESTEROL (mg)	SODIUM (mg)	FIBER (g)
Limes, fresh	½ medium	10	4	0	0	0	0.0	0	1	1
Loganberries, fresh	1 cup	75	18	½	1	1	0.0	0	0	8
Mandarin oranges, can	½ cup	46	12	1	1	0	0.0	0	6	1
Mangoes, fresh	½ medium	67	18	1	1	0	0.0	0	2	2
Melon balls, frzn.	1 cup	57	14	1	1	0	0.0	0	54	1
Mixed fruit										
dried	¼ cup	110	26	2	1	0	0.0	0	15	3
sweetened, frzn.	½ cup	123	30	2	2	0	0.0	0	4	2
Mulberries, fresh	1 cup	60	14	1	2	1	0.0	0	14	2
Nectarines, fresh	1 medium	67	16	1	1	1	0.0	0	0	2
Oranges, fresh	1 medium	62	15	1	1	0	0.0	0	0	3
Papayas, fresh	½ medium	59	15	1	1	0	0.0	0	5	3
Passion fruit, fresh	1 medium	17	4	0	0	0	0.0	0	5	2
Peaches										
fresh	1 medium	42	11	1	1	0	0.0	0	0	2
heavy syrup, can	½ cup	97	26	2	1	0	0.0	0	8	2
light syrup, can	½ cup	68	18	1	1	0	0.0	0	6	2
Pears										
fresh	1 medium	98	25	1½	1	1	0.0	0	0	4
heavy syrup, can	½ cup	98	26	2	0	0	0.0	0	7	2
light syrup, can	½ cup	72	19	1	0	0	0.0	0	6	2
Persimmons, native, fresh	1 medium	32	8	½	0	0	0.0	0	0	0
Pineapple chunks										
fresh	1 cup	76	19	1	1	1	0.0	0	2	2
heavy syrup, can	½ cup	99	26	2	0	0	0.0	0	1	1
light syrup, can	½ cup	66	17	1	0	0	0.0	0	1	1
Plantains, cooked	1 cup	179	48	3	1	0	0.0	0	8	4
Plums, fresh	1 medium	36	9	½	1	0	0.0	0	0	1
Pomegranates, fresh	½ medium	52	13	1	1	0	0.0	0	2	0
Prickly pears, fresh	1 medium	42	10	½	1	1	0.0	0	5	4
Prunes, dried	3 medium	60	16	1	1	0	0.0	0	1	2
Quince, fresh	1 medium	52	14	1	0	0	0.0	0	4	2
Raisins	¼ cup	124	33	2	1	0	0.0	0	5	2
Raspberries, fresh	1 cup	60	14	½	1	1	0.0	0	0	8
Rhubarb										
fresh	1 cup	26	6	½	1	0	0.0	0	5	2
sweetened, cooked	½ cup	139	37	2½	0	0	0.0	0	1	2
Starfruit, fresh	1 medium	42	10	½	1	0	0.0	0	3	3
Strawberries										
fresh	1 cup	50	12	1	1	1	0.0	0	2	4
sweetened, frzn.	½ cup	122	33	2	1	0	0.0	0	4	2
Tangerines, fresh	1 medium	37	9	½	1	0	0.0	0	1	2

FRUITS

ITEM	AMOUNT	CALORIES	CARBOHYDRATE (g)	CARBOHYDRATE CHOICES	PROTEIN (g)	FAT (g)	SATURATED FAT (g)	CHOLESTEROL (mg)	SODIUM (mg)	FIBER (g)
Tropical fruit, light, can	½ cup	80	21	1½	0	0	0.0	0	10	1
Watermelon, fresh	1 cup	49	11	1	1	1	0.0	0	3	1

MEATS

(Cooked w/o fat unless indicated.)

Beef

ITEM	AMOUNT	CALORIES	CARBOHYDRATE (g)	CARBOHYDRATE CHOICES	PROTEIN (g)	FAT (g)	SATURATED FAT (g)	CHOLESTEROL (mg)	SODIUM (mg)	FIBER (g)
Bottom round	3 oz.	187	0	0	27	8	2.5	82	43	0
Chuck roast										
arm	3 oz.	184	0	0	28	7	2.5	86	56	0
blade	3 oz.	213	0	0	26	11	4.5	90	60	0
Corned brisket	3 oz.	213	0	0	15	16	5.5	83	964	0
Eye of round	3 oz.	165	0	0	24	7	2.5	60	52	0
Filet mignon	3 oz.	179	0	0	24	9	3.0	71	54	0
Flank steak	3 oz.	176	0	0	23	9	3.5	57	71	0
Ground										
extra lean, 9%	3 oz.	192	0	0	23	10	4.0	41	82	0
lean, 16%	3 oz.	213	0	0	21	14	5.5	70	42	0
lean, 18%	3 oz.	238	0	0	24	15	6.0	86	76	0
regular, 21%	3 oz.	244	0	0	20	18	7.0	74	51	0
London broil	3 oz.	176	0	0	23	9	3.5	57	71	0
Porterhouse steak	3 oz.	183	0	0	22	10	3.5	59	59	0
Pot roast, round	3 oz.	234	0	0	24	14	5.5	82	43	0
Prime rib	3 oz.	333	0	0	18	28	11.5	72	53	0
Rib eye steak	3 oz.	191	0	0	24	10	4.0	68	59	0
Round steak	3 oz.	205	0	0	23	12	4.5	61	50	0
Rump roast	3 oz.	220	0	0	25	13	5.0	82	43	0
Short ribs	3 oz.	251	0	0	26	15	6.5	79	49	0
Sirloin steak	3 oz.	172	0	0	26	7	2.5	76	56	0
Sirloin tips	3 oz.	157	0	0	24	6	2.0	69	55	0
Stew meat	3 oz.	261	0	0	24	18	7.0	86	53	0
Strip steak	3 oz.	176	0	0	24	8	3.0	65	58	0
T-bone steak	3 oz.	174	0	0	23	9	3.0	50	60	0
Tenderloin, lean	3 oz.	179	0	0	24	9	3.0	71	54	0
Top round	3 oz.	153	0	0	27	4	1.5	71	52	0
Top sirloin	3 oz.	166	0	0	26	6	2.5	76	56	0
Veal										
chops, breaded & fried	3 oz.	194	8	½	23	8	2.5	95	386	0
cutlets/loin chop, braised	3 oz.	242	0	0	26	15	5.5	100	68	0
loin	3 oz.	149	0	0	22	6	2.0	90	82	0
patties, breaded & fried	3 oz.	228	7	½	18	14	4.5	86	153	0
shoulder	3 oz.	194	0	0	27	9	3.0	107	81	0
sirloin	3 oz.	143	0	0	22	5	2.0	88	72	0

MEATS
Game

ITEM	AMOUNT	CALORIES	CARBOHYDRATE (g)	CARBOHYDRATE CHOICES	PROTEIN (g)	FAT (g)	SATURATED FAT (g)	CHOLESTEROL (mg)	SODIUM (mg)	FIBER (g)
Game										
Beefalo	3 oz.	160	0	0	26	5	2.5	49	70	0
Bison/buffalo	3 oz.	122	0	0	24	2	1.0	70	48	0
Rabbit										
domestic	3 oz.	168	0	0	25	7	2.0	70	40	0
wild	3 oz.	147	0	0	28	3	1.0	105	38	0
Venison	3 oz.	134	0	0	26	3	1.0	95	46	0
Lamb										
Chops	3 oz.	184	0	0	26	8	3.0	81	71	0
Leg	3 oz.	219	0	0	22	14	6.0	79	56	0
Shoulder	3 oz.	235	0	0	19	17	7.0	78	56	0
Pork										
Chops										
broiled	3 oz.	179	0	0	24	8	3.0	67	54	0
fried	3 oz.	219	0	0	25	13	4.5	66	47	0
Ground	3 oz.	253	0	0	22	18	6.5	80	62	0
Ham										
cured, lean	3 oz.	134	0	0	21	5	1.5	47	1129	0
hocks	3 oz.	280	0	0	24	20	7.0	93	75	0
leg, fresh	3 oz.	232	0	0	23	15	5.5	80	51	0
picnic/shoulder roast	3 oz.	194	0	0	23	11	3.5	81	68	0
Loin	3 oz.	203	0	0	23	12	4.5	68	41	0
Spareribs, lean	3 oz.	199	0	0	22	12	4.0	73	54	0
Tenderloin, lean	3 oz.	139	0	0	24	4	1.5	67	48	0
Processed & Luncheon Meats										
Bacon	1 slice	36	0	0	2	3	1.0	5	101	0
Bacon bits										
imitation	1 T.	20	1	0	2	1	0.0	0	80	0
real	1 T.	30	0	0	3	2	1.0	5	250	0
Beef jerky	1 oz.	70	4	0	12	1	0.0	35	610	0
Beef sticks	1 (8.5 in.)	95	1	0	4	9	4.0	10	255	1
Bologna										
beef/beef & pork	1 oz.	88	0	0	3	8	3.5	16	278	0
light/Healthy Choice®	1 oz.	40	3	0	3	2	0.5	15	240	0
Braunschweiger	1 oz.	102	1	0	4	9	3.0	44	324	0
Canadian bacon	1 oz.	45	0	0	6	2	0.5	14	399	0
Corned beef, can	2 oz.	120	0	0	15	7	3.0	50	490	0
Corned beef hash, can	1 cup	420	33	2	17	24	11.0	55	1230	6
Deviled Ham® spread	¼ cup	150	0	0	9	12	3.5	35	460	0
Ham, chopped, can	2 oz.	90	0	0	9	6	2.0	30	620	0
Ham, deli, extra-lean	1 oz.	37	0	0	5	1	0.5	13	405	0
Headcheese	1 oz.	76	0	0	4	6	2.0	16	189	0

MEATS
Processed & Luncheon Meats

ITEM	AMOUNT	CALORIES	CARBOHYDRATE (g)	CARBOHYDRATE CHOICES	PROTEIN (g)	FAT (g)	SATURATED FAT (g)	CHOLESTEROL (mg)	SODIUM (mg)	FIBER (g)
Hot dogs										
beef/pork & turkey	1 (1.6 oz.)	143	1	0	5	13	5.5	29	458	0
Healthy Choice®	1 (1.4 oz.)	70	7	½	6	3	1.0	15	440	0
Liverwurst	1 oz.	92	1	0	4	8	3.0	45	244	0
Mortadella	1 oz.	88	1	0	5	7	2.5	16	353	0
Olive loaf	1 oz.	75	2	0	3	6	2.0	20	374	0
Pastrami	1 oz.	99	1	0	5	8	3.0	26	348	0
Pepperoni	1 oz.	141	1	0	6	12	4.5	22	578	0
Roast beef, deli	1 oz.	32	0	0	6	1	0.5	14	287	0
Salami										
beef	1 oz.	74	1	0	4	6	2.5	18	333	0
beef & pork/Genoa	1 oz.	110	0	0	6	9	3.5	29	518	0
Sandwich steaks, frzn.	1 (2 oz.)	175	0	0	9	15	6.5	40	39	0
Sausages										
bockwurst	1 (2 oz.)	174	0	0	8	16	5.5	33	627	0
bratwurst	1 (2 oz.)	171	1	0	8	15	5.5	34	316	0
breakfast	1 (0.5 oz.)	48	4	0	2	3	1.0	18	116	0
chorizo	1 (2 oz.)	258	1	0	14	22	8.0	50	700	0
Italian	1 (2 oz.)	183	1	0	11	15	5.0	44	523	0
kielbasa	1 (2 oz.)	176	1	0	8	15	5.5	38	610	0
knockwurst	1 (2 oz.)	175	1	0	7	16	6.0	33	573	0
Polish	1 (2 oz.)	185	1	0	8	16	6.0	40	497	0
smoked, beef	1 (2 oz.)	177	1	0	8	15	6.5	38	641	0
smoked, pork	1 (2 oz.)	221	1	0	13	18	6.5	39	851	0
summer	1 (1 oz.)	88	1	0	4	8	3.5	23	404	0
Vienna	1 (0.6 oz.)	47	0	0	2	4	1.5	8	152	0
Spam®, can										
lite	2 oz.	110	1	0	9	8	3.0	40	580	0
reduced sodium	2 oz.	180	1	0	7	16	6.0	40	580	0
regular	2 oz.	180	1	0	7	16	6.0	40	790	0
Specialty & Organ Meats										
Brains, pan fried	3 oz.	167	0	0	11	13	3.0	1697	134	0
Chitterlings, pork	3 oz.	258	0	0	9	24	8.5	122	33	0
Frog's legs	3 oz.	90	0	0	20	0	0.0	62	71	0
Hearts	3 oz.	149	0	0	24	5	1.5	164	54	0
Liver, pan fried	3 oz.	185	7	½	23	7	2.5	410	90	0
Oxtail	3 oz.	207	0	0	26	11	5.0	94	162	0
Pigs' feet, pickled	3 oz.	173	0	0	12	14	4.5	78	785	0
Sweetbreads	1 oz.	66	0	0	6	4	2.0	113	15	0
Tongue	3 oz.	241	0	0	19	18	7.5	91	51	0
Tripe	3 oz.	83	0	0	12	3	1.5	81	39	0

MILK & YOGURT
Milk & Milk Beverages

ITEM	AMOUNT	CALORIES	CARBOHYDRATE (g)	CARBOHYDRATE CHOICES	PROTEIN (g)	FAT (g)	SATURATED FAT (g)	CHOLESTEROL (mg)	SODIUM (mg)	FIBER (g)
MILK & YOGURT										
Milk & Milk Beverages										
Acidophilus milk										
2%	1 cup	130	13	1	8	5	3.0	20	170	0
skim	1 cup	100	15	1	10	0	0.0	5	150	0
Buttermilk										
dried	1 T.	29	4	0	3	0	0.0	5	39	0
lowfat	1 cup	110	13	1	9	3	1.5	15	260	0
skim	1 cup	90	13	1	9	0	0.0	0	220	0
Carb Countdown™ dairy beverage										
lowfat	1 cup	100	3	0	12	5	3.0	20	210	0
skim	1 cup	70	3	0	12	0	0.0	0	210	0
whole	1 cup	130	3	0	12	8	5.0	35	210	0
Chocolate milk										
lowfat	1 cup	158	26	2	8	3	1.5	8	153	1
skim	1 cup	144	27	2	9	1	0.5	4	121	1
whole	1 cup	208	26	2	8	8	5.5	30	150	2
Coconut milk, can										
lite	¼ cup	48	2	0	1	4	3.0	0	15	0
regular	¼ cup	93	2	0	2	9	9.0	0	9	0
Condensed milk, sweetened, can										
chocolate	2 T.	120	22	1½	2	3	1.5	10	70	0
fat free	2 T.	109	24	1½	3	0	0.0	3	41	0
whole	2 T.	123	21	1½	3	3	2.0	13	49	0
Eggnog, non-alcoholic										
2%	1 cup	191	17	1	12	8	4.0	194	155	0
whole	1 cup	343	34	2	10	19	11.0	150	137	0
Evaporated milk, can										
lowfat	½ cup	100	12	1	8	2	2.0	20	140	0
skim	½ cup	100	15	1	10	0	0.0	5	147	0
whole	½ cup	169	13	1	9	10	6.0	37	134	0
Filled milk	1 cup	154	12	1	8	8	7.5	5	139	0
Goat milk	1 cup	168	11	1	9	10	6.5	27	122	0
Human breast milk	1 fl. oz.	22	2	0	0	1	0.5	4	5	0
Instant Breakfast™, Carnation®										
can	10 fl. oz.	200	31	2	12	3	0.5	10	180	0
mix, no added sugar	1 pkt.	70	12	1	4	0	0.0	0	80	0
mix, regular	1 pkt.	130	28	2	5	0	0.0	0	100	0
prepared, w/ skim	1 cup	220	40	2½	13	0	0.0	5	230	0
Kefir										
1%, flavored	1 cup	160	21	1½	14	2	1.5	10	125	0
1%, plain	1 cup	110	8	½	14	3	1.5	10	125	0

MILK & YOGURT
Milk & Milk Beverages

ITEM	AMOUNT	CALORIES	CARBOHYDRATE (g)	CARBOHYDRATE CHOICES	PROTEIN (g)	FAT (g)	SATURATED FAT (g)	CHOLESTEROL (mg)	SODIUM (mg)	FIBER (g)
Kefir *(continued)*										
2%, flavored	1 cup	160	26	2	8	4	3.0	15	85	2
nonfat, plain	1 cup	85	13	1	8	0	0.0	5	120	0
Lactaid® milk										
1%	1 cup	110	13	1	8	3	1.5	15	125	0
skim	1 cup	80	13	1	8	0	0.0	0	125	0
whole	1 cup	150	12	1	8	8	5.0	35	125	0
Lowfat milk										
1%	1 cup	102	12	1	8	3	1.5	10	124	0
1%, protein fortified	1 cup	118	14	1	10	3	2.0	10	143	0
2%	1 cup	122	12	1	8	5	3.0	20	122	0
Malted milk drink	1 cup	228	30	2	9	9	5.5	34	172	0
Milk shake, w/ whole										
chocolate	1 cup	211	34	2	6	6	4.0	22	161	1
vanilla	1 cup	185	30	2	6	5	3.0	18	136	1
Ovaltine®, w/ skim	1 cup	170	30	2	10	0	0.0	5	185	0
Powdered milk, dry										
nonfat	¼ cup	61	9	½	6	0	0.0	3	93	0
whole	¼ cup	159	12	1	8	9	5.5	31	119	0
Rice Dream® beverage										
1%, chocolate flavored	1 cup	170	36	2½	1	3	0.0	0	115	0
1%, plain	1 cup	120	25	1½	1	2	0.0	0	90	0
1%, vanilla flavored	1 cup	130	28	2	1	2	0.0	0	90	0
Sheep's milk	1 cup	265	13	1	15	17	11.5	66	108	0
Skim milk	1 cup	86	12	1	8	0	0.0	5	127	0
Soy beverage										
1%, plain	1 cup	90	15	1	4	2	0.0	0	85	2
1%, vanilla	1 cup	130	19	1	7	3	0.5	0	125	3
nonfat, plain	1 cup	90	19	1	4	0	0.0	0	80	1
regular, plain	1 cup	140	14	1	11	5	0.5	0	105	0
unsweetened, plain	1 cup	90	5	0	9	5	0.5	0	30	4
Strawberry Milk, Quik®	1 cup	230	32	2	7	7	5.0	30	115	0
Whole milk	1 cup	150	11	1	8	8	5.0	33	120	0
Yogurt										
Flavored										
fat free, w/ aspartame	1 (6 oz.)	90	17	1	6	0	0.0	0	95	0
fat free, w/ aspartame, fruited	1 cup	120	21	1½	7	0	0.0	5	110	0
lowfat, fruited	1 cup	220	42	3	7	2	1.5	15	115	0
lowfat, w/ granola topping	1 (6.5 oz.)	220	46	3	6	2	1.0	5	110	1
Yoplait® Whips!®	1 (4 oz.)	140	25	1½	5	3	2.0	10	75	0
Plain										
fat free	1 cup	100	16	1	10	0	0.0	10	160	0

MILK & YOGURT
Yogurt

ITEM	AMOUNT	CALORIES	CARBOHYDRATE (g)	CARBOHYDRATE CHOICES	PROTEIN (g)	FAT (g)	SATURATED FAT (g)	CHOLESTEROL (mg)	SODIUM (mg)	FIBER (g)
Plain yogurt *(continued)*										
lowfat	1 cup	130	16	1	10	3	1.5	15	125	0
whole milk	1 cup	149	11	1	9	8	5.0	32	113	0
Soy										
flavored	1 (6 oz.)	160	29	2	4	2	0.0	0	20	1
plain	1 cup	120	22	1½	5	3	0.0	0	30	1
Yogurt Drinks & Squeeze Yogurts										
Drinkable yogurt	10 fl. oz.	240	44	3	10	3	2.0	10	150	3
w/ artificial sweetener	7 fl. oz.	80	15	1	5	0	0.0	0	85	0
GoGurt®	1 (2.25 oz.)	80	13	1	2	2	1.0	5	40	0

NUTS, SEEDS & PEANUT BUTTER

ITEM	AMOUNT	CALORIES	CARBOHYDRATE (g)	CARBOHYDRATE CHOICES	PROTEIN (g)	FAT (g)	SATURATED FAT (g)	CHOLESTEROL (mg)	SODIUM (mg)	FIBER (g)
Almond butter	1 T.	99	3	0	2	9	1.0	0	70	1
Almond paste	1 T.	65	7	½	1	4	0.5	0	1	1
Almonds	23	170	5	0	6	15	1.0	0	0	3
Brazilnuts	8	186	4	0	4	19	5.0	0	1	2
Cashew butter	1 T.	94	4	0	3	8	1.5	0	98	0
Cashews, salted	18	170	8	½	5	14	3.0	0	120	1
Chestnuts	3	62	13	1	1	1	0.0	0	1	1
Filberts/hazelnuts	20	176	5	0	4	17	1.5	0	0	3
Flax seeds	2 T.	95	7	0	4	7	0.5	0	7	5
Hickory nuts	10	197	5	0	4	19	2.0	0	0	2
Macadamias	11	204	4	0	2	21	3.5	0	1	2
Mixed nuts										
w/ peanuts, salted	27	170	6	½	6	15	2.5	0	110	2
w/o peanuts, salted	20	170	6	½	5	16	2.0	0	110	2
Peanut butter										
chunky/creamy	2 T.	190	7	½	7	17	3.5	0	150	2
natural	2 T.	190	7	½	8	16	2.0	0	125	3
reduced fat	2 T.	190	15	1	7	12	2.5	0	190	2
Peanuts										
Beer Nuts®	39	170	7	½	7	14	3.0	0	80	2
dry roasted, salted	39	160	6	½	7	13	2.0	0	190	2
honey roasted	39	150	8	½	7	12	2.0	0	95	2
Sweet N' Crunchy®	18	140	16	1	4	7	1.0	0	20	2
w/ oil, salted	39	170	6	½	7	14	2.0	0	115	2
Pecans	20 halves	196	4	0	3	20	2.0	0	0	3
Pine nuts	¼ cup	190	9	½	4	15	4.0	0	0	4
Pistachio nuts, salted	¼ cup	190	9	½	6	14	2.0	0	220	3
Poppy seeds	1 T.	45	2	0	2	4	0.5	0	2	1
Pumpkin/squash seeds	2 T.	36	4	0	1	2	0.5	0	46	0

NUTS, SEEDS & PEANUT BUTTER

ITEM	AMOUNT	CALORIES	CARBOHYDRATE (g)	CARBOHYDRATE CHOICES	PROTEIN (g)	FAT (g)	SATURATED FAT (g)	CHOLESTEROL (mg)	SODIUM (mg)	FIBER (g)
Sesame butter/tahini	1 T.	89	3	0	3	8	1.0	0	5	1
Sesame seeds	2 T.	103	4	0	3	9	1.5	0	2	2
Soynut butter	1 T.	93	6	½	3	6	1.0	0	66	1
Soynuts, salted	¼ cup	120	9	0	12	4	1.0	0	150	5
Sunflower seeds, salted	2 T.	104	2	0	4	10	1.0	0	102	1
Trail mix										
w/ chocolate chips	¼ cup	177	16	1	5	12	2.0	1	10	2
w/ fruit, tropical	¼ cup	142	23	1½	2	6	3.0	0	4	2
w/ seeds	¼ cup	173	17	1	5	11	2.0	0	86	2
Walnuts, chopped	2 T.	95	2	0	4	9	0.5	0	0	1

PASTA, RICE & OTHER GRAINS
(Cooked unless indicated.)
Pasta

ITEM	AMOUNT	CALORIES	CARBOHYDRATE (g)	CARBOHYDRATE CHOICES	PROTEIN (g)	FAT (g)	SATURATED FAT (g)	CHOLESTEROL (mg)	SODIUM (mg)	FIBER (g)
Cellophane noodles, dry	1 cup	190	50	3	0	0	0.0	0	0	0
Chinese noodles	1 cup	300	68	4	10	2	0.0	0	110	12
Chow mein noodles, can	1 cup	280	38	2½	6	12	2.0	0	460	2
Couscous	1 cup	176	36	2½	6	0	0.0	0	8	2
Egg noodles	1 cup	213	40	2½	8	2	0.5	53	11	2
Gnocchi	1 cup	268	33	2	5	13	8.0	35	141	2
Macaroni/pasta										
regular	1 cup	197	40	2½	7	1	0.0	0	1	2
whole wheat	1 cup	174	37	2½	7	1	0.0	0	4	4
Pasta & sauce, mix										
3 cheese rotini	1 cup	320	44	3	11	12	5.0	15	870	1
butter & herb	1 cup	300	42	3	9	13	4.5	65	710	2
cheddar broccoli	1 cup	330	51	3½	11	9	3.0	15	810	2
chicken	1 cup	270	40	2½	8	9	2.0	50	780	1
Pasta Roni®, box										
butter & garlic	1 cup	260	40	2½	8	8	2.0	5	760	2
fettuccine Alfredo	1 cup	460	48	3	11	25	6.0	10	1160	2
shells & cheddar	1 cup	310	40	2½	9	13	3.5	5	730	2
Ramen noodles, w/ seasoning	1 cup	190	25	1½	4	8	4.0	0	850	1
Ravioli, cheese, w/o sauce	9 (2 in.)	260	34	2	8	5	3.0	20	360	1
Rice noodles	1 cup	160	39	2½	0	0	0.0	0	8	0
Soba noodles	1 cup	113	24	1½	6	0	0.0	0	68	1
Spaghetti	1 cup	197	40	2½	7	1	0.0	0	1	2
Tortellini, w/o sauce										
w/ cheese	1 cup	333	49	3	15	9	4.5	47	400	3
w/ meat	1 cup	373	33	2	25	15	5.5	240	437	1

PASTA, RICE & OTHER GRAINS
Rice

ITEM	AMOUNT	CALORIES	CARBOHYDRATE (g)	CARBOHYDRATE CHOICES	PROTEIN (g)	FAT (g)	SATURATED FAT (g)	CHOLESTEROL (mg)	SODIUM (mg)	FIBER (g)
Rice										
Basmati	½ cup	107	22	1½	3	1	0.0	0	0	1
Brown	½ cup	108	22	1½	3	1	0.0	0	5	2
Fried	½ cup	135	17	1	3	6	1.0	21	131	1
Pilaf	½ cup	130	22	1½	2	3	0.5	0	76	1
Rice A Roni®, chicken										
reduced sodium	½ cup	140	26	2	4	3	0.5	0	350	1
regular	½ cup	155	26	2	4	5	1.0	0	565	1
Risotto, dry	¼ cup	150	37	2½	3	0	0.0	0	0	0
Spanish	½ cup	108	21	1½	2	2	0.5	0	147	2
White										
instant	½ cup	81	18	1	2	0	0.0	0	2	0
regular	½ cup	121	27	2	2	0	0.0	0	0	1
Wild	½ cup	83	18	1	3	0	0.0	0	2	1
Other Grains										
Barley										
pearled	½ cup	97	22	1½	2	0	0.0	0	2	3
whole	½ cup	135	30	1½	4	1	0.0	0	1	7
Buckwheat/kasha	½ cup	77	17	1	3	1	0.0	0	3	2
Bulgur	½ cup	76	17	1	3	0	0.0	0	5	4
Millet	½ cup	104	21	1½	3	1	0.0	0	2	1
Polenta										
fried, slice, w/ oil	1 (4 oz.)	199	16	1	2	14	2.0	0	300	0
fried, slice, w/o oil	1 (4 oz.)	80	16	1	2	0	0.0	0	300	0
w/ water & salt	⅔ cup	73	16	1	2	1	0.0	0	785	2
Quinoa, dry	¼ cup	159	30	2	6	2	0.5	0	9	3

POULTRY
(Cooked w/o fat unless indicated.)
Chicken
Breasts

ITEM	AMOUNT	CALORIES	CARBOHYDRATE (g)	CARBOHYDRATE CHOICES	PROTEIN (g)	FAT (g)	SATURATED FAT (g)	CHOLESTEROL (mg)	SODIUM (mg)	FIBER (g)
BBQ, w/ skin	3 oz.	162	2	0	20	8	2.0	62	181	0
breaded & fried, w/ skin	3 oz.	221	8	½	21	11	3.0	72	234	0
deli	1 oz.	33	1	0	5	1	0.5	14	338	0
fried, w/ skin, w/ flour	3 oz.	189	1	0	27	8	2.0	76	65	0
fried, w/o skin	3 oz.	159	0	0	28	4	1.0	77	67	0
roasted, w/ skin	3 oz.	168	0	0	25	7	2.0	71	60	0
roasted, w/o skin	3 oz.	140	0	0	26	3	1.0	72	63	0
Capon, roasted, w/ skin	3 oz.	195	0	0	25	10	3.0	73	42	0
Cornish hens										
roasted, w/ skin	3 oz.	221	0	0	19	15	4.5	111	54	0
roasted, w/o skin	3 oz.	114	0	0	20	3	1.0	90	54	0

POULTRY
Chicken

ITEM	AMOUNT	CALORIES	CARBOHYDRATE (g)	CARBOHYDRATE CHOICES	PROTEIN (g)	FAT (g)	SATURATED FAT (g)	CHOLESTEROL (mg)	SODIUM (mg)	FIBER (g)
Fingers, fried	6	310	18	1	15	20	4.0	50	680	2
Giblets, fried	3 oz.	236	4	0	28	11	3.0	379	96	0
Gizzards, simmered	3 oz.	130	1	0	23	3	1.0	165	57	0
Hearts, simmered	3 oz.	157	0	0	22	7	2.0	206	41	0
Hot dogs	1 (1.6 oz.)	116	3	0	6	9	2.5	45	617	0
Legs										
breaded & fried, w/ skin	3 oz.	232	7	½	19	14	3.5	77	237	0
fried, w/ skin, w/ flour	3 oz.	216	2	0	23	12	3.5	80	75	0
fried, w/o skin	3 oz.	177	1	0	24	8	2.0	84	82	0
roasted, w/ skin	3 oz.	197	0	0	22	11	3.0	78	74	0
roasted, w/o skin	3 oz.	146	0	0	24	5	1.5	79	81	0
Livers, simmered	3 oz.	134	1	0	21	5	1.5	537	43	0
Pâté, chicken liver, can	1 oz.	57	2	0	4	4	1.0	111	109	0
Patties, breaded & fried	1 (3 oz.)	242	13	1	14	15	4.5	51	452	0
Thighs										
breaded & fried, w/ skin	3 oz.	248	9	½	17	15	4.0	95	434	1
fried, w/ skin, w/ flour	3 oz.	223	3	0	23	13	3.5	83	75	0
fried, w/o skin	3 oz.	185	1	0	24	9	2.5	87	81	0
roasted, w/ skin	3 oz.	210	0	0	21	13	3.5	79	71	0
roasted, w/o skin	3 oz.	166	0	0	21	8	2.5	77	64	0
Wings										
fried, w/ skin, w/ flour	1 (1 oz.)	91	1	0	7	6	1.5	23	22	0
roasted, w/ skin	1 (1 oz.)	82	0	0	8	6	1.5	24	23	0
Game										
Duck										
roasted, w/ skin	3 oz.	287	0	0	16	24	8.0	71	50	0
roasted, w/o skin	3 oz.	171	0	0	20	10	3.5	76	55	0
Goose										
roasted, w/ skin	3 oz.	259	0	0	21	19	6.0	77	60	0
roasted, w/o skin	3 oz.	202	0	0	25	11	4.0	82	65	0
Ostrich										
ground	3 oz.	121	0	0	23	3	1.0	71	64	0
tenderloin	3 oz.	113	0	0	20	3	1.0	81	61	0
Pheasant										
roasted, w/ skin	3 oz.	205	0	0	26	11	3.0	81	45	0
roasted, w/o skin	3 oz.	151	0	0	27	4	1.5	75	42	0
Quail										
roasted, w/ skin	3 oz.	218	0	0	22	14	4.0	86	60	0
roasted, w/o skin	3 oz.	152	0	0	25	5	1.5	79	58	0
Turkey										
Bacon	2 slices	68	1	0	4	5	1.5	25	368	0
Bologna	1 oz.	56	0	0	4	4	1.5	28	249	0

POULTRY

Turkey

ITEM	AMOUNT	CALORIES	CARBOHYDRATE (g)	CARBOHYDRATE CHOICES	PROTEIN (g)	FAT (g)	SATURATED FAT (g)	CHOLESTEROL (mg)	SODIUM (mg)	FIBER (g)
Breast, deli	1 oz.	31	0	0	6	0	0.0	12	406	0
Dark meat										
roasted, w/ skin	3 oz.	184	0	0	23	9	3.0	77	68	0
roasted, w/o skin	3 oz.	157	0	0	24	6	2.0	75	70	0
Ground										
extra lean	3 oz.	120	0	0	26	2	0.5	45	80	0
lean	3 oz.	169	0	0	20	9	2.5	90	107	0
Ham, deli	1 oz.	37	0	0	5	2	0.5	19	275	0
Hot dogs	1 (1.6 oz.)	102	1	0	6	8	2.5	48	642	0
Light meat										
roasted, w/ skin	3 oz.	139	0	0	24	4	1.0	81	48	0
roasted, w/o skin	3 oz.	119	0	0	26	1	0.5	73	48	0
Pastrami, deli	1 oz.	40	0	0	5	2	0.5	15	296	0
Patties, breaded & fried	1 (3 oz.)	241	13	1	12	15	4.0	53	680	0
Sausages	1 (2 oz.)	93	0	0	11	6	1.5	43	470	0

RESTAURANT FAVORITES

Appetizers

ITEM	AMOUNT	CALORIES	CARBOHYDRATE (g)	CARBOHYDRATE CHOICES	PROTEIN (g)	FAT (g)	SATURATED FAT (g)	CHOLESTEROL (mg)	SODIUM (mg)	FIBER (g)
Breadsticks	1 medium	140	26	2	5	2	0.0	0	270	1
Bruschetta	1 (4 in.)	62	6	½	2	4	1.0	2	125	0
Buffalo wings	4	210	4	0	22	12	3.0	130	900	0
Clams casino	6	377	19	1	35	17	10.0	115	802	1
Crab cakes, fried	1 (4 oz.)	290	20	1	9	19	4.0	149	893	0
Cream cheese puffs	3	331	14	1	3	29	6.5	18	180	0
Focaccia bread	1 (6 in.)	271	47	3	7	6	1.0	0	446	3
Garlic bread	1 (4 in.)	322	38	2½	12	14	4.0	20	522	4
Jalapeño poppers	6	360	32	2	7	22	10.0	45	810	3
Mozzarella sticks, w/ sauce	4	378	28	2	19	22	12.0	24	2712	3
Mushrooms, fried	8	237	13	1	4	19	3.0	22	193	1
Nachos, deluxe	1 order	1048	91	5	46	57	23.0	109	2252	17
Oysters Rockefeller	6	170	10	½	8	10	2.0	46	392	0
Pork dumplings, fried	1 (3.5 oz.)	340	24	1½	13	21	6.0	29	346	1
Potato skins	6	500	30	1½	20	34	14.0	80	1020	8
Shrimp cocktail, w/ sauce	5	42	3	0	6	0	0.0	54	262	0
Spring rolls, w/ meat	1 (2.5 oz.)	127	10	½	6	7	2.0	41	336	1
Stuffed mushrooms	3	134	10	½	4	9	5.0	23	183	1
Wontons, w/ meat	1 (0.7 oz.)	61	4	0	3	4	0.5	13	83	0

Desserts

ITEM	AMOUNT	CALORIES	CARBOHYDRATE (g)	CARBOHYDRATE CHOICES	PROTEIN (g)	FAT (g)	SATURATED FAT (g)	CHOLESTEROL (mg)	SODIUM (mg)	FIBER (g)
Apple pie à la mode	1 (6 oz.)	433	58	4	5	21	8.0	29	292	2
Caramel apple bars	1 (5 oz.)	370	54	3½	4	18	3.0	25	200	1
Carrot cake, w/ icing	1 (4 oz.)	494	53	3½	5	30	6.0	61	279	1
Cheesecake	1 (3 oz.)	295	23	1½	5	21	11.0	51	190	0

RESTAURANT FAVORITES

Desserts

ITEM	AMOUNT	CALORIES	CARBOHYDRATE (g)	CARBOHYDRATE CHOICES	PROTEIN (g)	FAT (g)	SATURATED FAT (g)	CHOLESTEROL (mg)	SODIUM (mg)	FIBER (g)
Chocolate chip cookies	1 (2 oz.)	280	40	2½	3	13	8.0	40	85	2
Chocolate mousse cake	1 (3 oz.)	291	41	3	2	12	4.0	29	140	2
Chocolate peanut butter pie	1 (6 oz.)	653	64	4	12	39	19.0	27	319	3
Crème brûlée	¾ cup	347	35	2	7	20	11.0	311	125	0
Fortune cookies	1	30	7	½	0	0	0.0	0	22	0
Fudge brownie sundae	1 (8 oz.)	687	83	5½	9	38	11.0	62	486	3
Key lime pie	1 (4.5 oz.)	410	59	4	5	17	11.0	15	290	1
Smoothie	16 fl. oz.	320	70	4½	7	1	0.5	5	160	4
Tiramisu	1 (5 oz.)	368	33	2	9	22	13.0	187	291	0
Entrées										
American										
BBQ beef sandwich	1 (6.5 oz.)	392	39	2½	20	17	6.0	54	1056	3
BBQ pork sandwich	1 (6.5 oz.)	347	39	2½	23	10	3.0	52	889	3
BBQ ribs	8 oz.	700	36	2½	44	42	18.0	130	1240	0
Chicken fried steak	8 oz.	530	28	2	30	34	16.0	54	1336	2
Filet mignon	8 oz.	479	0	0	64	23	8.5	191	143	0
Fried shrimp	12 large	218	10	½	19	11	2.0	159	310	0
Grilled salmon	8 oz.	423	0	0	59	19	3.0	135	265	0
King crab legs	9 oz.	248	0	0	50	4	0.0	135	2735	0
Potato, w/ broccoli & cheese	1 (10 oz.)	1168	114	6½	28	71	18.0	52	1684	16
Prime rib	12 oz.	1334	0	0	74	113	47.0	289	211	0
Shrimp Creole, w/ rice	2 cups	611	51	3½	55	19	4.0	371	1310	3
Shrimp jambalaya	2 cups	611	51	3½	55	19	4.0	371	1310	3
Southwestern tuna wrap	1 (14 oz.)	950	53	3½	41	64	17.0	110	1230	4
Stuffed shrimp	2 cups	552	17	1	56	27	6.0	443	1388	1
T-bone steak	10 oz.	530	0	0	42	40	18.0	121	534	0
Turkey & cheese bagel	1 (11 oz.)	506	66	4½	34	11	5.5	56	1393	4
Asian/Chinese										
Beef & broccoli	2 cups	512	14	½	76	39	10.0	202	1473	5
Cashew chicken	2 cups	817	23	1½	54	57	9.5	121	1975	4
Chicken curry	2 cups	586	20	1	54	32	7.0	168	2376	4
Egg rolls, meatless	1 (2.5 oz.)	113	11	1	3	6	1.5	33	339	1
Kung Pao chicken	2 cups	818	22	1½	54	58	10.0	120	1976	4
Pork chow mein, w/ noodles	2 cups	869	62	3½	44	51	10.5	96	1631	7
Shrimp & snow peas	2 cups	439	19	1	38	23	3.0	295	2134	3
Stir-fry chicken & fried rice	2 cups	432	45	3	19	19	3.5	85	853	3
Sushi, w/ fish & vegetables	1 cup	238	48	3	9	1	0.0	11	344	1
Sweet & sour pork, w/ rice	2 cups	537	79	5	26	13	3.5	57	1813	3
Tofu & vegetable stir-fry	2 cups	293	34	1½	15	14	2.0	0	445	10
Italian/Mediterranean										
Calzones, w/ pepperoni	1 (6 oz.)	450	49	3	21	19	9.0	10	930	6
Chicken cacciatore	2 cups	916	26	2	84	51	13.0	320	1183	4

RESTAURANT FAVORITES
Italian/Mediterranean

ITEM	AMOUNT	CALORIES	CARBOHYDRATE (g)	CARBOHYDRATE CHOICES	PROTEIN (g)	FAT (g)	SATURATED FAT (g)	CHOLESTEROL (mg)	SODIUM (mg)	FIBER (g)
Chicken cordon bleu	8 oz.	483	9	½	46	28	15.0	191	489	1
Chicken Marsala	8 oz.	593	12	1	55	31	11.0	177	540	1
Chicken/veal parmigiana	8 oz.	466	29	2	36	23	8.0	115	929	1
Eggs Benedict	19 oz.	860	55	3½	35	56	23.0	525	1943	3
Fettuccini Alfredo	2 cups	1430	68	4½	31	119	71.0	340	1470	3
Gyros	½ pita	296	23	1½	15	15	7.5	55	604	1
Linguini, w/ pesto sauce	2 cups	706	83	5	23	31	7.0	18	425	6
Lobster Newburg	2 cups	1225	23	1½	60	100	59.0	738	1294	0
Moussaka	2 cups	474	26	1	33	26	9.0	193	863	7
Pasta, w/ carbonara sauce	2 cups	651	83	5	25	24	10.5	93	496	5
Pasta, w/ marinara sauce	2 cups	530	94	5½	17	9	1.0	0	1100	10
Seafood Alfredo	2 cups	1014	62	4	38	69	41.0	337	672	5
Shrimp scampi	2 cups	438	2	0	58	20	10.0	480	584	0
Spanakopita	8 oz.	387	37	2½	16	20	10.0	227	769	4
Stuffed grape leaves	4	212	7	½	7	17	4.0	52	65	1
Veal scallopini	8 oz.	608	2	0	42	46	13.0	146	900	0
Vegetarian lasagna	2 cups	720	70	4½	40	34	24.0	130	1740	4
Mexican										
Chimichangas, beef & cheese	1 (6.5 oz.)	443	39	2½	20	23	11.0	51	957	0
Enchiladas										
cheese	2 (6 in.)	639	57	4	19	38	21.0	88	1568	1
seafood	2 (6 in.)	529	43	3	25	29	17.0	83	1372	1
Fajitas										
chicken	1 (9 oz.)	520	53	3½	18	26	8.0	70	1300	4
steak	1 (9 oz.)	510	52	3½	21	25	8.0	50	1200	3
Huevos rancheros	1 (2 eggs)	410	24	1½	23	26	9.5	450	530	4
Quesadillas	1 (2 oz.)	199	21	1½	6	10	3.5	14	255	1
Rice & beans	2 cups	520	84	5	20	12	4.0	20	1440	12
Salads, w/ dressing										
Caesar	4 cups	338	20	1	8	25	5.0	7	725	3
Chicken Caesar	4 cups	655	23	1½	37	47	9.0	86	1728	4
Greek	1 (14 oz.)	441	18	1	13	37	14.0	67	1301	4
Niçoise	1 (12 oz.)	423	26	1½	19	28	4.0	36	1026	5
Oriental chicken	1 (9 oz.)	270	17	1	40	4	0.5	70	700	5
Tossed, w/ gorgonzola	4 cups	400	9	½	20	34	13.0	50	800	3
Side Dishes										
Garlic mashed potatoes	1 cup	209	18	1	3	14	8.0	33	132	3
Grilled vegetables	1½ cups	120	15	1	6	4	0.0	0	310	3
Oven roasted potatoes	1½ cups	260	50	3	6	6	1.0	0	300	4
Polenta	½ cup	163	21	1½	4	8	3.0	12	571	2
Ratatouille	1 cup	133	12	1	1	10	1.5	0	106	4
Risotto	½ cup	281	29	2	7	15	9.0	36	851	1

RESTAURANT FAVORITES
Side Dishes

ITEM	AMOUNT	CALORIES	CARBOHYDRATE (g)	CARBOHYDRATE CHOICES	PROTEIN (g)	FAT (g)	SATURATED FAT (g)	CHOLESTEROL (mg)	SODIUM (mg)	FIBER (g)
Soft pretzels	1 large	390	84	5½	12	1	0.0	0	1100	3
Soups										
Borscht	1 cup	73	7	½	3	4	2.5	8	498	2
Cheese	1 cup	626	28	2	36	42	26.0	132	1464	2
Chicken chili	1 cup	233	21	1½	14	12	7.0	43	1353	4
Chilled fruit	1 cup	99	25	1½	1	0	0.0	0	12	1
Clam chowder	1 cup	270	16	1	11	20	9.0	63	730	1
Egg drop	1 cup	73	1	0	8	4	1.0	103	729	0
French onion, w/ croutons	1 cup	260	27	2	12	12	6.0	18	1020	2
Gazpacho	1 cup	68	10	½	2	3	0.0	0	286	2
Hot & sour	1 cup	133	5	0	12	6	2.0	23	1563	0
Minestrone	1 cup	154	23	1½	6	5	0.5	0	790	4
Seafood stew	1 cup	173	9	½	23	5	1.0	95	359	2
Shrimp gumbo	1 cup	151	18	1	10	5	1.0	50	590	4
Tomato Florentine	1 cup	61	14	1	4	1	0.5	3	1035	3
Vichyssoise	1 cup	223	18	1	5	15	8.0	44	336	2
Wonton	1 cup	45	5	0	4	1	0.0	15	940	1

SALAD DRESSINGS
(For mayonnaise/Miracle Whip®, see "Fats, Oils, Cream & Gravy".)

ITEM	AMOUNT	CALORIES	CARBOHYDRATE (g)	CARBOHYDRATE CHOICES	PROTEIN (g)	FAT (g)	SATURATED FAT (g)	CHOLESTEROL (mg)	SODIUM (mg)	FIBER (g)
Bacon & tomato										
light	1 T.	32	0	0	0	3	0.5	1	176	0
regular	1 T.	70	1	0	1	7	1.5	3	140	0
Blue cheese										
fat free	1 T.	23	6	½	0	0	0.0	0	180	1
light	1 T.	40	1	0	1	4	1.0	0	190	0
regular	1 T.	77	1	0	1	8	1.5	3	168	0
Buttermilk	1 T.	75	1	0	0	8	1.5	3	120	0
Caesar										
fat free	1 T.	13	2	0	1	0	0.0	0	240	0
light	1 T.	17	3	0	0	1	0.0	0	162	0
regular	1 T.	55	1	0	1	6	1.0	5	145	0
Catalina®										
fat free	1 T.	25	6	½	0	0	0.0	0	175	0
regular	1 T.	70	4	0	0	6	1.0	0	195	0
Creamy cucumber										
light	1 T.	24	1	0	0	2	0.5	0	153	0
regular	1 T.	70	1	0	0	8	1.0	0	110	0
Creamy garlic	1 T.	55	1	0	0	6	1.0	0	180	0
Creamy Greek	1 T.	80	2	0	0	8	0.5	0	80	0
Creamy parmesan Romano	1 T.	70	1	0	0	7	1.5	5	155	0
Creamy peppercorn parmesan	1 T.	80	2	0	1	8	1.5	5	140	0

SALAD DRESSINGS

ITEM	AMOUNT	CALORIES	CARBOHYDRATE (g)	CARBOHYDRATE CHOICES	PROTEIN (g)	FAT (g)	SATURATED FAT (g)	CHOLESTEROL (mg)	SODIUM (mg)	FIBER (g)
Creamy poppyseed	1 T.	65	4	0	0	5	1.0	0	125	0
French										
fat free	1 T.	23	6	½	0	0	0.0	0	150	1
light	1 T.	22	4	0	0	1	0.0	0	128	0
regular	1 T.	67	3	0	0	6	1.5	0	214	0
Garlic & herb										
creamy	1 T.	55	1	0	0	6	1.0	0	180	0
regular, mix	1 T.	70	1	0	0	8	1.0	0	170	0
Green Goddess®	1 T.	65	1	0	0	7	1.0	0	130	0
Honey mustard	1 T.	75	2	0	0	8	1.0	0	120	0
Italian										
creamy	1 T.	55	1	0	0	6	1.0	0	125	0
fat free	1 T.	10	2	0	0	0	0.0	1	215	0
light	1 T.	16	1	0	0	1	0.0	1	118	0
regular	1 T.	69	2	0	0	7	1.0	0	116	0
regular, mix	1 T.	70	1	0	0	8	1.0	0	160	0
Oil & vinegar	1 T.	70	0	0	0	8	1.5	0	0	0
Ranch										
fat free	1 T.	24	5	0	0	0	0.0	0	177	0
light	1 T.	50	3	0	0	5	1.0	0	160	0
regular	1 T.	80	1	0	0	9	1.5	3	130	0
Russian										
light	1 T.	23	5	0	0	1	0.0	1	141	0
regular	1 T.	76	2	0	0	8	1.0	3	133	0
Sesame seed	1 T.	68	1	0	0	7	1.0	0	153	0
Thousand island										
fat free	1 T.	20	5	0	0	0	0.0	0	140	1
light	1 T.	40	4	0	0	3	0.5	5	125	0
regular	1 T.	55	3	0	0	5	1.0	5	155	0
Vinaigrette										
balsamic, regular	1 T.	45	2	0	0	4	0.5	0	150	0
red wine, fat free	1 T.	15	4	0	0	0	0.0	0	160	0
red wine, light	1 T.	23	2	0	0	4	0.0	0	155	0
red wine, regular	1 T.	45	1	0	0	5	0.5	0	235	0
Western®										
fat free	1 T.	8	6	½	0	0	0.0	0	130	0
light	1 T.	35	6	½	0	2	0.0	0	135	0
regular	1 T.	75	5	0	0	6	1.0	0	125	0

SALADS

ITEM	AMOUNT	CALORIES	CARBOHYDRATE (g)	CARBOHYDRATE CHOICES	PROTEIN (g)	FAT (g)	SATURATED FAT (g)	CHOLESTEROL (mg)	SODIUM (mg)	FIBER (g)
SALADS										
Caesar, w/ dressing	1 cup	204	7	½	7	17	4.5	14	453	1
Carrot-raisin	½ cup	202	21	1½	1	14	2.0	10	118	2
Chef										
w/ dressing	1 cup	312	9	½	17	23	7.5	111	924	2
w/o dressing	1 cup	178	3	0	17	11	5.5	93	496	2
Chicken, w/ mayo.	½ cup	268	1	0	11	25	3.0	48	201	0
Coleslaw										
w/ mayo.	½ cup	98	9	½	1	7	1.0	3	178	1
w/ vinaigrette	½ cup	41	7	½	1	2	0.0	5	14	1
Cucumber										
creamy, w/ mayo.	½ cup	59	5	0	1	4	3.0	9	13	1
w/ vinegar	½ cup	24	6	½	0	0	0.0	0	1	1
Egg, w/ mayo.	½ cup	292	1	0	8	28	5.5	290	232	0
Fruit, fresh	½ cup	51	13	1	1	0	0.0	0	0	2
Gelatin, w/ fruit	½ cup	73	18	1	1	0	0.0	0	30	1
Ham, w/ mayo.	½ cup	259	13	1	10	19	6.0	44	1094	0
Lobster, w/ mayo.	½ cup	75	5	0	6	4	0.5	56	157	1
Macaroni, w/ mayo.	½ cup	230	14	1	2	19	2.0	14	180	1
Pasta primavera	½ cup	152	26	2	4	4	1.0	0	311	2
Potato										
German style	½ cup	136	20	1	2	5	2.0	8	470	1
w/ eggs & mayo.	½ cup	179	14	1	3	10	2.0	85	661	2
w/ mayo.	½ cup	138	17	1	2	8	1.0	6	105	2
Seafood										
w/ mayo.	½ cup	164	2	0	13	11	1.5	66	176	0
w/ pasta, vinaigrette	½ cup	126	11	1	5	7	1.0	17	524	1
Shrimp, w/ mayo.	½ cup	141	3	0	13	8	1.5	103	196	0
Spinach, w/o dressing	1 cup	108	11	1	5	5	1.5	77	227	2
Tabbouleh	2 T.	30	3	0	1	1	0.0	0	63	1
Taco										
w/ salsa	1 (16 oz.)	420	33	1½	24	21	11.0	65	1400	11
w/ salsa & shell	1 (19 oz.)	790	73	4	31	42	15.0	65	1670	13
Three bean, w/ oil	½ cup	70	7	½	2	4	0.5	0	260	3
Tortellini, cheese	½ cup	189	14	1	5	14	3.0	23	561	2
Tossed, w/o dressing	1 cup	26	5	0	2	0	0.0	0	25	2
Tuna, w/ mayo.	½ cup	192	10	½	16	9	1.5	13	412	0
Waldorf, w/ mayo.	½ cup	205	6	½	2	20	2.0	10	117	2

SOUPS
Canned, prepared

ITEM	AMOUNT	CALORIES	CARBOHYDRATE (g)	CARBOHYDRATE CHOICES	PROTEIN (g)	FAT (g)	SATURATED FAT (g)	CHOLESTEROL (mg)	SODIUM (mg)	FIBER (g)
SOUPS										
Canned, prepared										
Bean										
w/ bacon	1 cup	170	25	1	8	4	1.5	0	870	8
w/ franks	1 cup	188	22	1	10	7	2.0	13	1093	6
Beef barley, w/ vegetables	1 cup	100	14	1	5	3	1.0	10	860	2
Beef broth										
low sodium	1 cup	38	1	0	5	1	0.5	0	72	0
regular	1 cup	15	1	0	3	0	0.0	0	890	0
Beef consommé	1 cup	20	1	0	4	0	0.0	0	810	0
Beef noodle	1 cup	83	9	½	5	3	1.0	5	952	1
Black bean	1 cup	170	30	1	8	2	0.0	0	730	10
Cheddar cheese*	1 cup	161	18	1	7	6	3.5	15	1012	1
Chicken alphabet	1 cup	80	11	1	3	2	1.0	10	880	1
Chicken & dumplings	1 cup	96	6	½	6	6	1.5	34	860	0
Chicken & rice	1 cup	70	12	1	2	2	1.0	0	850	0
Chicken broth										
low sodium	1 cup	30	1	0	4	1	0.0	0	140	0
regular	1 cup	20	1	0	1	1	0.0	0	770	0
Chicken gumbo	1 cup	56	8	½	3	1	0.5	5	954	2
Chicken noodle	1 cup	60	8	½	3	2	0.5	15	890	0
Chili beef, w/ beans	1 cup	170	21	1	7	7	3.5	13	1035	10
Chunky, Campbell's®										
beef, w/ white & wild rice	1 cup	150	24	1½	9	3	1.5	10	960	2
chicken broccoli cheese & potato	1 cup	190	14	1	7	12	4.0	20	960	1
chicken corn chowder	1 cup	240	19	1	8	15	5.0	25	800	2
chicken & pasta, w/ mushrooms	1 cup	90	14	1	7	1	0.5	10	850	1
classic chicken noodle	1 cup	130	16	1	9	3	1.0	20	880	2
grilled chicken, w/ veg. & pasta	1 cup	110	15	1	8	2	0.5	15	930	2
hearty vegetable, w/ pasta	1 cup	100	13	1	7	3	1.0	15	790	2
sirloin burger, w/ veg.	1 cup	180	17	1	10	8	5.0	20	890	3
steak 'n' potato	1 cup	130	18	1	10	2	0.5	15	920	2
vegetable	1 cup	130	22	1½	3	4	1.0	0	870	4
Clam chowder										
Manhattan	1 cup	78	12	1	2	2	0.5	2	578	1
New England*	1 cup	141	19	1	8	4	1.5	5	1022	1
Corn chowder*	1 cup	141	24	1½	5	3	1.0	5	662	2
Cream of asparagus*	1 cup	161	16	1	6	8	3.0	5	932	1
Cream of broccoli*	1 cup	141	18	1	6	5	2.0	10	812	1
Cream of celery	1 cup	100	9	½	1	7	2.0	0	870	1
Cream of mushroom										
condensed, lowfat	½ cup	70	9	½	1	3	1.0	0	900	0

SOUPS

Canned, prepared

ITEM	AMOUNT	CALORIES	CARBOHYDRATE (g)	CARBOHYDRATE CHOICES	PROTEIN (g)	FAT (g)	SATURATED FAT (g)	CHOLESTEROL (mg)	SODIUM (mg)	FIBER (g)
Cream of mushroom *(continued)*										
condensed, regular	½ cup	100	9	½	1	7	2.0	0	870	1
lowfat	1 cup	70	9	½	1	3	1.0	0	900	0
reduced sodium	1 cup	70	10	½	1	3	1.0	0	460	0
regular	1 cup	100	9	½	1	7	2.0	0	870	1
Cream of potato*	1 cup	141	20	1	6	4	3.0	15	942	1
Cream of shrimp*	1 cup	141	14	1	6	7	3.0	20	942	1
Double Noodle®	1 cup	110	17	1	4	3	1.0	15	830	1
Escarole	1 cup	25	3	0	1	1	0.0	0	930	1
French onion	1 cup	45	6	½	2	2	0.5	0	940	1
Gazpacho	1 cup	46	4	0	7	0	0.0	0	739	1
Green pea	1 cup	180	29	1½	9	3	1.0	0	870	5
Healthy Choice®										
chicken noodle	1 cup	110	16	1	7	2	0.5	20	480	3
chicken pasta	1 cup	110	18	1	6	2	0.5	5	480	2
chunky beef & potato	1 cup	110	20	1	7	1	0.0	10	480	2
creamy tomato	1 cup	100	22	1½	2	2	1.0	0	480	2
garden vegetable	1 cup	120	26	2	6	1	0.0	0	480	4
hearty chili beef	1 cup	180	31	1½	14	2	0.5	10	480	7
split pea & ham	1 cup	160	27	2	11	3	1.0	5	480	4
zesty gumbo	1 cup	100	16	1	6	2	1.0	20	480	3
Healthy Request®										
chicken noodle	1 cup	60	8	½	3	2	1.0	10	450	1
chicken rice	1 cup	80	13	1	2	2	1.0	5	420	1
cream of mushroom	1 cup	70	10	½	1	3	1.0	0	460	0
tomato	1 cup	90	18	1	1	2	0.0	0	450	1
vegetable beef	1 cup	90	15	1	4	2	0.5	5	480	2
Hot & sour	1 cup	162	5	0	15	8	2.5	34	1011	1
Lentil	1 cup	140	22	1	9	2	0.0	0	750	7
Lobster bisque	1 cup	130	11	1	6	6	3.0	70	990	0
Matzo ball	1 cup	110	13	1	3	5	2.0	35	710	3
Minestrone	1 cup	100	17	1	4	2	0.5	0	960	3
Mushroom	1 cup	80	10	½	2	3	1.0	0	920	1
Oyster stew*	1 cup	131	11	1	6	7	4.5	25	972	0
Pasta e fagioli	1 cup	170	19	1	7	7	2.5	10	1040	4
Pepperpot	1 cup	100	9	½	4	5	2.0	15	1020	1
Ratatouille	1 cup	266	12	1	2	25	3.0	0	329	1
Scotch broth	1 cup	70	9	½	3	2	1.0	5	880	2
Seafood chowder*	1 cup	131	15	1	11	3	1.0	20	692	0
Split pea, w/ ham	1 cup	180	28	1½	9	3	2.0	0	850	5
Tomato										
bisque*	1 cup	179	27	2	6	6	3.0	20	1002	0

SOUPS

Canned, prepared

ITEM	AMOUNT	CALORIES	CARBOHYDRATE (g)	CARBOHYDRATE CHOICES	PROTEIN (g)	FAT (g)	SATURATED FAT (g)	CHOLESTEROL (mg)	SODIUM (mg)	FIBER (g)
Tomato *(continued)*										
creamy, ready to serve	1 cup	130	26	2	3	2	1.0	5	760	2
reduced sodium	1 cup	90	18	1	1	2	0.5	0	450	1
regular, w/ milk*	1 cup	141	26	2	6	1	1.0	5	772	1
regular, w/ water	1 cup	90	20	1	2	0	0.0	0	710	1
w/ rice, ready to serve	1 cup	119	22	1½	2	3	0.5	2	815	1
Turkey noodle	1 cup	64	8	½	4	2	0.5	5	758	1
Vegetable	1 cup	82	13	1	3	2	0.5	2	810	0
Vegetable beef	1 cup	90	15	1	5	1	0.5	5	890	2
Vegetable broth	1 cup	20	5	0	0	0	0.0	0	330	0
Vegetarian vegetable	1 cup	90	18	1	3	1	0.0	0	860	2
Wild rice, w/ chicken	1 cup	70	9	½	3	2	0.5	10	900	1
Dehydrated										
(Prepared unless indicated.)										
Beef noodle	1 cup	40	6	½	2	1	0.5	3	1042	1
Bouillon, dry										
beef	1 cube	5	0	0	0	0	0.0	0	900	0
chicken	1 cube	5	0	0	0	0	0.0	0	1100	0
vegetable	1 cube	5	0	0	0	0	0.0	0	980	0
Chicken noodle	1 cup	100	17	1	3	2	0.5	10	740	1
Chicken rice	1 cup	58	9	½	2	1	0.5	2	931	1
Cream of vegetable	1 cup	100	12	1	2	5	1.5	0	870	1
Cup Noodles®										
beef	1 (14 oz.)	300	38	2	7	13	7.0	0	1110	9
chicken	1 (14 oz.)	300	38	2	6	13	7.0	0	1060	9
Cup-a-Soup®										
chicken noodle	1 (6 oz.)	50	8	½	2	1	0.0	10	560	0
chicken vegetable, w/ noodles	1 (6 oz.)	50	10	½	1	1	0.0	10	520	0
tomato	1 (6 oz.)	90	19	1	2	1	0.0	0	540	0
Leek	1 cup	70	9	½	2	3	1.0	0	810	0
Minestrone	1 cup	100	18	1	2	2	1.0	0	810	3
Mushroom	1 cup	96	11	1	2	5	1.0	0	1020	1
Onion	1 cup	35	6	½	1	1	0.5	0	790	0
Onion soup mix, dry	2 T.	35	6	½	1	1	0.5	0	790	0
Ramen noodle	1 cup	190	25	1½	4	8	4.0	0	850	1
Tomato	1 cup	103	19	1	2	2	1.0	0	943	1
Vegetable beef	1 cup	53	8	½	3	1	0.5	0	1002	1

* *Prepared with ½ cup 1% milk. If prepared w/ whole milk add*
  24 calories, 3 g fat, and 12 mg cholesterol. If prepared
  w/ skim milk subtract 8 calories and 1 g fat.

VEGETABLES

ITEM	AMOUNT	CALORIES	CARBOHYDRATE (g)	CARBOHYDRATE CHOICES	PROTEIN (g)	FAT (g)	SATURATED FAT (g)	CHOLESTEROL (mg)	SODIUM (mg)	FIBER (g)
VEGETABLES										
(For dried beans, peas, and lentils see Vegetarian Foods & Legumes.)										
Alfalfa sprouts, raw	½ cup	5	1	0	1	0	0.0	0	1	0
Artichokes										
boiled/steamed	1 medium	60	13	½	4	0	0.0	0	120	7
hearts, marinated	½ cup	58	7	½	2	3	0.0	0	244	2
Asparagus, cooked	½ cup	22	4	0	2	0	0.0	0	10	1
Bamboo shoots, raw	½ cup	20	4	0	2	0	0.0	0	3	2
Bean sprouts, raw	½ cup	16	3	0	2	0	0.0	0	3	1
Beets, pickled	½ cup	74	18	1	1	0	0.0	0	300	3
Bok choy, cooked	½ cup	10	2	0	1	0	0.0	0	29	1
Broccoli										
cooked	½ cup	22	4	0	2	0	0.0	0	20	2
cooked, w/ cheese sauce	½ cup	115	6	½	7	8	3.5	16	202	2
raw	½ cup	10	2	0	1	0	0.0	0	12	1
Brussel sprouts, cooked	½ cup	30	7	½	2	0	0.0	0	16	2
Cabbage										
Chinese, cooked	½ cup	11	2	0	1	0	0.0	0	55	1
green, cooked	½ cup	17	3	0	1	0	0.0	0	6	2
red, raw	½ cup	9	2	0	0	0	0.0	0	4	1
Carrots										
cooked	½ cup	35	8	½	1	0	0.0	0	51	3
raw	1 large	31	7	½	1	0	0.0	0	25	2
Cauliflower										
cooked	½ cup	14	3	0	1	0	0.0	0	9	2
raw	½ cup	13	3	0	1	0	0.0	0	15	1
w/ cheese sauce, cooked	½ cup	88	4	0	4	6	3.0	13	157	1
Celery										
cooked	½ cup	12	3	0	1	0	0.0	0	65	1
raw	1 stalk	6	1	0	0	0	0.0	0	35	1
Chinese-style, frzn.	½ cup	44	9	½	3	0	0.0	0	302	3
Chives, raw	1 T.	1	0	0	0	0	0.0	0	0	0
Corn, cooked										
cream-style, can	½ cup	92	23	1½	2	1	0.0	0	365	2
on the cob	1 (4 oz.)	122	28	2	4	1	0.0	0	19	3
w/ butter sauce, frzn.	½ cup	115	23	1½	3	3	1.5	5	216	2
whole kernel, can	½ cup	66	15	1	2	1	0.0	0	175	2
whole kernel, frzn.	½ cup	66	16	1	2	0	0.0	0	4	2
Cucumbers, raw										
w/ skin	½ medium	20	4	0	1	0	0.0	0	3	1
w/o skin	½ cup	7	1	0	0	0	0.0	0	1	0
Eggplant, cooked	½ cup	14	3	0	0	0	0.0	0	1	1

VEGETABLES

ITEM	AMOUNT	CALORIES	CARBOHYDRATE (g)	CARBOHYDRATE CHOICES	PROTEIN (g)	FAT (g)	SATURATED FAT (g)	CHOLESTEROL (mg)	SODIUM (mg)	FIBER (g)
Endive, raw	1 cup	9	2	0	1	0	0.0	0	11	2
Green beans, cooked										
French-style	½ cup	25	6	½	1	0	0.0	0	3	2
snap	½ cup	22	5	0	1	0	0.0	0	2	2
Green onions, raw	½ cup	8	2	0	0	0	0.0	0	4	1
Greens, cooked										
beet	½ cup	19	4	0	2	0	0.0	0	174	2
collard	½ cup	25	5	0	2	0	0.0	0	9	3
dandelion	½ cup	17	3	0	1	0	0.0	0	23	2
mustard	½ cup	11	1	0	2	0	0.0	0	11	1
turnip	½ cup	14	3	0	1	0	0.0	0	21	3
Hominy, cooked	½ cup	58	11	1	1	1	0.0	0	168	2
Italian-style, frzn.	½ cup	48	5	0	1	3	1.0	5	130	1
Jicama, cooked/raw	½ cup	23	5	0	0	0	0.0	0	2	3
Kale, cooked	½ cup	18	4	0	1	0	0.0	0	15	1
Kohlrabi, cooked	½ cup	24	6	½	1	0	0.0	0	17	1
Leeks, raw	¼ cup	14	3	0	0	0	0.0	0	4	0
Lettuce, raw	1 cup	7	1	0	1	0	0.0	0	5	1
Mixed, frzn.	½ cup	54	12	1	3	0	0.0	0	32	4
Mushrooms										
can	½ cup	30	4	0	3	0	0.0	0	440	2
fried	5 medium	156	11	1	2	12	1.5	2	112	1
raw	½ cup	12	2	0	1	0	0.0	0	2	1
Okra, cooked	½ cup	26	6	½	2	0	0.0	0	4	2
Onions										
can	½ cup	21	4	0	1	0	0.0	0	416	1
chopped, raw	½ cup	30	7	½	1	0	0.0	0	2	1
rings, breaded & fried	5	164	21	1½	2	9	2.0	0	321	1
Parsley, raw	¼ cup	5	1	0	0	0	0.0	0	8	0
Parsnips, cooked	½ cup	63	15	1	1	0	0.0	0	8	3
Pea pods, cooked	½ cup	34	6	½	3	0	0.0	0	3	2
Peas, green, cooked	½ cup	67	13	1	4	0	0.0	0	2	4
Peppers, raw										
bell, green/red/yellow	½ cup	20	5	0	1	0	0.0	0	1	1
chiles, green, diced	¼ cup	20	4	0	2	0	0.0	0	40	2
jalapeños	1	4	1	0	0	0	0.0	0	0	0
Pimentos, can	¼ cup	11	2	0	1	0	0.0	0	7	1
Potatoes, cooked										
au gratin, box	½ cup	113	17	1	2	5	1.0	0	488	1
baked, w/ skin	1 (4 oz.)	124	29	2	3	0	0.0	0	9	3
blintzes, frzn.	1 (2.3 oz.)	90	15	1	3	4	1.0	5	170	2
boiled, w/o skin	1 (4 oz.)	98	23	1½	2	0	0.0	0	6	2

VEGETABLES

ITEM	AMOUNT	CALORIES	CARBOHYDRATE (g)	CARBOHYDRATE CHOICES	PROTEIN (g)	FAT (g)	SATURATED FAT (g)	CHOLESTEROL (mg)	SODIUM (mg)	FIBER (g)
Potatoes *(continued)*										
French fries, frzn.	10 medium	100	16	1	2	4	0.5	0	15	2
hash browns, frzn.	½ cup	170	22	1½	2	9	3.5	0	27	2
instant, w/ marg. & milk	½ cup	160	18	1	3	8	1.5	0	460	1
knish, frzn.	1 (2 oz.)	200	19	1	4	12	2.5	55	130	1
mashed, w/ marg. & milk	½ cup	111	18	1	2	4	1.0	2	310	2
O'Brien, frzn.	½ cup	198	21	1½	2	13	3.0	0	42	2
pancakes, hmde.	1 medium	207	22	1½	5	12	2.5	73	386	2
pierogies, frzn.	3 (1.4 oz.)	180	34	2	5	2	0.0	5	420	2
scalloped, box	½ cup	98	16	1	2	4	1.0	0	465	1
scalloped, w/ ham, hmde.	½ cup	126	16	1	7	4	1.5	12	245	1
Tater Tots®, frzn.	9	170	21	1½	1	8	1.5	0	440	2
twice baked, w/ cheese	1 (5 oz.)	194	28	2	4	8	2.5	0	469	3
Pumpkin, can	½ cup	42	10	½	1	0	0.0	0	6	4
Radishes, raw	10	9	2	0	0	0	0.0	0	11	1
Rutabagas, cooked	½ cup	47	10	½	2	0	0.0	0	24	2
Salad greens, raw	1 cup	9	2	0	1	0	0.0	0	14	1
Sauerkraut, can	½ cup	22	5	0	1	0	0.0	0	780	3
Scallions, raw	1 T.	2	0	0	0	0	0.0	0	1	0
Shallots, raw	¼ cup	29	7	½	1	0	0.0	0	5	0
Spinach										
cooked	½ cup	21	3	0	3	0	0.0	0	63	2
creamed	½ cup	80	10	½	4	3	1.5	0	520	2
raw	1 cup	7	1	0	1	0	0.0	0	24	1
Squash										
acorn, cooked	½ cup	57	15	½	1	0	0.0	0	4	5
butternut, cooked	½ cup	47	12	1	1	0	0.0	0	2	3
spaghetti	½ cup	21	5	0	1	0	0.0	0	14	1
summer, cooked/raw	½ cup	18	4	0	1	0	0.0	0	1	1
winter, cooked	½ cup	40	9	½	1	1	0.0	0	1	3
zucchini, cooked	½ cup	8	2	0	0	0	0.0	0	1	1
zucchini, raw	½ cup	9	2	0	1	0	0.0	0	2	1
Succotash, cooked	½ cup	110	23	1½	5	1	0.0	0	16	4
Sweet potatoes										
baked, w skin	1 (4 oz.)	140	33	2	3	0	0.0	0	14	5
candied, frzn.	½ cup	276	67	4½	1	1	0.5	0	109	3
mashed, w/o fat	½ cup	172	40	2½	3	0	0.0	0	21	3
Swiss chard, cooked	½ cup	18	4	0	2	0	0.0	0	157	2
Tomatoes										
cherry, raw	6 medium	21	5	0	1	0	0.0	0	9	1
paste, can	½ cup	120	24	1½	8	0	0.0	0	80	4
puree, can	½ cup	50	12	1	2	0	0.0	0	499	3

VEGETABLES

ITEM	AMOUNT	CALORIES	CARBOHYDRATE (g)	CARBOHYDRATE CHOICES	PROTEIN (g)	FAT (g)	SATURATED FAT (g)	CHOLESTEROL (mg)	SODIUM (mg)	FIBER (g)
Tomatoes (continued)										
stewed, can	½ cup	35	9	½	1	0	0.0	0	220	1
sun dried	½ cup	70	15	1	4	1	0.0	0	566	3
whole, can	½ cup	23	5	0	1	0	0.0	0	178	1
whole, raw	1 medium	26	6	½	1	0	0.0	0	11	1
Turnips, cooked	½ cup	24	6	½	1	0	0.0	0	58	2
Water chestnuts, can	½ cup	35	9	½	1	0	0.0	0	6	2
Watercress, raw	½ cup	2	0	0	0	0	0.0	0	7	0
Wax beans, cooked	½ cup	22	5	0	1	0	0.0	0	2	2
Yams, baked/boiled	½ cup	79	19	1	1	0	0.0	0	5	3

VEGETARIAN FOODS & LEGUMES
(Cooked w/o salt unless indicated.)

ITEM	AMOUNT	CALORIES	CARBOHYDRATE (g)	CARBOHYDRATE CHOICES	PROTEIN (g)	FAT (g)	SATURATED FAT (g)	CHOLESTEROL (mg)	SODIUM (mg)	FIBER (g)
Aduki/adzuki beans										
dry, cooked	½ cup	147	28	1	9	0	0.0	0	9	8
sweetened, can	½ cup	351	81	5½	6	0	0.0	0	323	4
Bac-O's®	1½ T.	30	2	0	3	2	0.0	0	120	0
Bacon, vegetarian	2 (0.4 oz.)	45	2	0	6	2	0.0	0	360	0
Baked beans, vegetarian, can	½ cup	150	28	2	6	1	0.0	0	340	4
Black beans										
can	½ cup	110	17	½	7	1	0.0	0	400	7
dry, cooked	½ cup	114	20	1	8	0	0.0	0	1	7
Black eyed peas/cowpeas										
can	½ cup	92	16	1	6	1	0.0	0	359	4
dry, cooked	½ cup	80	17	1	3	0	0.0	0	3	4
Black turtle beans										
can	½ cup	109	20	1	7	0	0.0	0	461	8
dry, cooked	½ cup	120	23	1	8	0	0.0	0	3	5
Broad/fava beans										
can	½ cup	110	20	1	6	1	0.0	0	250	5
dry, cooked	½ cup	94	17	1	6	0	0.0	0	4	5
Burgers, vegetarian, frzn.										
Better'n Burgers®	1 (2.5 oz.)	100	6	½	13	2	0.0	0	310	3
Bocaburger®, original	1 (2.5 oz.)	90	6	½	13	1	0.0	0	340	4
Chik Patties®	1 (2.5 oz.)	160	1	0	11	6	0.5	0	430	2
Gardenburger®, original	1 (2.5 oz.)	120	7	½	14	4	0.0	0	300	4
Butter beans, can	½ cup	90	16	1	6	0	0.0	0	450	4
Calico beans, dry, cooked	½ cup	127	24	1	8	0	0.0	0	6	9
Cannellini beans, can	½ cup	100	18	1	5	1	0.0	0	270	5
Chickpeas/garbanzo beans										
can	½ cup	143	27	1½	6	1	0.0	0	359	5
dry, cooked	½ cup	134	22	1	7	2	0.0	0	6	6

VEGETARIAN FOODS & LEGUMES

ITEM	AMOUNT	CALORIES	CARBOHYDRATE (g)	CARBOHYDRATE CHOICES	PROTEIN (g)	FAT (g)	SATURATED FAT (g)	CHOLESTEROL (mg)	SODIUM (mg)	FIBER (g)
Chik'n Nuggets™, frzn.	4 (0.7 oz.)	180	17	1	15	6	0.5	0	570	2
Chili, vegetarian, can	1 cup	200	38	2	12	1	0.0	0	780	7
Chili beans, can	½ cup	110	24	1	7	1	0.5	0	360	7
Cranberry/Roman beans										
can	½ cup	108	20	1	7	0	0.0	0	432	8
dry, cooked	½ cup	120	22	1	8	0	0.0	0	1	9
Crowder peas, can	½ cup	110	18	1	7	1	0.0	0	500	5
Falafel patties	1 (0.6 oz.)	57	5	0	2	3	0.5	0	50	1
Great northern beans										
can	½ cup	70	17	1	6	0	0.0	0	490	6
dry, cooked	½ cup	104	19	1	7	0	0.0	0	2	6
Ground meat alternative										
fresh	2 oz.	50	4	0	8	0	0.0	0	270	2
frzn.	⅔ cup	80	4	0	10	2.5	0.0	0	210	2
Hot dogs										
tofu	1 (1.5 oz.)	60	2	0	8	3	1.0	0	240	0
veggie	1 (2 oz.)	80	6	½	11	1	0.0	0	580	1
Hummus	½ cup	210	25	1	6	10	1.5	0	300	6
Kidney beans										
can	½ cup	104	19	1	7	0	0.0	0	444	4
dry, cooked	½ cup	112	20	1	8	0	0.0	0	2	7
Lentils, cooked	½ cup	115	20	1	9	0	0.0	0	2	8
Lima beans										
baby, frzn.	½ cup	95	18	1	6	0	0.0	0	26	5
can	½ cup	95	18	1	6	0	0.0	0	405	6
dry, cooked	½ cup	108	20	1	7	0	0.0	0	2	7
Miso	2 T.	71	10	½	4	2	0.5	0	1254	2
Mung beans, dry, cooked	½ cup	106	19	1	7	0	0.0	0	2	8
Natto	½ cup	186	13	½	16	10	1.5	0	6	5
Navy beans										
can	½ cup	148	27	1	10	1	0.0	0	587	7
dry, cooked	½ cup	129	24	1	8	1	0.0	0	1	6
Pigeon peas										
can	½ cup	70	14	1	4	0	0.0	0	390	4
dry, cooked	½ cup	102	20	1	6	0	0.0	0	4	6
Pink beans, dry, cooked	½ cup	126	24	1½	8	0	0.0	0	2	4
Pinto beans,										
can	½ cup	103	18	1	6	1	0.0	0	353	6
dry, cooked	½ cup	117	22	1	7	0	0.0	0	2	7
Red beans, dry, cooked	½ cup	122	23	1	7	0	0.0	0	6	9

VEGETARIAN FOODS & LEGUMES

ITEM	AMOUNT	CALORIES	CARBOHYDRATE (g)	CARBOHYDRATE CHOICES	PROTEIN (g)	FAT (g)	SATURATED FAT (g)	CHOLESTEROL (mg)	SODIUM (mg)	FIBER (g)
Refried beans, can										
fat free	½ cup	100	18	1	6	0	0.0	0	480	6
regular	½ cup	120	22	1	6	2	0.0	0	560	5
Sausages, vegetarian, frzn.										
links	1 (2 oz.)	90	7	½	8	3	0.5	0	440	2
patties	1 (1.5 oz.)	109	4	0	8	8	1.5	0	378	1
Seitan, dry	½ cup	227	21	1½	32	2	0.0	0	30	3
Soy meal, defatted	½ cup	206	22	1	30	1	0.0	0	2	11
Soy protein										
concentrate	1 oz.	94	9	½	16	0	0.0	0	1	2
isolate	1 oz.	96	2	0	23	1	0.0	0	285	2
Soybeans										
green, cooked	½ cup	127	10	½	11	6	0.5	0	13	4
mature, cooked	½ cup	149	9	0	14	8	1.0	0	1	5
mature, roasted, salted	¼ cup	203	14	½	15	11	1.5	0	70	8
Split peas, dry, cooked	½ cup	116	21	1	8	0	0.0	0	2	8
Stakelets®, frzn.	1 (2.5 oz.)	140	6	½	12	8	1.0	0	480	2
Tempeh	4 oz.	240	21	1	18	9	1.5	0	0	8
Tofu										
firm, lite	3 oz.	30	1	0	5	1	0.0	0	70	0
firm, regular	3 oz.	50	2	0	6	3	0.0	0	30	0
flavored, baked	3 oz.	150	5	0	12	9	1.0	0	330	3
soft, regular	3 oz.	45	2	0	4	3	0.0	0	0	0
Turkey slices, vegetarian	3 (0.5 oz.)	50	3	0	10	0	0.0	0	100	0
TVP®, dry	¼ cup	80	7	½	12	0	0.0	0	2	4
White beans, dry, cooked	½ cup	124	22	1	9	0	0.0	0	5	6
Winged beans, dry, cooked	½ cup	126	13	1	9	5	0.5	0	11	2
Yeast										
brewer's	3 T.	75	8	½	12	0	0.0	0	30	0
nutritional	3 T.	116	13	½	16	0	0.0	0	63	6

Favorite Foods

ITEM	AMOUNT	CALORIES	CARBOHYDRATE (g)	CARBOHYDRATE CHOICES	PROTEIN (g)	FAT (g)	SATURATED FAT (g)	CHOLESTEROL (mg)	SODIUM (mg)	FIBER (g)

MyPyramid 2005

MyPyramid is part of an overall food guidance system that emphasizes the need for a more individualized approach to improving diet and lifestyle.

Additional information about USDA's MyPyramid is available at MyPyramid.gov. The 2005 Dietary Guidelines for Americans and consumer brochure are available at www.healthierus.gov/dietaryguidelines.

Know Your Numbers

Date	Cholesterol	LDL	HDL	Triglycerides	Blood Pressure	Weight	Other/Comments

Medications/Supplements

Start Date	Name of Medication & Dosage	Comments	Stop Date

Estimate your Daily Nutrient Goals in Three Easy Steps

Step 1

Determine your recommended calorie goal using the information below. If you want to lose between one-half to one pound per week, subtract 250-500 calories from the recommended ranges. For a balanced diet, women should not eat less than 1200 calories and men should not eat less than 1500 calories each day.

1500-1800 calories
Sedentary women and some older adults

1800-2400 calories
Active women and many sedentary men

2400-2800 calories
Active men and some very active women

Step 2

Locate your calorie goal on the left-hand side of the chart below. Read the chart across to the right to determine your other nutrient goals. Each nutrient goal is based on a percentage of your calorie goal. Three different levels for fat and two levels for saturated fat goals are listed. Your goal is to eat within the recommended ranges.

Step 3

Look at the bottom of the chart for cholesterol, sodium and fiber recommendations. If you have special nutrient needs, talk with your health care provider or registered dietitian for the amounts that are right for you.

Calorie Goal	Fat Grams			Saturated Fat Grams		Carbohydrate Grams	Protein Grams
	30%	25%	20%	10%	7%	50-60%	10-15%
1200	40	33	27	13	9	150-180	30-45
1500	50	42	33	17	12	188-225	38-56
1800	60	50	40	20	14	225-270	45-68
2000	67	56	44	22	16	250-300	50-75
2200	73	61	49	24	17	275-330	55-83
2500	83	69	56	28	19	313-375	63-94
2800	93	78	62	31	22	350-420	70-105

Cholesterol	Sodium	Fiber
300 milligrams	2400 milligrams	25 to 35 grams

If you have diabetes and are counting carbohydrate grams or carbohydrate choices, each has been provided for you in this book. The amount of carbohydrate grams and choices you can eat is based on your calorie goal.

Carbohydrate Goals for Diabetes

Calorie Goal	Carbohydrate Grams	Carbohydrate Choices
1200	150-180	10-12
1500	188-225	13-15
1800	225-270	15-18
2000	250-300	17-20
2200	275-330	18-22
2500	313-375	21-25
2800	350-420	23-28

Carbohydrate choices have been calculated using the 15-Gram Equation (15 grams of carbohydrate = 1 carbohydrate choice). We have done the calculating for you for all foods listed in this book. Since fiber is part of the total carbohydrate, when fiber was 5 grams or greater, it was subtracted from the total carbohydrate grams before calculating carbohydrate choices.

Carbohydrate Grams	Carbohydrate Choices
0-5	0
6-10	½
11-20	1
21-25	1½
26-35	2
36-40	2½
41-50	3
51-55	3½
56-65	4
66-70	4½
71-80	5

Looking for an Individualized Eating Plan?

A registered dietitian (RD) can help. To locate an RD in your area, contact The American Dietetic Association's referral service by calling 1-800-366-1655 or visit the website at www.eatright.org.

Desirable Levels:
Blood Lipids & Blood Pressure

	General Population	Diabetes	Coronary Heart Disease
Cholesterol	<200 mg/dL	<200 mg/dL	<180 mg/dL
LDL	<100 mg/dL	<100 mg/dL	<70-100 mg/dL
HDL	>40 mg/dL	>45 mg/dL (men) >55 mg/dL (women)	>55 mg/dL
Triglycerides	<150 mg/dL	<150 mg/dL	<150 mg/dL
Blood Pressure	<120/80 mmHg	<130/80 mmHg	<120/80 mmHg

Goals

Cholesterol: _____

LDL: _____

HDL: _____

Triglycerides: _____

Blood Pressure: _____

Weight: _____

References

Books and Periodicals

American College of Sport's Medicine. *ACSM's Resource Manual for Guidelines for Exercise Testing and Prescription,* Fourth edition. Philadelphia: Lippincott, Williams & Wilkins, 2001.

American Diabetes Association. *Clinical Practice Recommendations 2003.* The American Diabetes Association, 2003.

"Carbohydrate Counting." In *A Core Curriculum for Diabetes Education: Diabetes Management Therapies.* 4th ed. Chicago: American Association of Diabetes Educators, 2001.

Feller, Robyn M., *The Complete Bartender.* New York: Berkely Books, 1990.

Meilach, Dona Z., *The Best 50 Bar Drinks.* California: Bristol Publishing Enterprises, 2001.

Wheeler, Madelyn L., Marion Franz, Phyllis Barrier, et al. "Macronutrient and Energy Database for the 1995 Exchange Lists for Meal Planning: A Rationale for Clinical Practice Decisions," *Journal of the American Dietetic Association 96* (1996): 1167-1171.

Other

- Fast food franchise nutrition information, 2004.

- *The Food Processor, Nutrition & Fitness Software.* Version 7.92. Salem, OR: ESHA Research, 2001.

- Manufacturer's *Nutrition Facts* food labels.

- Seventh Report of the Joint National Committee on Prevention, Detection, Evaluation & Treatment of High Blood Pressure (JNC 7). NIH Publication No. 03-5233, 2003.

- Third Report of the National Cholesterol Education Program (NCEP) Expert Panel on Detection, Evaluation, and Treatment of High Blood Cholesterol in Adults (ATP III). NIH Publication No. 01-3670, 2001.

- United States Department of Agriculture. *MyPyramid,* 2005.

Calories Used Through Activity

Listed below are the number of calories used during 30 minutes of various activities. Calorie values are approximate and vary based on an individual's weight, exertion and skill level. Values were calculated for a 150-pound person. To adjust for your weight: divide your weight by 150, then multiply this number (your weight factor) by the calorie values on this chart.

Activity	30 minutes	Activity	30 minutes
Aerobic dance	215	Handball	430
Archery	125	Hiking	215
Badminton	161	Hockey, field/ice	287
Baseball/softball	179	Horseback riding	143
Basketball	215	Housework/cleaning	125
Bicycling, <10 mph	143	Hunting	179
Bicycling, 10-12 mph	215	Ice skating	251
Bicycling, >12 mph	287	Judo/karate	358
Bowling	107	Jumping rope	358
Boxing/sparring	322	Kayaking	179
Canoeing	125	Kick boxing/tae kwon do	358
Dancing	161	Mountain biking	304
Farming, driving tractor	89	Mountain/rock climbing	287
Fencing	215	Mowing lawn	197
Fishing	143	Painting, outside	179
Football	287	Pool (billiards)	89
Gardening	179	Racquetball	251
Golfing, w cart	125	Roller blading/skating	251
Golfing, w/o cart	161	Rowing machine	341
Golfing, walk & carry clubs	197	Running, 5mph	287

Calories Used Through Activity *(continued)*

Activity	30 minutes
Running, 8mph	483
Running, 10mph	573
Sailing	107
Scuba diving	251
Sitting	36
Ski machine	340
Skiing, cross-country, 4-5 mph.	287
Skiing, downhill	215
Sleeping	32
Snow shoeing	287
Snow shoveling	215
Soccer	251
Squash	430
Stair climbing	330
Standing	43
Stationary bike	179

Activity	30 minutes
Stretching	143
Swimming, fast	358
Swimming, slow	287
Table tennis (ping pong)	143
Tai chi	143
Tennis, doubles	215
Tennis, singles	287
Treading water	143
Volleyball	107
Walking, 3 mph.	125
Walking, 4 mph.	143
Water aerobics	143
Water-skiing	215
Weight training (moderate)	107
Weight training (vigorous)	215
Wrestling	215
Yoga	143

Index

HealthCheques™: A Self-Monitoring System

by Jane Stephenson, RD, CDE, and Diane Bader. Copyright 2004. Track calories, fat, carbohydrates, carb choices, protein, saturated fat, sodium, cholesterol or fiber on a daily basis using this easy-to-carry checkbook. Each checkbook set consists of a 112-page Food Counter that provides nutrient values for more than 1,500 foods. The lower portion is a Food & Activity Log to record the foods eaten and physical activity. Replace the Log as needed.

Diet-Free HealthCheques™: A Self-Enrichment System

by Jane Stephenson, RD, CDE and Jackie Boucher, MS, RD, CDE. Copyright 2000. An ideal system for those who do not need another "diet", yet want to enjoy food without guilt. Designed for the chronic dieter, binge eater, and stress eater, this tool focuses on 10 S.T.R.A.T.E.G.I.E.S. that give the individual the "why" and "how" behind developing a healthier relationship with food, self, activity, and weight. The 4-week Journal on the lower portion helps the individual track eating and activity habits, identify common feelings and situations that 'trigger' problematic eating behavior, and gauge satiety levels. Replace the Journal as needed.

HealthCheques™: A Meal-Planning System

by Jane Stephenson, RD, CDE. Copyright 2001. This meal-planning tool lets you decide what, how much, and when to eat. A full set includes the Food Exchange Guide, which lists all foods categorized by the six major Exchange Lists and a 4-week Food and Activity Journal. The Guide has extensive Fast Foods, Restaurant Foods, and Mixed Dishes sections. The Journal allows you to record blood glucose levels and all foods and beverages eaten throughout the day. Also provided is an easy checkbox system of tracking food exchanges, with room to record grams of carbohydrate and physical activity expended. Included are sample meal plans ranging from 1200 to 3000 calories, plus room to add your own individualized food plan. Replace the Journal as needed.

Any of the above sets can be ordered on page 125 or 127. Please call our toll-free number (800-322-5679) if you have any questions or would like to request a FREE color catalog.

REORDER FORM and Other Products from Appletree Press!

HealthCheques™ checkbook sets:
(see page 126 for product description)

A) **HealthCheques™: A Self-Monitoring System**
by Jane Stephenson, RD, CDE and Diane Bader
Copyright 2004.
Item #400   **$7.95 each: Send me _____ at $_____.**

B) **Diet-Free HealthCheques™: A Self-Enrichment System**
by Jane Stephenson, RD, CDE and Jackie Boucher, MS, RD, CDE.
Copyright 2000.
Item #420   **$7.95 each: Send me _____ at $_____.**

C) **HealthCheques™: A Meal-Planning System**
by Jane Stephenson, RD, CDE.
Copyright 2001.
Item #430   **$7.95 each: Send me _____ at $_____.**

HealthCheques™: Carbohydrate, Fat & Calorie Guide
Second Edition
by Jane Stephenson, RD, CDE
and Diane Bader.

Softcover, 128 pages.
Copyright 2004. A comprehensive pocket guide listing the calories, carbohydrate, protein, fat, saturated fat, cholesterol, sodium and fiber content of 4,000 foods. Includes carbohydrate choices.

**$7.95 each:
Send me _____ at $_____.**

SHIPPING INFORMATION:

Add: $2.00 for one book or checkbook

$3.00 for two books or book & checkbook $ _____

(Minnesota residents must add sales tax) 6.5% tax $ _____

TOTAL ENCLOSED $ _____

Circle Method of Payment: Check   Visa   MasterCard

Card Number _____Expiration Date _____

Name _____

P.O. Box and/or Street Address_____

_____

City, State and Zip Code _____

MAIL TO: **Appletree Press, Inc.**   Toll-free: 1-800-322-5679
Suite 125   Fax: (507) 345-3002
151 Good Counsel Drive   Phone: (507) 345-4848
Mankato, MN 56001   Website: www.appletree-press.com
